*"A brilliant mosaic of startling truths. The greatest adventure story never told."*
–Chris Brady

# INSIDIOUS

## The Rise of the Financial Matrix and the Fall of Economic Freedom

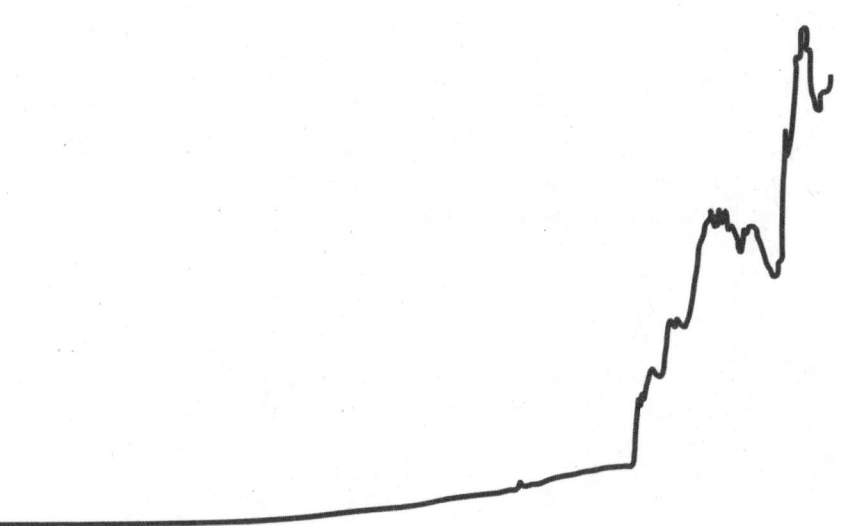

*New York Times Bestselling Author*

# ORRIN WOODWARD

The information presented in this book is for general educational purposes only, and provides information the authors believe to be accurate on the subject matter covered. It is sold with the understanding that neither the authors nor the publisher are providing advice for any particular portfolio or for any individual's particular situation, or rendering investment advice or other professional services such as legal or accounting advice. If expert assistance in areas that include investment, legal, and accounting advice are needed, please seek a competent professional's services.

This publication may make reference to performance data collected over various periods of time. Remember that past results do not guarantee future performance. Performance data, as well as laws and regulations, change over time, which could affect the applicability of the information presented in this book. Any data presented herein is used merely to illustrate the underlying principles.

This book is not to serve as the basis for any financial decision or as a recommendation of any specific investment.

No warranty is made with respect to the accuracy or completeness of the information contained herein, and both the authors and the publisher specifically disclaim any responsibility for any liability, loss, or risk, personal or otherwise, which is incurred as a consequence, directly or indirectly, of the use and application of any of the contents of this book.

Copyright © 2024 by Orrin Woodward

All rights reserved. No part of this book may be reproduced or transmitted in any form or by any means, electronic or mechanical, including photocopying and recording, or by any information storage and retrieval system, without the written permission of Obstaclés Press. Inquiries should be sent to the publisher.

Obstaclés Press and the Obstaclés logo are trademarks of Life.

Published by:
Obstaclés Press
200 Commonwealth Court
Cary, NC 27511

orrinwoodward.com

ISBN: 979-8-218-42082-6

First Edition, June 2024
10 9 8 7 6 5 4 3 2 1

Scripture quotations marked "KJV" are taken from The Holy Bible, Cambridge, 1769.

Scripture quotations marked "NIV" are taken from The Holy Bible, New International Version®, NIV®, Copyright© 1973, 1978, 1984, 2011 by Biblica, Inc.® Used by permission of Biblica, Inc.® All rights reserved worldwide.

Printed in the United States of America

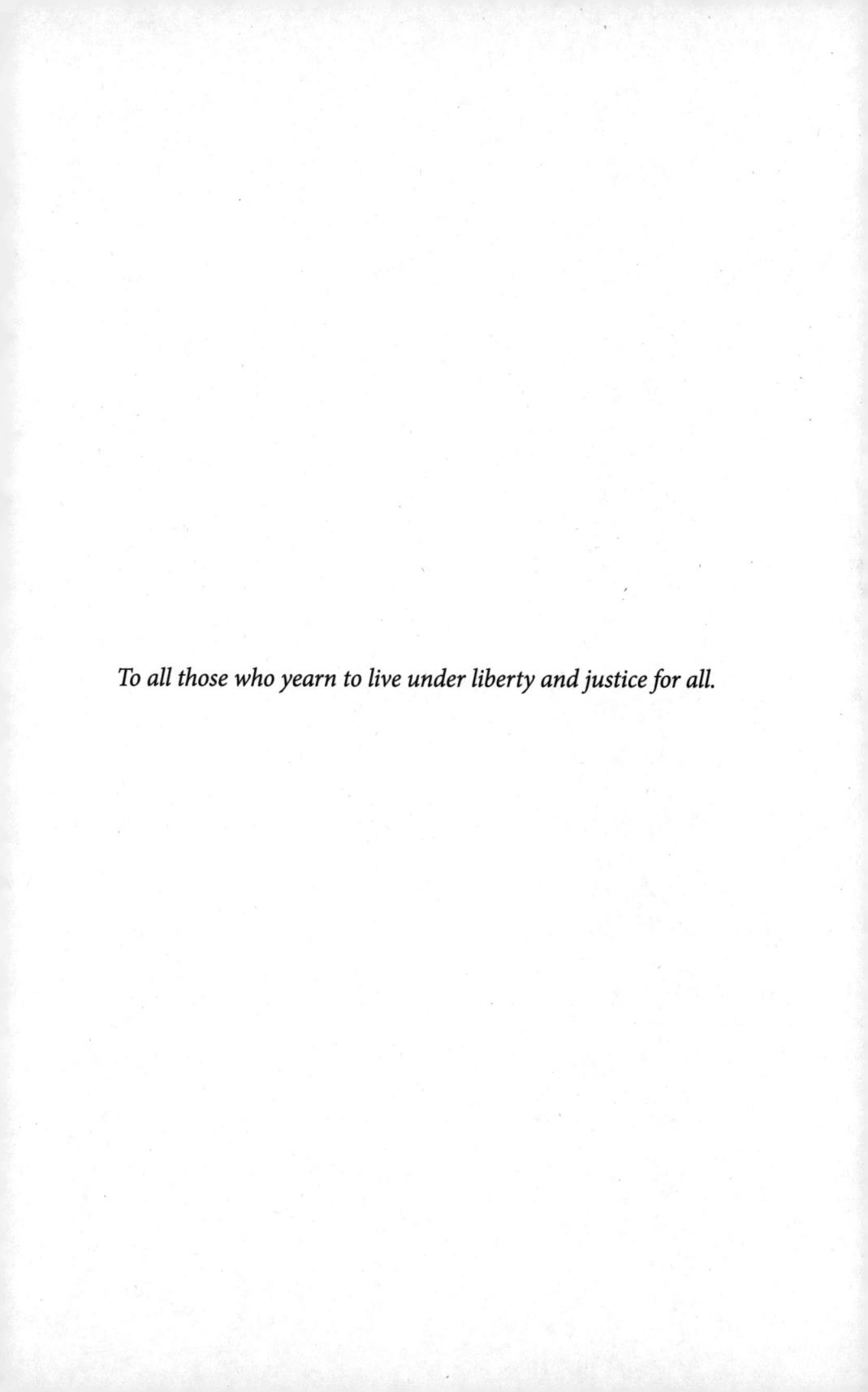

*To all those who yearn to live under liberty and justice for all.*

# **INSIDIOUS** [ in-sid-ee-uhs ]

1. intended to entrap or beguile.

2. stealthily treacherous or deceitful

3. operating or proceeding in an inconspicuous or seemingly harmless way but actually with grave effect

# CONTENTS

**Foreword**..................................................................9

**Preface**....................................................................13

**Introduction**............................................................19

**Chapter 1:**
The Financial Matrix Debt Explosion........................27

**Chapter 2:**
Force Market Versus Free Market Systems...............49

**Chapter 3:**
What is Money?.........................................................67

**Chapter 4:**
Legitimate Versus Illegitimate Banking.....................85

**Chapter 5:**
Fractional (or Fictional) Reserve Banking...............103

**Chapter 6:**
Medicis and Fuggers................................................119

**Chapter 7:**
Business Cycles........................................................135

**Chapter 8:**
Central Banks and the Gold Standard......................153

**Chapter 9:**
The Money War: Financial Power Versus State Power............171

**Chapter 10:**
Financial Power Wins the Money War..................................189

**Chapter 11:**
The Rise of the Financial Matrix............................................209

**Chapter 12:**
Money, Media, Management, and Monopolies......................229

**Chapter 13:**
Free Banking and the Bitcoin Standard.................................247

**Study Questions**........................................................................264

**Acknowledgments**....................................................................270

**End Notes**.................................................................................272

# FOREWORD

*Only small secrets need protection. Big secrets
are protected by the public's incredulity.*
–Joseph Goebbels, Chief Propagandist for the Nazi Party

At a Kenyon College commencement, writer David Foster Wallace began his speech with the story of two young fish swimming by an older one. "Morning boys," said the older fish. "How's the water?" After swimming a bit further, one of the younger fish asked the other, "What the hell is water?" Economics, and specifically, money, can be such a difficult subject precisely because it's so ubiquitous, surrounding us constantly and involved in nearly every aspect of our lives. We earn money, save it, spend it, invest it, lose it, stress over it, talk about it, and deal with it in one way or another every single day. We are so close to it that we have great difficulty seeing it clearly. We interact with a large, complex, global financial system all the time and yet we have almost no idea what it is, where it came from, or what it really does to us. If it's true to any degree that past is prologue, then a logical step toward making meaningful predictions is to understand financial history as a way of seeing clearly the monolithic financial system we swim in today, which is, in essence, our "water." This is important, and no mere academic exercise, because money impacts each and every one of us in crucial ways. Further, its complexity is a feature, not a bug, intentionally designed to obscure what is really going on.

The book you hold in your hands is not a dry academic treatise, but rather an adventure story. In fact, I would say it's the greatest adventure story never told. It reveals the tale of perhaps the largest con ever perpetrated against humankind. It's a story so sweeping, so compelling, so amazing, that many will wonder why it's never been shared this clearly, if ever, before. As this captivating narrative unfolds, the reader will be presented with a litany of keen insights. I sincerely believe this book will take the Austrian school of economics forward a notch or two. It will unblur lines of distinction others have either missed or conflated. It is chock full of memorable illustrations and models that are not only useful, but in at least one instance, ground-breaking. It peels back the curtain on the greatest financial fraud that is hidden in plain sight by giving a well-researched, expansive history of how we got here. And it comes not from the compromised world of academia but from the brutally rugged, honest and clear-eyed world of the entrepreneur.

After carefully reading through the manuscript at least three times during it's development, I became increasingly struck with the realization that almost nobody else could have written it. Very few people have the background, experience, perspective, scholarship, time, and inclination to suffer through the research required to assemble something like this. Even more importantly, very few people are free enough to write honestly without a conflict of interest, having to instead be careful to kiss the ring of whomever is providing the grant, funding, or tenure that is usually required for writing a book in this genre. Refreshingly, this work instead springs out of the raw passion of an offended entrepreneur, who, once confronted with the realities of how the financial system bilks trillions of dollars from unsuspecting hard-working people, could not leave well enough alone.

Specifically, in these pages author Orrin Woodward coins the term "The Financial Matrix." He presents a breakthrough conceptualization of the Free Market Mechanism (FMM), which economists have struggled to make clear for centuries. He in-

# FOREWORD

troduces us to the warring factions of State Power money and Financial Power money, a critical distinction that is almost always missed. He shows how governments serve the bankers, and not the other way around. He convincingly demonstrates that the so-called Business Cycle is due to Fractional Reserve Banking (FRB), not just fiat money in general. Crucially, Woodward articulates two types of inflation and their differing effects on the economy. And finally, built upon a clear understanding of the system we swim in today and how it came to be, he gives a reasonable, intelligent, and hopeful solution to unwind the mess.

Not everyone, however, will be thrilled with this work. As Upton Sinclair wrote, "It is difficult to get someone to understand something when their salary depends on them not understanding it." As readers will discover, much of the confusion around our financial system today is perpetrated by the system itself, one that employs armies of experts to whitewash its operations. This book unabashedly assaults such strongholds and slays those sacred cows. And when ivory towers are threatened, one can count on the tusks coming out. But this book does not seek harmony, it seeks to expose the truth, and that is always a revolutionary act.

How refreshing it is, indeed, when something real and true cuts through the noise of negative fear-mongering on one side, and worshipful fawning on the other, and provides actual intelligent analysis and insight. For anyone with even a slight interest in their own financial future, this book is crucial. It is a brilliant mosaic of startling truths.

*Force and fraud are the two cardinal virtues in war.*
—*Thomas Hobbes*

# PREFACE

## What is the Financial Matrix?
*The truth sets you free after it ticks you off.*

The 1999 science fiction movie *The Matrix*[1] portrayed an artificial intelligence (AI) computer system tapping into human energy to control the world. While the storyline is fiction, its insights into human nature are not. The AI network achieved its power over the people with mass support. But why would people promote their own enslavement? After all, the AI system had declared war upon humanity. To answer this paradox, we will begin with the English philosopher Thomas Hobbes, who demonstrated that the nature of warfare included two cardinal virtues—force and fraud. Although force can overwhelm an opponent temporarily, fraud is the only way illegitimate gains can be permanently sustained. In fact, this is what the AI computers in the movie concluded. They didn't force people to follow their illicit and autocratic rule; instead, they *fraudulently seduced* them into it. The computers created an elaborate simulation that offered illusory freedoms to make slavery's reality more palatable to the victims. The key to successful long-term fraud is to alter human perceptions so that pleasant fictions are believed while living with unpleasant realities. Frauds, in effect, help people accept the unacceptable. *The Matrix* fooled people into believing a false perception (liberty and justice) instead of the true reality (energy slaves to power the system). Interestingly, once a perception is altered, the truth becomes difficult to believe. This is one of the key insights in *The Matrix* movie—that most people prefer comfortable lies over uncomfortable truths.

The term "Financial Matrix," which will be used throughout this book, was coined in honor of this insight. There really is a system that runs the world; the difference from the movie is that the source of oppression is the financial system, not artificial intelligence. Indeed, the more I studied the global financial system, the more shocking the parallels became between the movie and reality. For instance, both matrices create an illusion that people are free and the system is just, even though the global Financial Matrix controls people by siphoning wealth and the global AI system in the movie controls people by siphoning energy. The Financial Matrix is the real system of control that enslaves billions of people. It does this by lending fake money to be paid back by real labor, all while making us believe that we are free. It's time to close the chasm between perception and reality.

Several scenes from *The Matrix* speak directly to the Financial Matrix. For example, Morpheus warned Neo about exposing the truth too fast to people still in the system:

That system is our enemy. But when you're inside, you look around; what do you see? Businessmen, teachers, lawyers, carpenters. The very minds of the people we are trying to save. But until we do, these people are still a part of that system…not ready to be unplugged. And many of them are so inured, so hopelessly dependent on the system that they will fight to protect it.

Just like the movie, the Financial Matrix thrives upon fraud backed by force. It has, as Morpheus told Neo:

*Pulled the wool over the people's eyes, blinding them to the truth…That you are a slave, Neo. Like everyone else, you were born into bondage, born into a prison that you cannot smell or taste or touch. A prison…for your mind…Unfortunately, no one can be…told what the [Financial] Matrix is…You have to see it for yourself.*[2]

# PREFACE

I now place two pills in front of you, dear reader: take the blue pill and remain asleep in the Financial Matrix, or take the red pill and awaken to the truth, "no matter how deep the rabbit hole goes." Neo chose the red pill and learned the uncomfortable truths that set him free. Remember, avoiding the truth does not change it. The Financial Matrix has a plan to control your future, just like John Perkins, author of *Confessions of an Economic Hit Man*, described its plans to control developing nations' futures:

*This (financial) empire, unlike any other in the history of the world, has been built primarily through economic manipulation, through cheating, through fraud, through seducing people into our way of life, through economic hit men...My real job...was giving loans to other countries, huge loans, much bigger than they could possibly repay...So we make this loan, most of it comes back to the United States (banks), the country is left with a lot of debt plus interest, and they basically become our servants, our slaves.*[3]

It's time to expose the plunderous nature of our current financial system. This truth will either humble power, or power will crush truth. The truth is that the Financial Matrix is a global system of debt control, an insidious parasite feeding upon the world's economic system, that relies upon ignorance and apathy in order to increase its power and profits. This book will cure ignorance, and together we must address apathy, as Edmund Burke allegedly observed: "All that is necessary for the triumph of evil is that good men [and women] do nothing."[4] It's time to do something, and it starts by shining light upon this evil. We do not fight evil with evil, for if we become evil to defeat evil, then we haven't truly defeated evil but rather have been defeated by it. Moreover, we cannot beat something with nothing. Thus, we must follow Buckminster Fuller's advice: "You never change things by fighting the existing reality. In order to change something, you need to build a new model that makes the existing one obsolete."[5] It's time to build a better money model to replace the Financial Matrix, an insidious global money system that is the most pervasive system of tyranny ever created to enslave humanity. It's time for people to awaken to the true peril by banishing both ignorance and apathy; it's time to restore an honorable money and banking system; and finally, it's time to let freedom ring again throughout the world.

*This would be a much better world if more married couples were as deeply in love as they are in debt.*
—Earl Wilson

# INTRODUCTION

**Our Personal Story**
*The higher we climbed, the more we saw.*

"Orrin, you promised me." These words spoken to me over thirty years ago still, to this day, stir my soul. My lovely bride had just called me out. And, despite my rationalizations, I knew she was right. I had promised Laurie she could be a stay-at-home mom when we started having children, but the reason I was hesitating was because we could barely pay our bills with both of us working. How in the world were we going to survive on just one income, especially with baby expenses added in? The financial fear was paralyzing. How could I keep my promise to Laurie while still remaining financially solvent?

Laurie's boldness exposed the moral issue. I knew I had made her a promise, but I couldn't imagine her coming home from work under our current financial circumstances. Of course, I tried to be a good husband and ignore the growing angst so I could celebrate with Laurie, but as the due date drew closer, my fears only expanded. On one hand, my parents taught me to keep my word, and I could not deny I had given Laurie my word. On the other hand, however, my parents taught me to pay my bills, and I could not deny that our finances were in shambles. Talk about being stuck between a rock and a hard place! Even with both of us working (me as an engineer and Laurie as an accountant), we had $32,000 of debt outside of our mortgage. And it wasn't like we were living way above our means in our 982-square-foot house and high-mileage used cars.

I didn't see a way to keep my word to Laurie and, at the same time, remain fiscally above water. Thus, self-deception took over, as I convinced myself that Laurie loved her accounting job too much to think about quitting it. The crazy thing was that I told that story so many times that I believed it. Fortunately, my lovely bride terminated my delusions when, one night, just before I was leaving for my MBA class, she asked when she should put in her two weeks' notice. I was stunned, but I repeated my well-rehearsed story that our current financial situation made it impossible at this time. She listened intently, shook her head, and said, "Orrin, you promised me." Ugh. Laurie's truth bomb was really discombobulating! I attempted to deflect its impact by suggesting a delayed implementation plan. Again, Laurie listened and shook her head, repeating, "Orrin, you promised me." Ah! This pesky fact was really getting annoying! Laurie is one wise lady, and she knew her facts would eventually trump my rationalizations. I mumbled the story one more time, but even I wasn't buying it anymore. Laurie waited for me to finish, looking deeply into my eyes and directly into my soul, before saying, "But Orrin, you promised me." That was it—game, set, and match to Laurie Woodward. Painful though it was, the truth Laurie proclaimed was about to set us free!

Looking back, I now realize Laurie had more faith in us than I did, and her faith was what strengthened mine. Yes, the financial challenge remained, but the moral one was removed. I made a promise to Laurie, and I intended to keep it. While driving to class that night, I asked a lot of questions, which led to us taking a new financial journey that ultimately, many years later, made this book a reality. Where did we go wrong financially? Were we the only couple being broken on the financial wheel? Why did it seem that we served money more than it served us? And finally, how would we break out from our present financial prison? Although our parents taught us to work hard, get good grades at

## INTRODUCTION

good schools, and enter well-paying professions, it wasn't working financially. After all, if results were the key to success, then the four US patents, a national technical benchmarking award, and promotion to senior engineer at age of twenty-five should have done the trick. Also, even my 19 percent raise (when the average that year was 3 percent), wasn't enough, for we simply could not afford to lose Laurie's salary and still pay our bills.

Because Laurie was for sure coming home, we began with the end in mind and created a new financial path to provide for our family without her income. This would require finding new mentors who achieved better financial results and learning the principles they used to achieve them. Finally, I believed the same systematic mindset I had applied to build manufacturing systems to produce fuel pumps could also be used to build leadership systems to produce leaders. "In God we trust; all others must have data" was no longer just my engineering mantra, but it became the standard operating procedure for our financial futures. From now on, Laurie and I would not follow the herd, for we were going to live the life we always wanted, and it began by taking the road less traveled.

Success is like walking through a minefield, and the key to its navigation is to learn from experience, preferably someone else's. We didn't have the time or money to repeat mistakes others had made, so we consumed the best leadership and financial principles we could find and combined them with my systems training so that we could learn faster. Success is hard even with proven principles, but it's practically impossible without them. As John Wayne stated, "Life is tough, even tougher when you're stupid." Laurie and I shot for the moon by living below our means, and pouring everything extra into personal, professional, and business development. For the next five years, even though we worked very hard, we still failed more than we succeeded. However, as Vince Lombardi emphasized, "The harder you work, the harder it is to surrender," and we knew that by working hard and smart, we were too invested to ever surrender.

Finally, in the sixth year of our entrepreneurial journey, we struck gold. Sure, we had dialed in our financial, leadership, and business systems, but the hand of God was evident throughout our leadership community. Whereas when our financial journey began, nobody would have cared to listen to a thing we had to say, by this point we were filling basketball arenas with committed community members. Perhaps Proverbs 16:9 describes our journey best: "A man's heart plans his way, but the LORD directs his steps," and we were stepping into an entirely new financial peer group. Over the next seven years, Laurie and I built income streams that many months surpassed seven figures. In the process, we purchased dream estates in Michigan and Florida and experienced the lifestyle of the rich and famous, jet-setting around the globe for business and pleasure. This lifestyle is what introduced us to billionaires, top bankers, business CEOs, members of Congress, presidential advisors, well-known speakers, and top religious leaders. It was our discussions and relationships with them that helped us piece together the truth. I still cannot believe that two naive middle-class kids, without any previous connections, who just a few years before couldn't rub two nickels together, obtained inside access to American power centers. I now recognize that God provided us with wealth beyond our imaginations to help us see the elites' financial fabrications.

We built wealth by teaching entrepreneurs how to build businesses and live the American Dream. The only way we knew how to do that was by satisfying customers in the free market system. However, when the wealth doors opened to us, we discovered there is one set of rules for the people and another set for the elites. Whereas people in the free market must practice the Golden Rule, "Do unto others as you would have them do unto you," to achieve success by serving others, the elites practice the

## INTRODUCTION

Power Rule, "He who has the gold makes the rules," to achieve bigger 'success' by plundering others. In short, Laurie and I discovered we were in the wrong place with the wrong people who followed wrong philosophies. Although we had made it to the top by applying Golden Rule principles, we discovered the elite's application of Power Rule principles like those practiced in the movie *The Firm*; except it wasn't a firm, but an international Financial Matrix that demanded to be served.

At first, we laughed it off, assuming it was mere idle boasting, but the more we listened, the more convinced we became that these people were not fooling around. It became readily apparent that a Power Rule agenda controlled the global political and economic systems, and the Golden Rule was just perception to cover the Power Rule reality. And once privy to the specific billionaire Power Rule plans in our field, we not only refused to go along, but even worse (in their eyes), suggested Golden Rule fixes if they expected us to continue working with them. Of course, the billionaires were not amused, and it took nearly three years and fifty million dollars to extricate ourselves from their circle.

Somehow, by God's grace, Laurie and I, and most of our world-class leadership community, remained together and united. Although we certainly were not naive kids anymore and now saw the world with eyes wide open, the ordeal didn't make us bitter. Instead, it provided the motivation to make things better. We knew the Golden Rule free market system was the only path forward to liberty and justice, but we also now knew the elites preferred Power Rule plunder because it's easier and more lucrative. We vowed to learn precisely how the elites used Power Rule philosophies to achieve their control over the political and economic systems. Fortunately, the clues collected from our many conversations with people in positions of power, some with regular Oval Office access, all helped jump-start our research. Now, more than fifteen years later, we have put together how the international Financial Matrix achieved global hegemony over the political and economic systems worldwide. The people deserve to know the truth, and what they do with the truth will determine their destiny.

To God be all the glory, for without Him directing our steps, this book would not have been possible. He provided Golden Rule mentors that inspired us to pursue financial freedom and then exposed us to Power Rule realities to urge us to learn the rest of the story. Finally, because we were financially free, I was blessed with the time necessary to research, think, and eventually write this book. The goal is to share what the Financial Matrix is, why it was created, and how it works, culminating with a plan to restore liberty and justice for all. Our money system is fraudulent, a potent mixture of nonsense, half-truths, and outright lies, designed to plunder the people so the elites can enjoy absolute profits and total power. My prayer is that when enough people learn the truth, they will no longer tolerate subjugation to the Financial Matrix, and as a result, future generations will experience liberty and justice for all.

*Rather go to bed supperless, than rise in debt.*
—Benjamin Franklin

# –1–

## The Financial Matrix Debt Explosion
*You will know them by their fruit.*

Over the years I've listened to speakers and read books that referred to the "Boiling Frog" syndrome, an urban legend describing how a frog can be slowly boiled alive. Of course, if you try to throw a frog into a pot of boiling water, it will immediately jump out. However, if placed into lukewarm water with the temperature raised slowly over time, the frog will not perceive the danger, and by the time it does, it will have lost its strength to jump out and will boil to death. I cannot imagine a better analogy for what has occurred in America in the last fifty years. If the Financial Matrix had loaded today's astronomical debt on top of every American all at once, the people would never have let it stand. There would have been public protests and political demands, and the Financial Matrix would have received its waking papers. Instead, the debt temperature slowly increased each year, compounding a little here, and then a little there until the reality set in that America has forty-six times as much debt (two trillion to over ninety-three trillion dollars) in just over fifty years. Like the boiling frog, Americans are boiling in debt, and pathetically not even trying to jump out. The rest of this chapter spells out how, in practically every economic area, the Financial Matrix has annually increased debts until we can no longer resist and have begun to boil.

While America may be leading the debt explosion, the world is following in our wake. In 2020, according to the IMF Database, world debt "observed the largest one-year debt surge since World

War II, with global debt rising to $226 trillion as the world was hit by a global health crisis and a deep recession...Global debt rose by 28 percentage points to 256 percent of GDP."[1] Although world debt is gigantic, the growth in America's debt is even more alarming. As mentioned above, it has increased from two trillion to over ninety-three trillion dollars since 1971! While debt used to be a small part of the modern economy, it now *is* the economy. What happened in 1971 that caused such an avalanche of debt? The short answer is that the Financial Matrix happened. In 1971, the Federal Reserve central bank achieved its dream: the legal permission to commit monetary fraud by creating unlimited amounts of money out of thin air. Since that time, the Federal Reserve has created dollars to lend to national central banks, who then lend them to the nation's banks, and these banks then lend them to governments, businesses, and households. In other words, since 1971 the banks have created money out of thin air, loaned it to us, and we labor to pay it back.

No wonder debt is snowballing around the globe as the Financial Matrix gets wealthy beyond measure and exploits its outrageously advantageous position. Consider a family given exclusive rights to use Monopoly game money as real money to loan to anyone, anywhere in the world, and make interest in real money on those loans. We wouldn't be shocked to learn that they were extremely wealthy fifty years later, nor would it be surprising that the world had a lot more Monopoly money debt as a result. None of us would play under those rules, and yet for over fifty years, we have lived in a world economy playing precisely such a game. In upcoming chapters, we will cover how the Financial Matrix achieved this staggering economic power, but in this chapter we will narrow in on how this debt is impacting people like you and me—specifically how the exponential increase in debt is destroying our opportunities, liberties, and global justice.

# THE FINANCIAL MATRIX DEBT EXPLOSION

Creating money out of thin air is fraud. It's called counterfeiting for us and is an imprisonable offense. However, the Financial Matrix is legally permitted to do this worldwide. The Financial Matrix is a complex worldwide network of private central banks and big money interests that are allowed to create and loan money to the world. This outlandish sanction to create and lend endless amounts of money not only produces unlimited profits but also unlimited power because, as the Bible explained, "The borrower is slave to the lender." This means that when we are indebted, we are essentially indentured—the fruit of our labor belongs to someone else. At the same time, the lender has gained an unrestricted upper hand. Private fiat money (meaning money created out of nothing and given value by mere dictate) has thereby given the Financial Matrix unrestrained might over nations, corporations, and households. Ezra Pound recognized this when he noted, "Wars in old times were made to get slaves. The modern implement of imposing slavery is debt."[2] Americans are now debt slaves, and the world is following our lead.

**USD RELATIVE PURCHASING POWER (1913-2019)**

Shaded areas indicate U.S. recessions    Source: U.S. Bureau of Labor Statistics    fred.stlouisfed.org

## Inflation: Artificially Expanding the Money Supply

We will discuss inflation in more detail in upcoming chapters, but this fraudulent expansion of the money supply benefits the Financial Matrix while plundering everyone else. As the money supply increases, the value (or purchasing power) of the dollars already in circulation falls, as more dollars are fighting for the same amount of goods. This hurts the poor and middle class the most. Since 1971, the purchasing power of the American dollar has decreased by 98 percent. That is not a typo! A person holding one hundred dollars today would have the equivalent purchasing power of two dollars in 1971. This is a hidden theft of every person's wealth.

**Inflation and Wealth Inequalities**

The Financial Matrix has achieved complete control over the global economy through lending out counterfeit money. In the most lopsided special deal ever created, the Financial Matrix receives compound interest on counterfeit money from practically every nation, company, and person worldwide. Anyone on fixed incomes or those who are not connected to the financial elites are on the outskirts. The Financial Matrix monetary inflation creates artificial winners and losers, and perpetual inflation creates big gains for the insiders and big losses for everyone else. Economist Jonathan Newman aptly described how monetary expansion creates an unfair playing field through what is known as the Cantillon Effect:

*Murray Rothbard called Richard Cantillon the "father of modern economics." One of Cantillon's greatest insights involved the uneven effects of monetary expansion. New money enters the economy at a particular point—the first spender of new money acquires goods from the market, and those sellers may now use the money to increase their demands for goods, and so on. The money ripples out from its origin, providing real benefits to those closest to the center. As the new money is spent, prices rise, meaning those whose incomes rise later in this spending chain (or never) are the "losers" in this process.*[3]

# THE FINANCIAL MATRIX DEBT EXPLOSION

Newman shared a chart that tracked the growth of bank credit and the total net worth of the top 1 percent, which confirmed that all the benefits from the monetary expansions are flowing to the financial elites and their cronies. The Financial Matrix has created a legalized counterfeiting and credit expansion system that flows immense benefits to the financial elites, subsidized by the rest of us. As the total bank credits (debt to the people) expand, so too does the wealth of the elites on a nearly one-to-one basis.

## TOP 1% WEALTH COINCIDES WITH MONEY CREATION

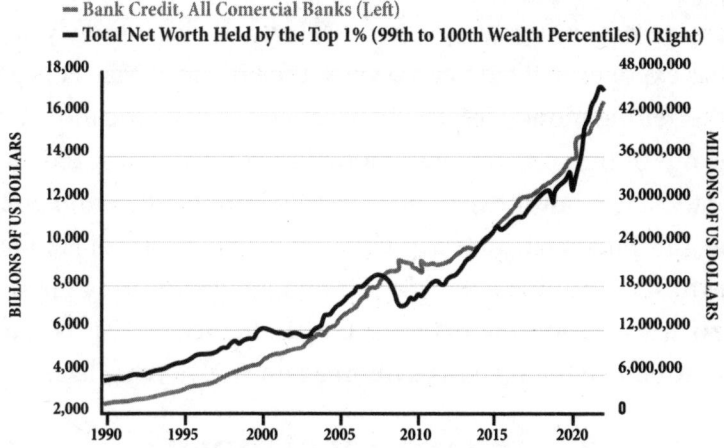

Source: Board of Governors of the Federal Reserve System (US)

## Inflation Protects the Financial Matrix

The right to fraudulently counterfeit money, however, is about more than just profits for the Financial Matrix. After all, in any economic downturn, the Financial Matrix knows that it can counterfeit any amount of money necessary to rescue the big banks and big businesses it owns. The "too big to fail" entities, in other words, are protected from economic consequences while the rest of the economy suffers. The Financial Matrix enjoys private profits during economic booms and then socializes the losses during economic busts. Imagine running a business where, any time you are short of cash, you can simply counterfeit more on command. It doesn't take an economic genius to understand that this is an unfair special deal for the few at the expense of the many. For instance, during the 2008–2009 Great Financial Crisis and later during the COVID-19 shutdowns, the Financial Matrix created trillions of counterfeit dollars to rescue the banking system from imminent collapse. The graphic below reveals how stable the base money supply was when it was based upon precious metal money, for it was essentially a flatline from ancient Egyptian times until the 1960's, since the above-ground total gold supply only increases at approximately 2 percent per year or less. However, as the graphic displays, the base money supply has exponentially increased since the Financial Matrix began counterfeiting money (replacing precious metal as the monetary base) out of thin air. The base money supply has expanded consistently since, but it exploded upwards in both 2008 and 2020, when the Financial Matrix purchased 'toxic assets' of dubious value to save the global banking system. Evidently, the Financial Matrix learned nothing from the Great Financial Crisis because it had to rescue the banking system again twelve years later.

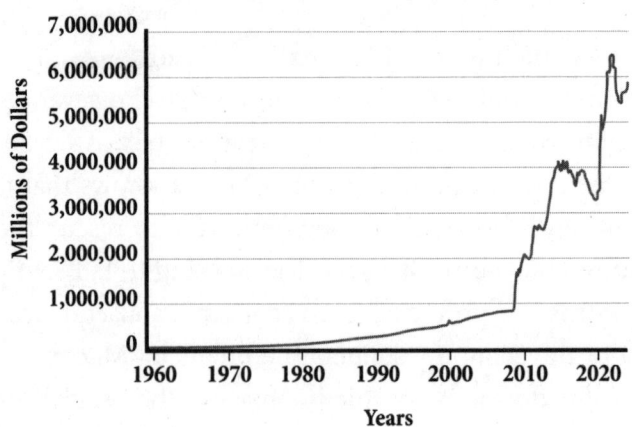

## Inflation and Flatline Income

The Financial Matrix has plundered the wealth of all who are not in on their scam, which the money supply chart reveals. Although the world's total gold supply accumulated for over four thousand years, by 1960 the total amount barely made it onto the graphic. However, since the birth of the Financial Matrix's global counterfeiting operation, the base money supply has fraudulently increased nearly six million times beyond the gold supply! The Financial Matrix is a legalized global counterfeiting outfit that has turned the people of the world into capital subjects for life. Interestingly, this is the very thing that President Abraham Lincoln warned about in his 1861 Annual Message to Congress:

*There is not of necessity any such thing as the free hired laborer being fixed to that condition for life. Many independent men everywhere in these States a few years back in their lives were hired laborers. The prudent, penniless beginner in the world labors for wages awhile, saves a surplus with which to buy tools or land for himself, then labors on his own account another while, and at length hires another new beginner to help him. This is the just and generous and prosperous system which opens the way to all, gives hope to all, and consequent energy and progress and improvement of condition to all. . . Let them beware of surrendering a political power which they already possess, and which if surrendered will surely be used to close the door of advancement against such as they and to fix new disabilities and burdens upon them till all of liberty shall be lost.*[4]

The Financial Matrix has fulfilled President Lincoln's prophecy by plundering the people's productivity gains, closing the door to advancement for billions of people worldwide. Indeed, the Pew Research graphic is the smoking gun that reveals the Financial Matrix's crime against humanity. As we discussed, 1971 was the coming-of-age party of the Financial Matrix, when the global banking cartel was given the legal right to create counterfeit money not backed by anything but government force. In the free market system, as productivity levels increase, so too do the wages of the people. And before 1971, the Pew Graphic shows that the people were rewarded as their productivity increased. However, after 1971, even though productivity continued to increase at about the same rate, workers no longer received commensurate wage increases. The Financial Matrix, in other words, is an insidious system that inflates the money supply for profits and protection, paid for by plundering the increases in the people's productivity.

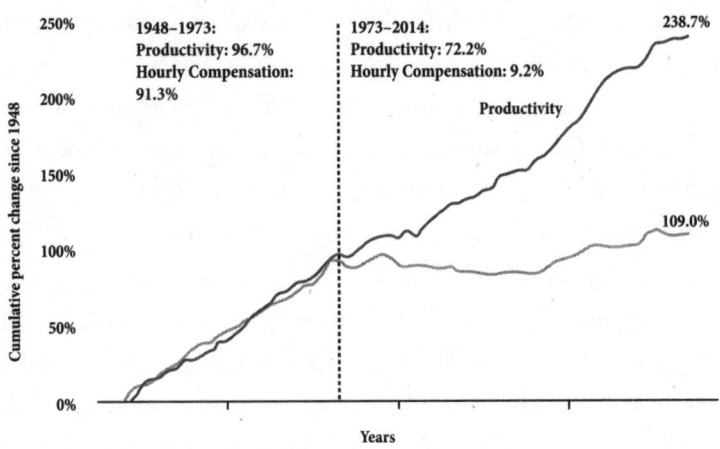

Note: Data are for average hourly compensation of production/nonsupervisory workers in the private sector and net productivity of the total economy. "Net Productivity" is the growth of output of goods and services minus depreciation per hour worked.

Source: Pew Research Center

### American Debt Data

Let's examine American debt data because it is readily available, understanding that most other nations have similar trends. According to 2022 Statista.com, America's total debts are $93.5

# THE FINANCIAL MATRIX DEBT EXPLOSION

trillion, which is broken down into three main categories: government, business, and household. A trillion is a very large number—a million times a million. There are many illustrations people have come up with to attempt to explain just how big a trillion dollars is. Consider this one: You would have to burn through $31.71 per second for a full year to reach one billion dollars, and then continue to squander money at this rate for another one thousand years before you would spend one trillion dollars! Americans, in other words, are consuming a ton of debt. The $93.5 trillion in total American debts, at just 6 percent interest, means $5.5 trillion in annual interest payments. This is real money that has to be paid to real bond holders and lenders. It is not some abstract number that doesn't mean anything. This figure represents over twice what the IRS collects in taxes each year. Moreover, this $5.5 trillion only services the interest and doesn't touch the principal. Effectively the Financial Matrix has trapped the American economy (and the world's) in a monetary vise and tightens it every year. America is like Mike Campbell in Ernest Hemingway's novel *The Sun Also Rises*, who was asked, "How did you go bankrupt?" and answered, "Two ways, gradually and then suddenly."[5]

The next graphic displays how the Financial Matrix has leveraged fiat debt-money to gain profit and power over governments, corporations, and people worldwide. *The Matrix* movie illustrated how appearances are just as important as reality for most people, and as long as people can look successful, apparently most will tolerate debt-slavery. These debts, however, must be paid by human productivity siphoned off from every household—a problem that grows worse over time. If debt has increased forty-six times in just over fifty years, this means the amount of production being siphoned into the Financial Matrix has also increased approximately forty-six times. And as the graphic shows, the increased burden of payments for government debts, business debts, and household debts ultimately lands on the people themselves. That's because it's the people who pay higher taxes to fund indebted governments, higher prices to fund indebted corporations, and higher monthly payments to fund their own indebted households.

## FINANCIAL MATRIX CASHFLOW

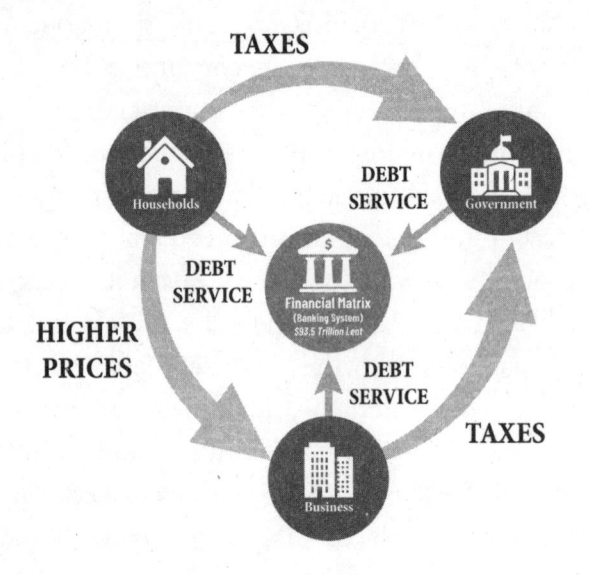

*Diagram: Cashflow between Households, Government, and Business, all connected to the Financial Matrix (Banking System) $93.5 Trillion Lent, with flows labeled TAXES, DEBT SERVICE, and HIGHER PRICES.*

So much for the flow of funds. Now let's consider the structure. The Financial Matrix is at the top of a power pyramid, followed by governments and corporations they own. The bottom of the pyramid is the people who, of course, must labor to make enough money to buy from the Financial Matrix corporations, pay taxes to the Financial Matrix governments, and pay debts owed to Financial Matrix banks. This is the new American dream, now a nightmare, thanks to unlimited debt-money first permitted in 1971.

# THE FINANCIAL MATRIX

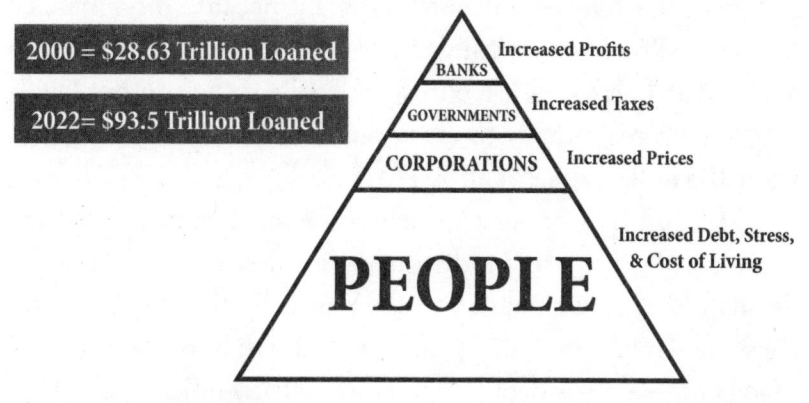

2000 = $28.63 Trillion Loaned

2022 = $93.5 Trillion Loaned

BANKS — Increased Profits
GOVERNMENTS — Increased Taxes
CORPORATIONS — Increased Prices
PEOPLE — Increased Debt, Stress, & Cost of Living

**The Financial Matrix**

The Financial Matrix creates fiat money for little cost, but enjoys high profits. As the philosopher Thomas Hobbes observed, the two cardinal virtues of war are force and fraud. The Financial Matrix essentially declared economic war upon the world by practicing *private fraud* backed by *public force*. And since money is essential to the modern economy, and every nation, company, and individual worldwide must obtain this money from the Financial Matrix, there is no question who won the economic war. The Financial Matrix dictates the terms that the borrowers must follow or risk defaulting on their loans. When individuals default, the force side of the Financial Matrix's war kicks in. The defaulter, by law, loses the previous payments submitted plus the original asset. Therefore the reality is that anything 'owned' with debt is not truly owned because bankers can take it away until it is paid for in full. Although the Financial Matrix wants debtors to believe they are owners (so they will feel free and prosperous), if a payment is missed, debtors soon learn who truly owns the asset. The Financial Matrix has the full support of the laws of government to enforce debtor compliance, with defaulters receiving downgraded credit ratings, and repeat offenders running the risk of financial excommunication. A fair arrangement would be one in which both parties have skin-in-the-game. The current money system is not only unfair but fraudulent because the Financial Matrix is allowed to lawfully create fake or unearned money to lend, while borrowers are punished legally if they do not legitimately earn real money to repay them. So one side has no risk, while the other carries it all.

To see just how hungry for debt these three entities—government, corporations, and individuals—are, let's dig into just a few details of how they operate to their own detriment. As we review each area impacted by debt, we will see how the Financial Matrix turns up the debt temperature little by little in each area, but when all areas are combined, the boiling water has cooked America's liberty and justice. And with every increase in debt, the Financial Matrix strengthens its grip and control over everything in the boiling water.

**Government Debts**

Governments do not earn money, but they do spend it profusely. Consequently, when government debt grows, a steady stream of tax revenue from the people must be secured in order to service it. In America, this tax load includes federal income tax, Social Security, sales tax, state income tax, property tax, and local taxes, as well as a bewildering list of fees and licenses that cause the average family to work until after July 4th (ironically known as "Independence Day") to earn enough to cover their complete tax burden before they get to keep the first dollar for their own needs.

The magnitude of this tax load is bad enough on its own. But there is more. The Financial Matrix also ensures governments are less accountable even as they grow more powerful. Borrowing allows the government to act without the people's consent because, unlike tax increases, which require the passing of laws by elected officials, borrowing can be done entirely without restraint. To reiterate: taxes, as described above, are already high. But that is not the only stream of input the government has at its disposal to feed its spending addiction. The government can simply borrow the funds it needs beyond its tax revenues and leave future generations responsible for the bill of the burden of such debt and its interest.

**Business Debts**

Businesses have also fallen in love with debt. Instead of the tried-and-true profitable method of reinvesting long-term earnings, debt (and the pressure for publicly traded companies to focus on their stock price) has forced businesses to live for today. This has created a highly unstable environment wherein businesses must grow sales now to service growing debts. And when debt overwhelms even giant entities, the company becomes a debt zombie—one of the walking dead—that survives by government handouts. Think about how absurd it was for so many businesses with billions of dollars in annual revenues to need COVID-19 bailout money within weeks of the government-enforced shutdown. How do billion dollar companies exist without any money in reserve? This is our new debt reality. Even worse, this business debt is ultimately paid by the people through the resulting higher prices and/or inferior products. Debts and taxes incurred by businesses, in other words, result in higher prices paid by consumers, period. This makes the people fully responsible for business debt, along with government debt discussed above. Now we can see why this explosion in debt is so disastrous to everyday people's living standards, for they must pay the debts for both debt-addicted governments and businesses.

### Total Personal Debts

Finally, in addition to having to carry the burden of both government and corporate debts, consumers must also pay their own debts. According to *The Ascent*[6] (average American debt is up in nearly every category compared to 2020. In late 2022, total household debts (not even including student and medical) surpassed $17 trillion, a $2.5 trillion increase since 2020.

### American statistics organized by debt category are:
- Average mortgage debt: $236,443
- Average credit card debt: $5,733 (Many households have multiple cards.)
- Average home equity loan: $41,045
- Average outstanding student loan balance: $37,650 (Many households have multiple members with loans.)
- Average auto loan debt: $22,612 (Many households have multiple cars.)

By combining the average monthly costs for the household mortgage, cars, home equities, credit cards, and student loans, the typical American household today is paying interest on nearly $350,000 of total debt. However, that same American household only earns $105,000 annually, which means debts are over three times larger than average income. While interest rates can range anywhere from 5 percent to 25 percent, even choosing a conservative average rate of 7 percent results in over $2,000 per month to service household debts.

As debts increase, the financial gerbil wheel, so to speak, speeds up. First, the $2000 drain on financial resources prohibits opportunities to move ahead by investing. Second, debt is like walking on thin ice, for if the household income diminishes in any way (through lost jobs, health troubles, or other financial challenges), the ice cracks and the household begins drowning in debt. To the point, 60 percent of US bankruptcies are caused by unforeseen medical issues that cut incomes due to lost work hours, paired with medical expenses averaging around $10,000. The Financial Matrix has siphoned, through debt, the necessary reserves families need to protect themselves when unforeseen events arise. To understand just how fast household debt is expanding, let's take a quick look at each area.

**Mortgage Debts**

Since the beginning of 2022, the average monthly mortgage payment has doubled from around $1,500 to almost $3,000 because the thirty year mortgage rate has increased from 3 percent to over 7 percent.[7] We are talking about twice the payment for the same size house! How did this happen? The Federal Reserve jacked up interest rates to address the inflation caused by the creation of so many fraudulent dollars during COVID-19, and of course, the American households are the ones who pay for it.

**Credit Card Debts**

According to the New York Federal Reserve, Americans' total credit card balance is $1.079 trillion in the third quarter of 2023.[8]

**TOTAL OUTSTANDING CREDIT CARD BALANCES**

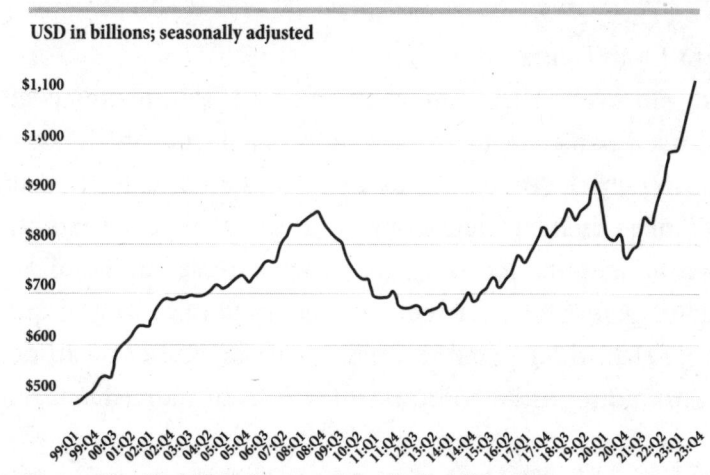

USD in billions; seasonally adjusted

Source: New York FED Consumer Credit Panel/Equifax

That's another increase upon the record $1.031 trillion from the second quarter of 2023, leaving the total balance the highest since the Fed began tracking it in 1999. Credit card balances spiral upward when people pay the minimum on their statement because of unexpected expenses or when the overall debt burden no longer allows payments toward the principal and interest is all that can be paid. According to a consumer protection official, Nessa Feddis:

*The minimum is really useful if people are a little short of income in a particular month—for example, when they're in between jobs or they recently had a large expense. But it's not something that should be routine. In part, that's because the minimum is usually so low that it just barely exceeds the interest charges that accrue each month on your balance. When you're just paying the minimum, it could take years—in some cases, decades—to pay off your full balance. Paying only the minimum could also send up red flags to other lenders, suggesting that you struggle to repay debts.*[9]

Paying the minimum payments is now punishing families even more when we consider that the average credit card interest rate has increased from 12 percent in 2015 to 19 percent in 2023.

**Student Loan Debts**

A recent Wells Fargo study discovered that millennials and Gen Z need half their total income to pay debts, which is why, as a University of Arizona study revealed, half of college graduates still need financial help from family members two years after completing school. Increasing debt is what caused millennials to be the first generation in American history to have a lower quality of life than their parents. Total American student loan debt is an astounding $1.76 trillion, which is even more than credit cards, and continues to climb as new borrowers enter college. Perhaps the worst aspect of student loans is the fact that they cannot be relieved even when someone files for bankruptcy. Student loans are exempt from such protections. Thus, as total student loan debt is increasing at nearly 28 percent per year since the turn of the 21st century, more and more students are taking on a permanent commitment, one that might take them the rest of their lives to pay. In a 1987 *New York Times* op-ed,[10] then Secretary of Education William Bennett described why student loan debt began its exponential rise, writing, "If anything, increases in financial aid in recent years have enabled colleges and universities blithely to raise their tuitions, confident that Federal loan subsidies would help cushion the increase. Federal student aid policies do not cause college price inflation, but there is little doubt that they help make it possible." Bennet's analysis back then has been proven true today. This is another example of the Law of Unintended Consequences, wherein a government intervention is meant to help students but actually hurts them by indebting them into the Financial Matrix even before they have graduated. For instance, Al Lord, the mastermind behind Sallie Mae's (the government sponsored for-profit entity) meteoric rise and fall, admitted in a Wall Street Journal article that colleges raised tuition because they knew students could access student loans secured by Sally Mae. Shockingly, according to writer Mark J. Drozdowski:

*Not only were universities conspirators in this scheme, but many also directly profited from Sallie Mae's soaring stock prices. Early investors in Sallie Mae included Harvard, Yale, Princeton, MIT, Notre Dame, Stanford, and Wellesley College, among others. A 1980 Harvard Crimson article noted that Harvard and Brown University ranked among the five largest shareholders of Sallie Mae stock at the time. These universities essentially became part of Sal-*

lie Mae's sales force, notes the Wall Street Journal article. *And for good reason: The more they raised tuition, the more loans students absorbed. More loans meant more fees, interest, and commissions for Sallie Mae, driving up the company's stock and directly benefiting shareholders, including universities themselves.*[11]

Universities win, bankers win, and Sally Mae wins, while students take it on the chin. This is yet another example of how the Financial Matrix uses the state to enforce its debt claims, in this case, for life. Of course, this is a massive conflict of interest, but since the foxes run the hen house, student debts continue to rise.

**Car Loans**

Auto loan rates were greatly affected by the COVID-19 pandemic and its impact upon the U.S. economy. According to the St. Louis Fed,[12] since 2020, the nation's auto-loan balance jumped 28 percent and now totals more than $1.5 trillion, which makes it the fastest-growing type of consumer debt in the U.S. Although the federal government may help people qualify for loans, the people still have to pay them. And with car loans increasing even faster than student loans and credit cards, the growing debt burden on those same American families is growing unbearable.

Now that we have discovered how debt has damaged prosperity, let's see how it has impacted peace of mind. Debt has more than just financial ramifications.

**Debt Angst or Denial**

Angst is defined as a feeling of deep anxiety or dread, typically an unfocused one about the human condition or the state of the world in general. When someone is drowning in debt, it should not be surprising that what follows is anxiety, dread, and an inability to focus. Interestingly, angst can build through debt-denial. Even though, unlike the American government, we may avoid thinking about debt, we cannot avoid its consequences. We simply cannot spend more than we make for long, though many try. Compulsive spenders may ignore the bottom line by rejecting self-discipline, but this only ensures they experience outside discipline, including credit denials, foreclosures, legal actions, and harassing phone calls from debt collectors.

**Stress**

The opposite of denial is stress, where we try to face the issue without a plan. We should certainly think through our finances, but once we have the plan in place, we should then use all our mental energy to execute the plan, not beat ourselves up for past financial sins. Unfortunately, when stress is not handled properly, it takes its toll on our most important relationships. For example, in 2023 CNBC[13] reported that 54 percent of divorced Americans claimed that debt was one of the trigger points for their divorce because it caused "increased stress and tension within the relationship" that ultimately led to divorce. When we consider that the National Institute of Mental Health estimates that forty million Americans suffer from anxiety and that financial worries are one of the leading catalysts, it's clear that increasing debt is not just about financial well-being. In fact, stress from debt can become chronic if not handled properly, which in turn increases potential drug or alcohol use to cope with it. Worse, as stress builds, life can become so painful that, according to a study published in 2021 by the *American Journal of Epidemiology*, people are twenty times more likely to make an attempt on their lives. And if not to such extremes, stress can at least take a toll on our physical health.

**Anger**

For many people, as debt increases, so does anger. In medical circles, this phenomenon is called Debt-Anger Syndrome. Instead of denying or stressing about debts, some people get mad. They begin by hating the creditors who continually send them bills and then transfer that emotion to the mailman who delivers them. Next, the anger is passed on to the boss, who doesn't pay a high enough wage, or to spouses who don't work enough. These debt-angry folks can also blame their kids, who never seem to have enough and don't stop asking for money. Anger can cause all kinds of issues, for it not only ruins relationships, but the physiological effects can lead to migraines, heart disease, and even reduced resistance to infections.

**Mental Depression**

Because none of these (denial, stress, anxiety, and anger) resolve the underlying issue, as bills continue to stack up, hope is finally lost and depression results. A 2020 Kaiser Family Foundation Health Tracking Poll found that households with income or job loss experienced at least one adverse mental health effect.[14] These included difficulty sleeping or eating, increases in alcohol consumption or substance use, and worsening chronic conditions. There is no such thing as hopeless situations, but there can be hopeless people *in* situations. Depression can exacerbate debt issues because depressed people seek to alleviate stress by doing activities that further increase debt, such as going on shopping sprees or taking vacations; nonetheless, the problems remain when they return. This vicious cycle continues to spin, with debt causing pain and pain causing even more debt, while the Financial Matrix continues to profit.

Is increasing debt and angst truly the extent of our futures? Are these calamitous results on our lives just part-and-parcel of living in the modern world? There must be a better way.

*Every individual is continually exerting himself to find out the most advantageous employment for whatever capital he can command. It is his own advantage, indeed, and not that of society, which he has in view. But the study of his own advantage naturally, or rather necessarily, leads him to prefer that employment which is most advantageous to society.*
—*Adam Smith*

# –2–

## Force Market Versus Free Market Systems
*You can't beat something with nothing.*

We cannot just criticize the Financial Matrix for drowning the world in debt, but we should also find an alternative economic model that provides liberty and justice for all. To accomplish this, we must learn the difference between the two foundational economic systems: *force markets*, which use what we might call Power Rule Philosophies (PRP), and *free markets*, which use what we will call Golden Rule Philosophies (GRP). The key difference between the two economic systems is how they generate profits, with PRP relying upon plunder and GRP relying upon production. In the book *The City of God*, Augustine said justice is what separates good governments from criminal gangs:

*Remove justice, and what are kingdoms but gangs of criminals on a large scale? What are criminal gangs but petty kingdoms? A gang is a group of men under the command of a leader, bound by a compact of association, in which the plunder is divided according to an agreed convention. If this villainy wins so many recruits from the ranks of the demoralized that it acquires territory, establishes a base, captures cities, and subdues peoples, it then openly arrogates to itself the title of kingdom, which is conferred on it in the eyes of the world, not by the renouncing of aggression but by the attainment of impunity. For it was a witty and truthful rejoinder which was given by a captured pirate to Alexander the Great. The king asked the fellow, "What is your idea in infesting the sea?" And the pirate answered, with uninhibited insolence, "The same as yours, in infesting the earth! But because I do it with a tiny craft, I'm called a pirate; because you have a mighty navy, you're called an emperor."*[1]

Augustine compares and contrasts economic systems based upon ethical considerations. Whereas the force market PRP is an unethical system of institutionalized injustice because the elites plunder people by violating their human rights (life, liberty, and property), the free market GRP is an ethical system of institutionalized justice because the people freely produce and exchange with each other while respecting human rights. The determining factor is how the government's monopoly of force is applied, for the same state power used to organize justice (the systemic protection of life, liberty, and property) can just as easily be used by the state to organize injustice (the systemic violation of life, liberty, and property). The state, according to economist Ludwig von Mises, was defined as the governmental power within a specific territory designed to ensure justice: "The state is essentially an apparatus of compulsion and coercion. The characteristic feature of its activities is to compel people through the application or the threat of force to behave otherwise than they would like to behave."[2]

This is the paradox of the state: any power strong enough to protect rights is also strong enough to violate them. Interestingly, author Albert Jay Nock drew a distinction between government and the state, noting that governments had limited powers that protected people's rights, whereas states had unlimited powers that violated them.[3] By maintaining this distinction, we notice that for the Western nations, the twentieth century is the history of limited-power governments transforming into absolute-power states. Renowned sociologist Franz Oppenheimer, after more than fifty years of studying nation-states, concluded:

# FORCE MARKET VERSUS FREE MARKET SYSTEMS

*The State...is a social institution, forced by a victorious group of men on a defeated group, with the sole purpose of regulating the dominion of the victorious group over the vanquished, and securing itself against revolt from within and attacks from abroad...this dominion had no other purpose than the economic exploitation of the vanquished by the victors. No primitive state known to history originated in any other manner.[4]*

Throughout history, in other words, the elites have practiced Power Rule Philosophies to direct the state's absolute power to plunder the people. Nock observed:

*In proportion as you give the state power to do things for you, you give it power to do things to you...All the power [the state] has is what society gives it, plus what it confiscates from time to time on one pretext or another; there is no other source from which state power can be drawn.[5]*

Perhaps no one understood this better than French political philosopher Bertrand de Jouvenel, who described how adopting the perspective that unethical elites habitually seek to plunder the people is the master code that unlocks world history:

*Whoever does not wish to render history incomprehensible by departmentalizing it—political, economic, social—would perhaps take the view that it is in essence a battle of dominant wills, fighting in every way they can for the material which is common to everything they construct: the human labor force.[6]*

After a lifetime of studying power, de Jouvenel concluded that when the elites who rule seek to profit unjustly from this power, then the state has unethically institutionalized injustice instead of justice. This is the Financial Matrix today, the most powerful institutionalized injustice ever created by mankind, which controls the nation-states worldwide in order to secure global profits and power over the people.

In contrast, a genuine free market must be an unhampered economy, one without any state intervention within its natural processes. Austrian economist Richard Ebeling defined such a free economy with eight characteristics:

1. *All means of production are privately owned.*
2. *The use of the means of production is under the control of private owners, who may be individuals or corporate entities.*
3. *Consumer demands direct how the means of production—land, labor, and capital—will be used.*
4. *Competitive forces of supply and demand determine the price of consumer goods and the various factors of production, including labor.*
5. *The success or failure of individual and corporate enterprises is determined by the profits or losses these enterprises earn, based on their greater or lesser ability to satisfy consumer demands in competition with their rivals in the marketplace.*
6. *The market is not confined to domestic transactions and includes freedom of international trade, investment, and movement of people.*
7. *The monetary system is based on a market-determined commodity (e.g., gold or silver), and the banking system is private and competitive, neither controlled nor regulated by the government.*
8. *The government is limited in its activities to the enforcement and protection of individual life, liberty, and honestly acquired property.*[7]

The topic of economics can perhaps be intimidating to the uninitiated because there are many terms and concepts not dis-

# FORCE MARKET VERSUS FREE MARKET SYSTEMS

cussed in our daily lives. However, we naturally understand economics much better than we probably realize. In fact, most of us routinely interact with the four main aspects of the free market—money, demand, supply, and price. When we go to work to earn money, we help build the supply of products and services in the market. With the money we earn, we go to the store or online and look at market prices before purchasing the items we desire, which causes our household demand to be recorded as money "votes." Producers then respond to the demand of these votes and produce more or less as needed. So as you can see, in just three sentences, we have confirmed that each of us is more connected with the economic system and understands the four major components of the free market rather well. The important things to understand about economics are not obscure or difficult, and they should not be made so by ivory tower theorists. What makes the free market so effective is that it needs no centralized controller or overeducated elites to intervene because the four factors (supply, demand, price, and money) are all created and self-regulated by the free market system itself. The number one thing the government can do to support the free market is to leave it alone and ensure others leave it alone, by protecting liberty and justice for all market participants. The free market can record people's economic 'votes' as market prices for the products and services in demand, and entrepreneurs then compete to supply these 'voters' with their market demands, and those who do so successfully are rewarded accordingly.

Not surprisingly, the Financial Matrix has no intention of leaving the market alone, for it profits greatly by intervening in the economy and converting the free market into a force market. Most of us are not aware of these market interventions and are thus easily led astray by those who blame the free market for the troubles the force market actually created. This is the gap between perception and reality that the Financial Matrix exploits.

Until we understand how the free market system operates, we will not comprehend how the Financial Matrix is damaging it with its insidious force and fraud activities. The government is supposed to punish fraud in the free market, not protect it. After all, the legitimate use of force in the market is to ensure everyone enjoys liberty and justice by preventing any mafia-like market participants from coercing others against their will. Just like in sporting events, everyone must play by the same rules, a situation enforced by an impartial referee. If someone attempts to commit fraud against another market participant, the government should ideally punish the offender for breaking the law. In situations where the government does take sides, the referee is then supporting one team at the expense of the others, resulting in an unfair contest. The force market is a rigged game because the referee is no longer neutral but rather an active participant on the side of certain market actors. Absurdly, the Financial Matrix then blames the free market for problems caused by its force market interventions, which it uses to justify even more interventions.

In a free market, people exchange goods and services when the perceived gain is better than the perceived give. The free market consists of hundreds of millions of "win-win or no deal" decisions by its participants. We either value what we are gaining more than what we are giving, or we simply won't do the deal. This results in a series of win-win transactions occurring freely without compulsion. All of this can happen without the interference of elite economic planners, government officials, regulators, or any other types of force interventions. The free market, when left free, operates smoothly and efficiently.

**Free Markets, Fuel Systems, and Self-Regulation**

How does this freely operating market of millions of exchanges work so well on its own? It does so by freely responding

## FORCE MARKET VERSUS FREE MARKET SYSTEMS

to prices. The free market is a self-balancing process that equalizes the supply and demand of every product and service around a responsively moving price point. Adam Smith famously said it is like there is an "invisible hand" balancing the market. This astonishing self-regulating mechanism, or "invisible hand," actually operates through the four features mentioned earlier: 1) Money, 2) Demand, 3) Supply, and 4) Price. As stated, this is best achieved without external interference in any part of the process. The key to understanding the free market is to visualize these four features dynamically interacting to balance supply and demand at a price point without centralized control. The challenge is that supply and demand curves, which are typically used to teach this topic, do not adequately depict the dynamic nature of market signals and how entrepreneurs utilize them to identify opportunities. In order to come up with an easier-to-understand way to illustrate how the free market system truly works, I returned to my automotive fuel system roots.

For the first fifteen years of my adult life, I worked as a systems engineer at General Motors. Serving as a technical consultant, product engineer, and process engineer in the fuel systems department, I applied systems thinking routinely. My first assignment was to benchmark (competitively analyze) every major fuel system design from every global manufacturer. This, along with great engineering mentors, helped me gain expertise in fuel systems, which led to four patents and winning the first-ever National Technical Benchmarking award in our division's storied history. Whereas most people think linearly, a cause-and-effect mindset in which A leads to B and results in C, in systems theory, by contrast, sometimes C can cause A or a combination of A and C can result in B because the world is usually more systems than simple. Systems are not linear because they do not operate in a straight line; instead, they function in loops of individual inputs. Each part of the system is interdependent, meaning an event in one part of the loop interacts with every other part. In systems theory this is called a feedback loop. And when studying any system, the effect of the feedback loop must be recognized, or wrong conclusions will result. Although this may sound more complicated than linear thinking, the reality is that systems are all around us, and most of the challenges we face in modern life have resulted from someone applying linear thinking to a systemic problem.

I state my systems pedigree to emphasize that modern economists, for the most part, are failing to think systemically, focusing on data calculated in a linear fashion, while neglecting the underlying system from which the data was generated. For instance, the "school" or category of economic thought known as Keynesian economics studies every particular tree while missing the overall forest. Instead, if the economy were to be studied as a whole to discover the separate but interacting systems before examining the individual parts, the systemic nature would be revealed. This would help the economics profession escape the Keynesian cul-de-sac it's currently trapped in, and allow a return to the main thoroughfare. The more I studied the free market from this systems perspective, the more I discovered that it operated similarly to the fuel systems I designed and tested as a systems engineer.

Allow me to demonstrate what I mean. Let's briefly examine how a fuel system functions so we can compare it to the free market. An electric pump in the gas tank flows fuel through the fuel line to the fuel rails atop the engine. The spring-loaded fuel regulator opens at a set pressure to flow the excess fuel from the fuel rails back to the fuel tank. The constant pressure in the fuel rail allows the finely calibrated fuel injector to open, spraying pressurized gas into the cylinder, and then the spark plug will ignite. This controlled explosion is what moves the cylinder, which turns the crank and creates the engine's power. The fuel system, like a true free market economy, is a balanced system. As such, if any of the parameters fluctuate, the entire system becomes unstable. In a fuel system, for instance, faulty regulators, clogged fuel filters, or low battery voltage can cause the set parameters to fluctuate, and the fuel system is suboptimized or fails to power the engine at all. To blame the self-regulating fuel system itself for fluctuations caused by a failing component would be foolish. Systems thinking, as we will see, is the key to understanding how the usually balanced and self-regulating free market wobbles and fails when the Financial Matrix imbalances a key component part, namely, the money supply.

## AUTOMOTIVE FUEL SYSTEM

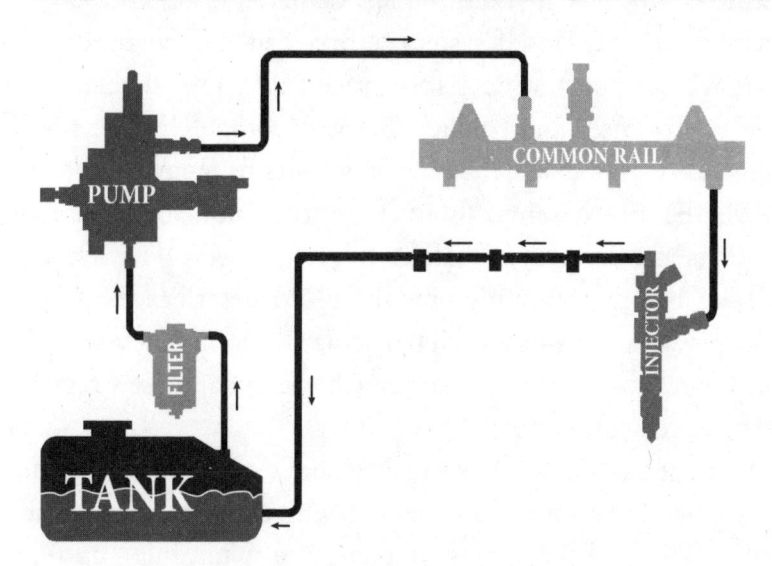

**Free Market Mechanism (FMM)**

By considering fuel systems, a breakthrough idea occurred to me regarding how to visually illustrate the operation of a free market system. Let's call it the Free Market Mechanism (FMM), a mental model that illustrates how the spontaneously ordered free market system dynamically self-regulates without the need for any centralized control. My hope is that this will prove an infinitely better illustration for free market dynamics than the overworked but little-understood supply and demand curves of old.

## FREE MARKET MECHANISM

**SUPPLY IN**
Land, Labor, Capital, Time & Entreprenuership

**DYNAMIC FLOAT**

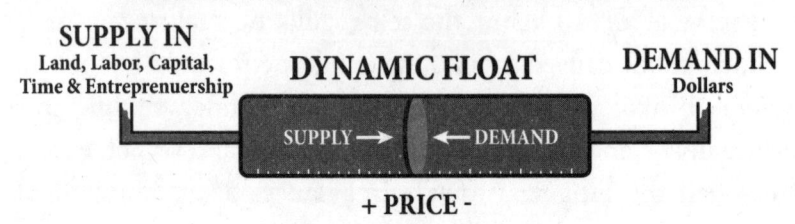

SUPPLY → ← DEMAND

**DEMAND IN**
Dollars

+ PRICE -

The Free Market Mechanism (FMM) explains how the four features of the free market (money, demand, price, and supply) interact within a closed system to arrive at the dynamic equilibrium price point, which is the price where total demand and total supply meet and balance. Because complex markets have many sub-components, the economy contains many component FMMs that are systemically interconnected to supply the final products and services for sale to buyers. However, for simplicity sake, before examining how the FMM describes the overall economy, let's study how each particular FMM interacts with the four aspects of the free market to achieve dynamic self-regulating balanced equilibrium.

To begin, as we discussed briefly above, consumers communicate their desire for supply by showing up with money ready to buy things. If the supply market price is too high, customers walk away from the transaction and supply is not cleared. In contrast, if the demand market price is too low, sellers walk away from the transaction, and the supply is not cleared. Somewhere in between these two points is the market equilibrium price where the lowest final seller price matches the highest remaining buyer price. This results in the market being cleared of inventory because the total supply is sold to the buyers willing to pay the

## FORCE MARKET VERSUS FREE MARKET SYSTEMS

market price. In this way, millions of products and services all over the globe achieve an equilibrium price that satisfies both buyers and sellers.

The willingness of a buyer to make a purchase is represented as a money flow into the demand side of the Free Market Mechanism (FMM) shown in the diagram. There are millions of such inflows. The Free Market Mechanism (FMM) recognizes these inflows as the total cumulative money on the demand side. Items more in demand have higher money flows, and those less in demand have lower money flows. The FMM market price is visually represented by a dynamic float. The demand and supply flows move the dynamic float left or right until a dynamic equilibrium is achieved. This is the price point where total demand would clear the total supply from the market. The FMM displays how an increasing supply, with constant demand, causes the dynamic float to move right until pressures equalize at a lower price. Conversely, with increasing demand and constant supply, the dynamic float moves left until pressures equalize at an increased price. This dynamic float concept models the dynamic price in a free market in the way it self-regulates until the price at which buyers and sellers agree is reached.

Looking at the supply side, total supply flow is created by entrepreneurs who perceive opportunities to profit from price signals. These bold market participants, who see opportunities where others see obstacles, combine land, labor, and capital innovatively to supply society with marketable goods and services. Successful entrepreneurs profit by satisfying customers, whereas unsuccessful entrepreneurs suffer losses from not satisfying customers. Entrepreneurs build leadership teams that see, create, and leverage opportunities to build value and profit by keeping total costs below the total revenues. Notice that success in a free market is completely dictated by entrepreneurs' abilities to satisfy customers. Profits are the reward for accurately predicting the future demand and supply needs of society and supplying them, while losses are the punishment for inaccurate predictions and poor execution.

### Free Market Mechanism (FMM) and Law of Markets

The FMM visually illustrates J. B. Say's Law of Markets (also known as Say's Law[8]), which states that the free market economy is a dynamically balanced system wherein a buyer must first produce something of value in order to receive something of value in exchange. Within a balanced system, in other words, you must give in order to get. This implies that the true effective demand in an unhampered economy is the result of previous acts of production. So, as the FMM shows, in an unhampered economy, there cannot be a chronic imbalance between demand and supply because the production of economic goods is what creates the effective demand for them in the first place. It is important to understand this truth: true wealth in a society increases with its production of goods and services. To quote J.B. Say: "A product is no sooner created, than it, from that instant, affords a market for other products to the full extent of its own value." Without increased production (supply), it doesn't matter what the demand is because no production is available to be purchased.[7]

The FMM brings Say's Law to life, driving home the point that the economy is a closed, balanced, and self-regulating physical system in which all interactions among the economic actors are accomplished internally. Although human beings can greatly increase the use and value of physical resources within a closed economic system, all economic resources are limited. Money, as will be discussed in the next chapter, is also a physically limited resource (think gold and silver), a highly marketable and scarce resource that sets the market value of all other marketable items in terms of monetary units for exchange purposes. In a closed system, just as the supply of physical and mental goods and services cannot be created without effort, neither can physical commodity money (gold and silver) be created without effort. This is the reason the free market is naturally in balanced equilibrium (as illustrated by the FMM): nothing is added from outside the system, and everything within the system will find its equilibrium price point where supply and demand are balanced. Thus, Say's Law teaches us that human beings must labor to create supply from limited physical resources that are in demand and then exchange these for money, which is itself a limited valuable resource. Without external interference (force and fraud), the closed physical economic system, as displayed by the FMM, balances around the market price. In fact, only when external force and fraud are added (the unhampered free market is now a manipulated hampered market) into the closed economic system by outside interventions will systemic gluts and shortages appear. If the government regulates market prices, for instance, it would be like an external hand holding the dynamic float in place and refusing to let it balance the supply and demand at the market price, which would predictably imbalance the two factors.

Not surprisingly, the Keynesian economists, who supported Financial Matrix interventions into the free market economy, sought to refute Say's Law; otherwise, they knew that Say's Law would refute them. To do so, they allege Say's Law taught that economic disequilibrium was impossible and then point to disequilibrium within the manipulated economy to "refute" Say's Law. However, Say's Law never said supply and demand imbalances are impossible, but only that in an unhampered economy, the self-regulating features (as displayed by the FMM) quickly rebalance the system. In fact, the "chronic disequilibrium" occurring in the modern economy is due to outside force and fraud interventions within the otherwise naturally balanced and self-regulating economic system. Say's Law teaches that in an unhampered economy, the dynamically balanced and self-regulating system can only have chronic imbalances when one of the four features of the free market system is being manipulated. We will discuss this further in future chapters, but for now it is vital to understand the fundamental principles behind Say's Law so that we can identify the Keynesian economic errors. In a 1950 article, Ludwig von Mises elaborated: "The Keynesians tell us that his immortal achievement consists in the entire refutation of what has come to be known as Say's Law of Markets. The rejection of this law, they declare, is the gist of all Keynes's teachings; all other propositions of his doctrine follow with logical necessity from this fundamental insight and must collapse if the futility of his attack on Say's Law can be demonstrated."[9] We will utilize the Free Market Money Mechanism to demonstrate the robustness of Say's Law and how the state and bankers used Keynesian fallacies regarding it to justify external force and fraud interventions to profit themselves while damaging the free market.

## The Free Market Balanced System is a Decentralized, Interdependent, and Spontaneous Order

The Free Market Mechanism (FMM) displays how the free market money system produces a dynamic, spontaneous, and self-equilibrating balanced system under liberty and justice for all. As mentioned previously, each product and service has its own FMM. Thus, in the large and complex global markets, many first-order consumer FMM goods utilize many second-order FMMs to supply component parts (such as components for an automobile) for the final consumer FMM. Thus, the Free Market Mechanism (FMM) models how the free market measures the independent actions from millions of market participants responding to market signals to create an interdependent system without the need for external interference. This global system is a spontaneous order that has a constantly growing number of

FMMs that dynamically adjust prices to balance supply and demand in real time, without an all-powerful centralized controller.

The truth is that no controller could achieve this. Who would be so foolish to believe one could track subtle price signal cues from hundreds of billions of FMMs within the modern economy at any given instant to achieve market equilibrium? If just one prediction failed (in reality, all would fail), the imbalance from that one failure not being correct would instantly imbalance the entire market, for systems do not operate independently. In consequence, just as one stalled car can back up an entire highway system, so too can all interventions within the balanced free market cause the economy to malfunction and sputter. Of course, the market is never in perfect equilibrium, which is why entrepreneurial profits (and losses) arise, which end up correcting maladjustments. However, statism (any system in which centralized governments seek to interfere in the free operation of markets) fails because no single entity has the global omniscience necessary to make the appropriate adjustments to balance supply and demand at the market price for every single item on the market. Thus, centralized controllers' claims are tomfoolery writ large. Only the decentralized actions of billions of independent actors in the free market system can measure the total accumulated desires of the people and communicate these accumulated market desires to entrepreneurs, who profit by ensuring a supply is available for every single product at the market price.

**Free Market Versus Force Market Case Study**

One of the best examples that communicates the radical difference in results between force market PRP and free market GRP is post-World War II Germany. After the war, Germany was formally and forcefully divided, with the eastern side using the force market economic policies of the Soviet Union and the western side following the more free-market-oriented policies of the United States and its allies. The free market revived West Germany's debilitated economy, but East Germany's force market languished as long as it endured. As the next chart reveals, West Germany's free market economy more than doubled the productivity of East Germany's force matrix (socialist) economy.

**WEST GERMANY vs. EAST GERMANY: CAPITALISM VS SOCIALISM**

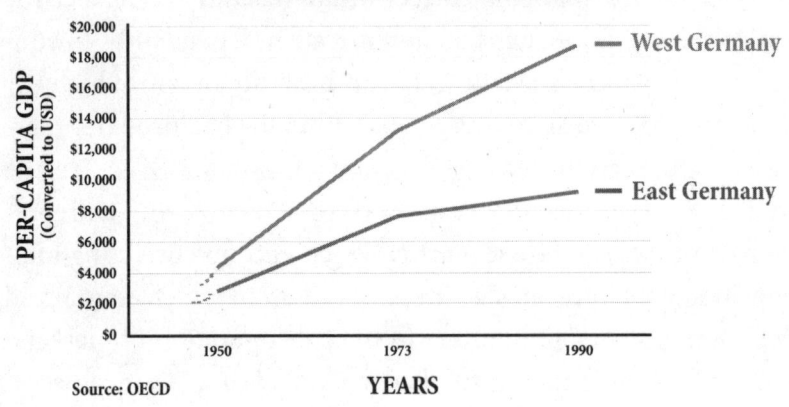

Source: OECD

Economic output, however, doesn't tell the story as well as a particularly colorful example. The Germans are some of the most car-loving people in the world, and their Autobahn is legendary for having no posted speed limits. And it is in the area of automobiles that the true colors of the two systems are most startlingly revealed. In a country artificially split between the Soviet socialist side (the east) and a free market one (the west), a unique comparison was presented to the world when the Iron Curtain was lifted in 1989.

At that time, the BMW 3 Series sedan, engineered and produced in West Germany, was one of the most popular and technologically sophisticated cars in the world, featuring fuel injection, anti-lock brakes, electronic controls of all sorts, traction control, and an exhaustive list of automotive innovations. In laughable contrast, from East Germany came the Trabant, a hopelessly un-

## FORCE MARKET VERSUS FREE MARKET SYSTEMS

derpowered two-stroke car made from recycled waste with no tachometer, turn signals, seat belts, or even a fuel gauge! This little beauty topped out at a whopping sixty miles per hour, but it took twenty-one seconds to get there! What's more, there was a ten-year waiting list for any "lucky" would-be purchaser, because the centralized process of production was so hopelessly inefficient. Moreover, the styling on this 1990 Trabant looks like it was designed in the 1960s and has been never upgraded since.

No matter the type of intellectual clothing elite media pundits, university professors, and other peddlers of socialist principles use to dress up their ideas, such defunct concepts are never anything more than rotting skeletons underneath. The bankruptcy of socialism could never have a better poster child than the hapless Trabant. This is true not only because the contrast between the BMW and the Trabant was so laughable, but because they were both produced at the same time by people having the same language, heritage, and culture who had suffered equally during the war and, in many cases, were even of the same families. But the free market system revitalized West Germany's economy, while its East Germany rival, through its centralized policies, was an economic mess.

*Gold is the money of kings, silver is the money of gentlemen, barter is the money of peasants—but debt is the money of slaves.*
—Norm Franz

# –3–

## What is Money?
*Money makes the world go around.*

The average person in a lifetime works over ninety-thousand hours to earn money, yet hardly anyone really knows what money is. Sure, they can earn it, spend it, save it, lend it, and borrow it, but what exactly is it? The lack of clarity around money is not an accident, for the Financial Matrix makes profits from the difference between people's perceptions and reality. For this reason, it is important for us to learn what money actually is, why it was created, and how it works.

Money, as it was originally created, was an economic blessing. It greatly expanded the number of voluntary exchanges in the economy and as a result, increased society's wealth. We will examine how the Financial Matrix abused this blessing of money, but it will be helpful if we first understand how free market money worked and the economic benefits that resulted. Prior to the invention of money, transactions would have been cumbersome, for they involved bartering of goods and services. This made for slow and clunky market exchanges due to what economists called indivisibility and the lack of coincidence of wants. Without money, for instance, how would you pay someone for helping you build a house? You couldn't give them a portion of the house as payment. You probably also couldn't trade them enough chickens or apples, either, supposing they were even desired by your home builder. The breakthrough occurred when market participants discovered what might be called an indirect exchange. Instead of swapping one good directly for another and dealing with the awkward mismatches and indivisibility of what was being traded, market actors put a neutral, valuable good in the middle instead. Goods and services could then be traded for this intermediary good first, and then that same good could again be used for the next transaction. The question, then, was: what good (or commodity) would be universally valuable for such intermediary use? Through a process of trial and error, merchants realized certain commodities were more in demand than others. These special products were the most marketable commodities, which were eventually called money. In consequence, all transactions could now be completed using this intermediary money, and the merchants started pricing all products and services in relation to this most popular commodity. The money economy was thus born. Money, as the most marketable commodity in the marketplace, expanded trade and markets, production, and the specialization of skills beyond anything previously imaginable. Everyone began accepting money because they knew they could exchange it for items they desired. This made trades possible between practically all parties and items within the marketplace. Murray Rothbard described how the most marketable commodity became even more marketable when it became money:

> Once a commodity begins to be used as a medium of exchange, when the word gets out, it generates even further use of the commodity as a medium. In short, when the word gets around that commodity X is being used as a medium in a certain village, more people living in or trading with that village will purchase that commodity since they know that it is being used there as a medium of exchange. In this way, a commodity used as a medium feeds upon itself, and its use spirals upward until, before long, the commodity is in general use throughout the society or country as a medium of exchange. But when a commodity is used as a medium for most or all exchanges, that commodity is defined as being a money.[1]

## WHAT IS MONEY?

Some of the commodities historically used as money include beads, seashells, feathers, big rocks, tobacco, cattle, and salt. Over time, however, precious metals, wherever they were available, had the widest market. People from every culture seemed to accept gold, silver, and copper as money. Beginning in ancient Egyptian times, precious metals were weighed on scales to complete transactions. This improved trade over the barter system we discussed, but it still required time, trust, and scales to weigh the metals in order to calculate payment. The next humongous leap ahead in the development of money occurred when the king of the ancient kingdom of Lydia invented coins. Lydia was the first to issue universal pieces of precious metal (made of stamped electrum, a naturally occurring gold and silver alloy) with the value of the precious metal content directly imprinted on the face. Now merchants could trade without weights and scales because they could readily identify the value of the coins based upon the king's stamp and known precious metal weights. There are two major ramifications to this enormous breakthrough. First, the weight of the precious metal in a piece of money became the key to commodity money. The second is the involvement of the government in the issuing of money, to which we will return with force and fury later in this book. For now, it's enough to see that this invention of coined money massively expanded markets and prosperity across the ancient world.

In nearly every nation and civilization, two precious metal commodities rose head-and-shoulders above all other money types wherever available: gold and silver. Originally, gold and silver were cherished for their ornamental value, being worn as a symbol of wealth and power; therefore, they were in demand as commodities well before they became money. Gold and silver became the free market choice for money because they met the three essential qualities of legitimate money: 1) a convenient medium of exchange, 2) a consistent measure of value, and 3)

69

a safe store of value. Coins were lightweight, easily identified, and accepted by nearly everyone in the marketplace. Precious metal money was also a consistent measure of value since the total global supply of gold and silver is fairly small, and cannot be increased as easily as other commodities. The total supply of gold in the world, for instance, usually expands by less than a couple percentage points per year at the most, even with laborious and technology-laden mining the world over. As a result, precious metal money has been rare and valuable since the beginning of recorded history. Finally, gold and silver are durable, portable, divisible, uniform, scarce, acceptable, and stable, all of which is why people across the world have used these two precious metals to transact exchanges.

Precious metal commodity money transformed the world's power structure. Whereas medieval power was based on the aristocracy's control of the *land* to direct serfs to exchange production for protection, the precious metal physical money economy directed people to exchange production for money and then use that money to buy other people's production. Thus, a land system based on a few people owning and securing the land and everyone producing to live had been replaced by a *money* system in which everyone produced to earn money for future exchanges in order to live. By the 14th century, the medieval feudal age was dying and the money economy was rising. Commerce and trade exploded throughout Christendom as people used their physically limited time, money, and skills to produce market goods in exchange for physically limited precious metal money. Author John Flynn explained the economic shift:

> *Transport companies were formed, and navigation canals were opened. These peddlers were changing the face and stirring the heart and lungs of Europe. They made it possible for the beekeeper in some remote Thuringian manor to exchange his honey for a*

*few ounces of pepper or cinnamon from the spice islands of Asia. Through their profit and coin-hunting expeditions, it became possible for the fustian weaver of Augsburg to buy the products of the silversmith of Florence, the silks of Venice, the brocades of Lahore, and the perfumes of Alexandria. Two great streams began to flow around Europe: one a stream of goods made up of every sort of product of every clime; the other a stream of money coined in the little mints of hundreds of petty princes. These fustian makers and wool weavers and tool mongers began to have a wider market for their wares, and they began to produce more. Men flocked to the towns.*[2]

## The Weight of the Matter

The use of precious metal money led to every item or service in the marketplace being priced based upon monetary units. A price is simply the ratio of the two quantities exchanged in any transaction. The weight of the precious metal involved in money was the key; the units we refer to still today (the dollar, pound, mark, franc, etc.) originally were names referring to the weight of gold or silver in the money. For instance, the 'pound sterling' in England was exactly one pound of silver, whereas the 'dollar' was the name used to describe the one-ounce silver coin minted by the 16th-century Bohemian count named Schlick, who lived in Joachimsthal (Joachim's Valley). These coins were called "Joachimsthalers," which was eventually shortened to "thalers," which was then pronounced "dollar" when they began to circulate in America.

Since precious metal commodity money was originally measured by weight, each money unit could be directly compared to another money unit. For instance, in the nineteenth century, the dollar was defined as 1/20 of a gold ounce, the pound sterling was defined as 1/4 of a gold ounce, and the French franc was established at 1/100 of a gold ounce. Thus, the exchange rates between different commodity monies were automatically set by the respective weights of the gold or silver contained in the coins. If one dollar is 1/20 of a gold ounce, for example, and the pound is 1/4 of a gold ounce, then we know that the pound is always exchanged for five dollars based upon the weight of the matter. Exchange rates were thus fixed between coins, allowing for quick international settlements. This is the only role that governments need to play in free market precious metal money; setting the weight of precious metal content in its money and guarding against fraudulent misrepresentation of that set amount. From there the market can determine exchange rates between national currencies.

Money, as we discussed in the last chapter, must be stable in supply because, through price action, it measures the variation in supply and demand of goods in the marketplace. If the measuring stick itself is allowed to vary in length, it cannot do a very good job of performing its function of measuring. This is why the free market prefers precious metals like gold and silver, whose supply is stable because their above-ground quantities cannot easily be expanded. With this in mind, the U.S. Bureau of Weights and Measures performs the only true role the government should rightfully have in free market money because it sets the uniform precious metal content standard for the nation's coins. The value of the dollar, in other words, like all other precious metal national currencies under commodity money, was originally derived from the weight of precious metal content it contained (remember the silver' dollar?). The dollar, pound, franc, etc. were not independent monetary entities that could be manipulated at will by the banking system or state but rather contained set weights of gold or silver. The precious metal content was what made the money standard.

Predictably however, as precious metal money began circulating throughout Europe the temptation to cheat overwhelmed many rulers. And since governments had quickly picked up on Lydia's lead and decided to reserve the coining of money for themselves alone, when tempted to cheat they also already had the means to do so with no one to stop them.

## Debasement: The First Expansion of Money Supply

The Roman Empire was actually the first to cheat in a big way on its own issuance of money. Rome's monetary policy, in reality, was a disaster and a great example of what not to do. Emperor Nero, in the middle of the first century A.D., initiated the monetary debasement of the Roman precious metal coins, which continued in one form or another for centuries until the empire collapsed. Debasement is the oldest and most labor-intensive method of expanding the money supply (increasing the total number of coins in the market) by reducing the precious metal content in each coin. The overall amount of precious metal remains the same, but the number of coins in circulation grows. This is accomplished by melting down the old coins and re-minting them with cheaper alloy metals as filler. The coins claim to contain the same amount of precious metal, but they don't. Like all frauds, this began slowly, and then picked up speed. Practically every subsequent Caesar collected the previous Caesar's coins and restamped them with his own image. Although getting the new Caesar's likeness on the coins was the ostensible public reason for reminting the coins, the private and much more profitable reason was debasement. In effect, these progressive and continuing debasements gradually destroyed Roman money.

Roman debasements increased the money supply (total coins available), which led to price inflation as the supply, demand, and prices (the Free Market Mechanism from the previous chapter) recalibrated for each market item to the new total money supply. The people had little recourse against this loss of purchasing power because the Caesars had a monopoly on the money throughout the vast Roman Empire. For instance, the silver denarius coin (see the graphic below) began with 95 percent silver content, but the final one issued less than two hundred years later contained only 0.5 percent silver content. So one coin turned into 190 coins after its final debasement, an expansion of the Roman money supply of 19,000 percent in just three centuries! No wonder the money of the Roman Empire collapsed through hyperinflation. Things got so bad that the Caesars refused to accept the debased money they created for tax payments and demanded actual agricultural goods instead.

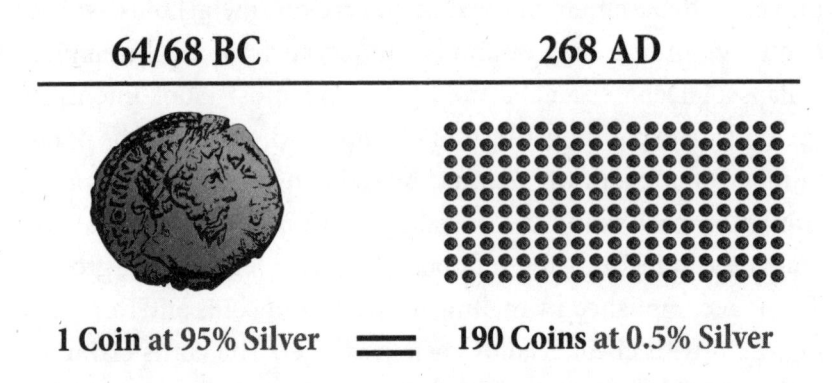

## 64/68 BC         268 AD

**1 Coin** at 95% Silver   =   **190 Coins** at 0.5% Silver

Despite this stark example from the ancient world, kings and kingdoms throughout the Middle Ages could not resist the temptation to grab wealth, power, and glory on-the-cheap by debasing their own currencies as well. Economist Richard Ehrenberg observed, "Many princes, both in the Middle Ages and later in the sixteenth and seventeenth centuries, did a roaring business in currency depreciation."[3] There was no central authority strong enough to assert itself over Christendom and stop this fraud, and local authority lacked either courage, wisdom, or the morality to stop the cheating. Although these debasements certainly enhanced the rulers' profits and power temporarily, just like in Roman times, they could not last without consequences. For one thing, there were competitive coins in the marketplace, so when a sovereign debased his coins, merchants would settle accounts in one that, relative to the others, retained its purity. For another, since debasement was not a secret, merchants weighed the coins to check for debasement, and if detected, coins were devalued in exchange accordingly. These two factors gradually slowed debasements because the fraud was public and no state was big enough to have a money monopoly that could force people to use it. Altogether, the debasements made people distrust state leaders, which damaged the glory, profit, and power of each kingdom. The fraud, in other words, boomeranged back upon the fraudsters themselves. Despite the debasements, the revolution of coined money continued to grow Europe's economy, and the expanded wealth increased people's quality of life.

## Free Market Mechanism and Debasement Inflation

The reason free market money should always be a scarce and limited physical resource is because it must be the most stable factor of the four free market mechanism features. As we said before, money automatically measures the fluctuations in demand and supply in a market to determine the dynamic equilibrium price. And any measuring device must be unchanging in order to be accurate. Therefore, when state rulers debased the money supply, they were causing the most important component of the free market to become corrupted. The economy suffers because money measures the total demand for every market item and communicates this data as price signals to entrepreneurs to prioritize profitable production plans. This is why money debasement is ruinous, for it not only fraudulently benefits the counterfeiters by artificially increasing the money supply, but it also falsifies the price signals used by entrepreneurs.

Debasement artificially adds to the money supply. This is a real problem since money is what is used in practically every market transaction, and if that supply is artificially increased, the counterfeiters who produce and are first to put this money into circulation benefit the most because they are effectively exchanging fake money for real goods. Therefore, whenever sovereigns (kings, etc.) or bankers artificially expand the money supply, they fraudulently plunder a portion of society's total economic goods at least equivalent to the percentage increase in the total money supply. In other words, when the manipulators double the money supply, they can use this fraudulent money to command over half of the economic resources in society. The reason it's not exactly half of the resources in this case is because it takes time for prices to adjust to the increased money supply, and thus the money manipulators purchase goods at the pre-inflated prices (this is the Cantillon effect we mentioned earlier) when first exchanging with the counterfeited money.

Debasement leads to inflation, which flows more money into the demand and supply sides of the FMM. However, the distortion on the demand side flow occurs instantaneously, since the demand flow is measured completely in money 'votes,' whereas the supply side increases more slowly as money (capital) is just one of the factors that creates the supply flow. In consequence, the Free Market Mechanism demonstrates how inflation increases demand faster than supply, which moves the dynamic float to the left, causing an increase in the market price. Thus, the FMM confirms what economist Milton Friedman emphatically stated: "Inflation is always and everywhere a monetary phenomenon."[4] To summarize, whenever the amount of money in circulation is artificially increased, the result is always an increase in prices. Valuables did not get more valuable; prices just went up.

The Free Market Mechanism (FMM) demonstrates the key attributes of how a free market economy ought to work. First, money must be stable in supply because its function is to measure the variation in demand and supply of goods and services, and result in a price point derived in monetary units. This is why

## WHAT IS MONEY?

stability is the sine qua non of the money supply, for without stability, money cannot perform its proper function in the free market. Looking even closer, we see that the FMM further shows that the total quantity of money (so long as it is stable) is not important. As long as there is a sufficient quantity of divisible money in the system so that it can record variations between demand and supply and arrive at a market price, then it has done its job. *Money itself is not wealth, but only the measure of wealth.* Therefore, an artificial increase in the total money supply does not increase the wealth in society. It only transfers wealth from the rightful owners to the fraudulent money creators in the amount inflated.

To illustrate this point, let's consider a silly example in which a fraudulent merchant convinces the U.S. government to change the definition of one yard from three feet to two. The merchant then purchases yards of cloth in England, where the yard is still measured at three feet, and then sells it in America, where the yard is now two feet. Sure, he could claim he legally sold you ninety "yards" of cloth, but you only have sixty yards (two-thirds as much) because the merchant has manipulated the definition of the yard's measurement. Notice that no additional wealth has been created, only a transfer of wealth from the rightful owner to the fraudulent manipulator.

In a similar fashion, the artificial expansion of the money supply is defrauding the monetary units, and even though you are still paid in dollars, your defrauded dollars are worth less than before just like the defrauded yard is a smaller measurement than before. This is fraud, has always been fraud, and will always be fraud. As Leviticus 19:35–36 states, "You shall do no wrong in judgment, in measures of length or weight or quantity. You shall have just balances, just weights." The debasement of coins way back in the ancient world began a series of fraudulent monetary interventions into what should have been and always remained a closed and physically limited free market economy. This debasement has grown in sophistication, scope, method, and manner over the years. It converts money, the most marketable, physically limited commodity used to measure the value of all other commodities and services, into a metaphysical sign that can more easily than ever be fraudulently manipulated by the powerful to plunder the people's wealth. Author David Hawke emphasized the inherent danger when physically limited commodity money is converted into metaphysical unlimited signs:

> *Since money is not a material object but a sign, it is certainly possible for it to breed. Signs only achieve their meanings within the human mind, and…the significance of signs can be multiplied infinitely. But while it is possible to multiply money in this way, it is morally undesirable to do so. And, it is morally undesirable because it violates logic, being incompatible with the essence of money. For Aristotle, money did not possess value because it was value; value was not an accidental attribute of money but its essence. Value itself does not have a value, and therefore cannot fluctuate in value. In other words, money is logically and ethically barren in essence, even though it is not necessarily so in practice.*[5]

If money measures the price signals entrepreneurs use to direct society's scarce resources, then when the variation in the quantity of money alters those signals, the distorted results ruin entrepreneurs' ability to make profitable supply side decisions. This is why monetary stability, what economists call "sound money," is essential for the proper functioning of the free market. Debasement, in other words, does more than just rob people of their wealth. It also introduces dislocations and distortions that interfere with the free operation of the market system.

The biggest development in money in the twentieth century was the complete conversion of limited physical commodity money (coins and paper backed by precious metals) into unlimited fraudulent metaphysical signs (paper fiat money backed by nothing). This conjuror's trick essentially separated money's perception (signs or symbols) from its physical reality (precious metals). Rulers ever since have sought to convince society that it gains when counterfeit money is created, but the only ones who gain are the counterfeiters themselves. When economist Elgin Groseclose studied such money fraud, he proclaimed: "Everywhere was an ignorant and foolish desire constantly to increase the number of units of money in one's possession, without reckoning what those units might represent."

### The Free Market Mechanism (FMM) and Banking

So far we have discussed how government manipulation of the money supply through debasement causes inflation and robs the people of their wealth. But there is another force at work in the world that also corrupts our money and results in not only inflation and decreased purchasing power but also wild swings of "boom and bust" cycles. In short, it's called commercial banking. The very function of lending, as practiced in today's world, is inflationary and a money supply distorter of the highest magnitude. Commercial banking should follow the same principles every other business follows under liberty and justice for all. While banking performs an essential and legitimate role in the free market, a financial partnership between banks and central governments, as we will see, has declared economic war against the people using monetary force and fraud.

Just as we looked at the operation of the free market of goods and services using the diagram of the Free Market Mechanism (FMM), we will do so again as applied to legitimate banking. Only by seeing the elegance of how the demand and supply of money equalize around the market price of money (interest rate) to balance the total money saved with the total money borrowed, without the need for any centralized control, can we then understand just how corrupt the actual banking system operates today.

# BANKING SYSTEM FMM

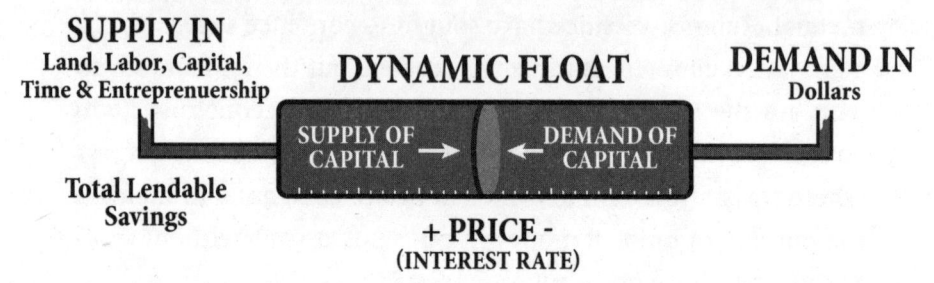

**SUPPLY IN**
Land, Labor, Capital,
Time & Entreprenuership

**DYNAMIC FLOAT**

**DEMAND IN**
Dollars

SUPPLY OF CAPITAL → ← DEMAND OF CAPITAL

Total Lendable Savings

+ PRICE -
(INTEREST RATE)

The demand for money in the Money FMM is represented by the total 'money bids' (interest rate bids) of those who desire to borrow money. Each buyer (borrower) has the highest interest rate he is willing to pay, and if the price is higher than that, he will not borrow money. However, if the price is right, the borrower will purchase the money at the agreed upon price, which is the interest rate. The supply side of the Money FMM represents the total amount saved by savers who are willing to forgo the use of saved money for a period of time in order to earn interest on their money. Bankers are matchmakers, for they connect people who have saved money (supply) with those who want to borrow money (demand), and they profit from the difference in rates of interest paid to the savers and charged to the borrowers. The FMM dynamic float moves left or right based upon the fluctuations in total demand and supply for money until the market price is reached. This is the price of money (the interest rate), where the total supply of money saved and total demand for money to borrow are equal. Naturally, when savers increase the total supply of money, with the demand remaining constant, the interest rate lowers. In contrast, if supply decreases and demand remains constant, the interest rate increases. The key point is that the dynamic float reaches the equilibrium market price (interest rate) by balancing supply and demand flows at the equilibrium pressure without any need for centralized control of the money supply, as with any other product or service. Sound familiar? Money, in other words, although it is used to measure the value of other commodities, is still itself a free market commodity and needs no outside intervention in order to arrive at its price to lend/borrow. Outside intervention can only damage the natural, dynamic balancing operations of the market.

We are now hovering over why the Financial Matrix exists today; namely, to centralize control over the money supply and therefore control the economy. Even though the Free Market Mechanism clearly illustrates that the money system balances itself like every product and service, the Financial Matrix has achieved a level of centralization and control that would make Karl Marx, the father of Communism, blush. The reality is that centralized money, despite what we are told, has nothing to do with market efficiencies and everything to do with economic war (force and fraud) designed to build absolute profits and power at the people's expense. Centralized control over the market never ends well, but the money controllers cannot let go of their centralized manipulations without losing their profits and power. This should remind the reader of the kings of old who couldn't help themselves when it came to debasing their own currencies for personal gain. The reason centralized control cannot work well and almost never lasts is because human beings do not have God-like omniscience to assimilate the billions of free market actions necessary to balance the economy (that the free market achieves in a decentralized fashion perfectly well on its own). To add even more insult to this injury, when manipulation of the money supply occurs, the entire economic system is affected by wild and destructive swings called Business Cycles (to be discussed in an upcoming chapter). Most disingenuous of all, not only do centralized manipulators refuse to accept responsibility for such damage to the economy, but they also go even further by blaming the free market itself for the imbalances their interventions caused in the first place! This would be like a car owner pouring water into the gas tank, then driving the car until it fails, and blaming the car company for a lack of quality.

To restore the free market system under liberty and justice for all, we must eliminate every single intervention within the economy, starting with the money manipulations that led to the growth and entrenchment of what we've been calling the Financial Matrix. We must learn how the bank-state partnership created the financial power that has parasitically fed off the production of the people. Ever since the time when money launched the modern age, we have been misled into believing that the free market is good in most areas, but in the monetary field, centralized control is better. Unfortunately, many otherwise very intelligent people accept this faulty premise without question. However, if we truly want freedom, it's time to jettison this false assumption and restore free market money and banking.

*I do not think you can trust bankers to control themselves. They are like heroin addicts.*
—Charlie Munger

# –4–

## Legitimate Versus Illegitimate Banking
*Compound interest is the 8th wonder of the world.*

Banking is an old profession. In fact, the Egyptian and Babylonian temples were practicing grain deposit banking before money was even invented. The money revolution, however, spread banking throughout the ancient world, and it was introduced into Europe by the Greeks. Next, the Romans built distinct buildings to formalize banking as an institution by removing them from the religious temples. As the Roman Republic expanded, almost all government spending was transacted through institutional banks that grew in power as the Romans did. In fact, Julius Caesar acknowledged this fact when, shortly after becoming Imperator, he created laws to allow bankers to confiscate borrowers' land if they defaulted. This was a major ruling that shifted creditors upward and debtors downward in the Roman social hierarchy.

With the collapse of the Roman Empire, money and banking went into hibernation during the feudal agricultural age, and only reawakened when the new Middle Eastern Crusader kingdoms began trading with the Byzantine Empire and the Italian city-states. Italian merchants played an essential role in returning money and banking to Europe by developing international relationships along the trade routes between the East and West. These new international merchant bankers built profits by facilitating and financing the production and trade of commodities, connecting the growing international economy. Naturally, the growing wealth also advanced status, and banker families (many from peasant origins), along with the commercial cities, increased in influence. The Italian banker families became a new class of moneyed aristocracy in the banking centers, which included Florence, Lucca, Siena, Genoa, Rome, and Venice. These merchant bankers quickly realized that the profits achieved from lending money were significantly better than those in traditional business fields, but only insiders knew why.

Although ethical money and banking are a blessing to the world, the dismal truth is that the reintroduction of banking into the West also reawakened fractional reserve banking (FRB), the original sin of the banking profession. We will reserve the full explanation of this unethical money racket for the next chapter, but for now understand that fractional reserve banking is a fraudulent expansion of the money supply that results in the siphoning off of society's resources. Fractional reserve bankers produce more banknotes representing the commodity money stored in their vaults than they actually have on deposit there. This enables them to create fraudulent loans out of thin air for which the borrower pays principal and interest. Soon, bankers realized that transactions could be completed using just the metaphysical symbols—the banknotes only—while the commodity money—the precious metal coins—remained stored in the vaults.

Once metaphysical signs could be lent in place of actual physical money, bankers had discovered a perfect scam. What was to stop them from lending out more metaphysical signs (banknotes) than physical money? The slickest part was that only the bankers themselves would know if there was actual money in the vaults to back the money symbols loaned to borrowers. Bankers now had the power to create an unlimited quantity of symbols from the metaphysical world and charge interest for them to be paid with borrowers' limited production from the physical world. This was the seed of the unlimited profits and power the bankers' would gradually obtain. Fractional reserve banking consumes

## LEGITIMATE VERSUS ILLEGITIMATE BANKING

people's wealth because they agree to exchange actual production for made-up symbols. As a result, bankers are essentially transformed into false money gods, controlling everything with their symbols.

Great minds from Augustine, Aristotle, Goethe, and Calvin recognized that banker profits were out-of-this-world, and suspected fraud was accounting for them, but disagreed upon what the legitimate and illegitimate aspects of banking actually were. This confusion allowed both the legitimate and fraudulent aspects of banking to thrive together, giving bankers the opportunity to institutionalize fractional reserve banking fraud. In time, economic control over the people passed from the *feudal* aristocracy to the new *financial* aristocracy. Whereas the feudal aristocracy had previously seized the physical land people needed in order to produce and exchange, the financial aristocracy now seized the metaphysical symbols (debt-money) people needed to produce and exchange. And since metaphysical symbols are easier to create than physical land is to seize, the result of the battle between the upstart financial aristocrats and feudal aristocrats was never in doubt.

The bankers understood that once people were conditioned to accept metaphysical symbols in place of precious metal money, then whoever owned the money symbols would in time own the world's production. And this is exactly what occurred. The people no longer exchanged physically limited production for physically limited money, but instead exchanged physically limited production for metaphysically unlimited symbols, owned by the bankers. Alas, the feudal aristocracy's fraudulent land monopoly was replaced by the financial aristocracy's fraudulent money monopoly, with the feudal serfs becoming financial serfs. The new financial aristocracy achieved this through an intentional deception designed to secure unfair and unlawful gain. The deception is effective because people have been conditioned to believe money signs are commodity money, instead of realizing that the metaphysical money signs were only ever supposed to represent actual physical commodity money allegedly backing them. Interestingly, the great Greek philosopher Aristotle was onto this. Unfortunately, though, his insights came with a confusion of terms that allowed bankers to thrive anyway. Although Aristotle claimed to be attacking usury, in reality he was talking about the FRB money fraud, the creation of more money symbols than physical money. Aristotle contended that the problem with bankers (what he called usury) was the artificial increase of the money supply. However, we lend our friends money all the time, and this does not increase the money supply. Only FRB lending does that because it creates more money signs than physical money. As a result, Aristotle brilliantly identified the FRB money fraud over twenty-three hundred years ago because it "unnaturally" makes "money breed."

Unfortunately, although Aristotle masterfully exposed the FRB money fraud, he obscured his brilliant insights by incorrectly categorizing the fraud as usury:

*"Usury [FRB] is most reasonably hated because its gain comes from money itself and not from that for the sake of which money was invented. For money was brought into existence for the purpose of exchange, but interest increases the amount of money itself [actually FRB did that], and this is the actual origin of the Greek word: offspring resembles parent, and interest is money [increases the money supply] born of money; consequently this form of the getting of wealth is of all forms the most contrary to nature."*[1]

Simply replacing what he called 'usury' with the term 'fractional reserve banking,' Aristotle would have had an open-and-shut case against a fraud that has prospered increasingly to this day. Aristotle recognized that money symbols were not part of the physical world, but were merely metaphysical representations of the physical money. Aristotle wonderfully explained why the money supply cannot be artificially expanded because it turns the measure of value in society into something of value for those willing to commit money fraud.

The banking and monetary fields have perpetuated their fraud through an intentionally misleading use of ordinary language. Indeed, nearly three centuries ago, philosopher John Locke noted that the achievement of human knowledge is often hampered by the use of words without fixed meanings. This leads to needless argumentation that only muddles the matter even more because of the unacknowledged ambiguity within the key terms. In other words, before we can have a logical discussion on any subject, we must identify any discrepancies in working definitions and seek to resolve them. Once this is accomplished, the ability to reason and discern fact from fiction will greatly improve upon the subject matter entailed. This is why we must carefully define the various terms in economics and banking before we can have a reasonable discussion. For instance, the free market, interest income, usury, fractional reserve banking, and capitalism have been mishmashed together by so many authors, in such a variety of ways, that it becomes difficult to determine what each author is meaning by the terms he or she is using. While we define the free market as an "unhampered" market under liberty and justice for all, many others use the terms "free market" and "capitalism" interchangeably. However, this leads to the muddling of terms, for many other authors refer to capitalism and fractional reserve banking interchangeably. The more these terms are confused, the more beneficial it is for the Financial Matrix, whose fraud thrives under the difference between perceptions and reality. I believe in the free market but oppose fractional reserve banking, and without properly defining the terms and understanding the important distinctions between them, the defense of the free market could be mistaken for a defense of FRB capitalism, and nothing could be further from my intent. This is to the Financial Matrix's advantage, of course, for when authors seek to defend legitimate aspects of money, banking, and the economy under a term defined differently by different authors, then the same terms used to defend legitimate functions can also be used to defend illegitimate functions. Hence, in the upcoming chapters, we will define our terms clearly so that we can eliminate confusion and logically discuss and reason.

Perhaps the best example of the confusion of terms is the various definitions of the word usury. The medieval theologians forbade usury and defined it as the taking of interest on any loan. Others, however, such as Aristotle, defined usury as the practice of fractional reserve banking. And finally, most churches today define usury as an unethically high rate of interest that unfairly enriches the lender. One term—with three definitions—none of which accurately describes the actual definition of Biblical usury. In consequence, we have four functional definitions for the same term! How can we carry on a logical discussion when the terms themselves are so confounded?

The concept of usury can be traced back nearly four thousand years, and throughout history, it has been condemned, prohibited, and restricted for ethical reasons. The great religions of the world were the most visible and vocal critics, including Hinduism, Buddhism, Judaism, Islam, and Christianity. The Catholic Church strongly condemned usury, and because theologians referenced Old Testament texts like "Do not charge a fellow Israelite interest," and New Testament ones like "Love your enemies: do good, and lend, hoping for nothing thereby," they concluded that earning interest on any loans was sinful usury. Christian councils from the 4th century A.D. upward consistently denounced usury, and by 800 A.D., the emperor Charlemagne turned the church's prohibition into the law of Christendom. This anti-usury move-

## LEGITIMATE VERSUS ILLEGITIMATE BANKING

ment gained momentum throughout the Middle Ages, reaching its peak in 1311 when Pope Clement V made the ban on usury absolute by declaring all secular law in favor of usury to be null and void. Clearly, it behooved the early merchant banks to keep the practice of earning interest on loans hidden from view.

Christian bankers faced a real dilemma. If the above definition of usury were true, and interest profits from loans were illegitimate, then the lender faced eternal consequences for committing a mortal sin. After all, lending at interest was the banker's main source of profit, and without the ability for enterprises to legitimately borrow money, the commercial revolution would be endangered. Even though practically everyone agreed that making interest on a loan was usury, few agreed upon why it was sinful. One popular argument stated that the usurer was selling time to the borrower, and theologians argued this was not possible because God created and owned time; therefore, the usurer cannot sell what he does not own. Theologians further argued that the usurer accepted money but gave nothing and concluded that lenders were committing metaphysical fraud by selling something they did not own while receiving what was owned by another. Here is another example of using excellent reasoning while confusing the terms. This assertion against usury is actually a superb refutation of fractional reserve banking, but not the earning of interest. By replacing the term "usury" with "fractional reserve banking" in this example, the argument would read: fractional reserve bankers lent money but gave nothing; therefore, lenders were committing metaphysical fraud by selling something they did not own while receiving what was owned by another. The great minds were making logical defenses against fraud, but then mistakenly classifying all lending as fraud under the distracting term "usury." This confounding of terms would have serious ramifications as banking developed. Much of the resistance against usury was in reality resistance against fractional reserve banking fraud, but due to the uncertainty in definitions, it was difficult to pinpoint the differences between legitimate and illegitimate banking.

These theologians were insightful original thinkers, but their Biblical definition of usury—earning interest on any loan—missed the mark. The Old Testament law given to Moses and the passages on usury written by David, Ezekiel, and Nehemiah described loans given to people who were poor at best and near starvation at worst. These people were financially flattened and in no position to repay loans with interest, with some not capable of paying back the principal. God expected the Israelites to respond with love and charity towards their unfortunate neighbors and not gain from their pain. Naturally, God expects the same from Christians today. Several New Testament parables provide the Biblical position on usury and interest. For example, in the Parable of the Talents, Matthew 25:24–27, Jesus teaches:

*He also who had received the one talent came forward, saying, "Master, I knew you to be a hard man, reaping where you did not sow, and gathering where you scattered no seed, so I was afraid, and I went and hid your talent in the ground. Here, you have what is yours." But his master answered him, "You wicked and slothful servant! You knew that I reap where I have not sown and gather where I scattered no seed? Then you ought to have invested my money with the bankers, and at my coming I should have received what was my own with interest."*

In these verses Jesus is rebuking the lazy steward for burying his talent when he could have at least given it to bankers to receive interest on the principal. If earning interest on any loan was truly usury, then why would Jesus Christ rebuke the lazy steward for not committing the damnable sin? Noted theologian Walter Kaiser captured the key difference between usury and honest interest when he wrote: "The fact that interest was approved for ventures that did not try to circumvent one's obligation to the poor is reinforced by Jesus' allusion and apparent approval of taking interest on commercial loans in Luke 19:23 and Matthew 25:27."[2] Thus, the prohibition against usury is not a prohibition against earning interest but instead a prohibition against demanding a "pound of flesh" from those who are in need of charity. Kaiser concluded his thoughts with: "the use of money for commercial or international ventures, and the security of a reasonable rate of interest, was a different matter from the requirement of aiding one's destitute brother." The Bible clearly differentiates between those who need freely provided charity and those who need free market loans. Usury, in consequence, protects against win-lose transactions where the rich take advantage of the poor, but does not prohibit banks from profiting by lending money in a win-win fashion in the free market.

Now we can see why the medieval church's total ban on earning interest was so damaging, for it drove the Italian Christian bankers to hide honest profits in dishonest ways. And since they did this through using abstract symbols and secret calculations, manipulating exchange rates, charging "late fees," and crediting "gifts," the bankers soon discovered it was a short step from hiding what should have been legitimate profits from church authorities to also hiding illegitimate profits as well. The free market aligns with Scripture in that the lending of money and earning of interest under liberty and justice is not an issue. However, fractional reserve banking is an anathema to both the free market and the Bible because it fraudulently counterfeits money to lend to others at profit, violating the very principles of liberty and justice for all. In free market banking, the lender is not selling time but merely exchanging present money for future money, with a fee (interest) that recognizes the time value of money. Just as a bird in hand is worth two in the bush, so too is money spent today worth more than money possibly spent tomorrow. The future is unpredictable, since only God knows the future like the present. And because everyone else experiences an increase in uncertainty as the time horizon expands, there is a cost associated with every delay. Therefore, delayed gratification is a cost, and if the borrower expects the legitimate lender to suffer that cost, he must be willing to pay the price for it. The borrower, in effect, pays interest for the inconvenience of the lender, who is delaying the use of his money, so that the borrower can enjoy the convenience of using the lender's money now. Thus interest charged in such a situation is a free market balancing of the accounts between legitimate lenders and their borrowers.

Honest banking provides a free market service and should be rewarded like other free market businesses. However, there is no reason for banking to receive ten times or one hundred times (or more) rewards than other business ventures. The new merchant banks performed three main functions: financing trade and commerce, foreign exchange, and maritime insurance. Profits could be made through all three functions, but by far the most profitable aspect for merchant bankers was the financing of loans. Ethical bank loans occur when bankers loan their own capital to borrowers or acquire the right to loan other people's capital for a specific time period and interest rate. The lender profits in this example from the gap between the interest rate paid to depositors who surrendered use of the funds, and the interest rate paid by borrowers who get to use the funds over the same time period. In essence, legitimate banks are matchmakers who connect savers with borrowers for profit. They make money by paying a lower rate of compound interest to savers (who forgo the use of their money temporarily) and charging a higher rate of interest to borrowers (who need other people's money temporarily). This is a profitable business, but nowhere near the astronomical levels of wealth and status achieved by the merchant bankers who illegitimately added fractional reserve banking into the mix to become the financial masters of the world.

Before studying honest and dishonest banking practices any further, we should understand how banks can earn legitimate compound interest by lending money. Albert Einstein, after studying compound interest, marveled: "Compound interest is the eighth wonder of the world. He who understands it, earns it…he who doesn't pays it."[3] What astounded Einstein was how quickly compound interest surpassed the growth levels expected with linear thinking. When money is allowed to compound for great lengths of time, the interest accumulated surpasses the principal by such an extent that it is no longer comprehensible. According to economist William Goetzmann, who studied clay tablets from the ancient world, the most likely origin of compounding calculations involved the birthrate of cattle compounded over time. While this constituted an interesting thought experiment, it neglected to include real-life factors like premature deaths, diseases, disasters, and predators, to name a few. Without these limiting factors, compounding becomes increasingly separate from reality. This is why the compounding of anything physical calculated beyond a handful of years no longer represents real world returns. Nothing in the physical world compounds indefinitely, for there are natural limiting factors that work against endless growth, but in the metaphysical world, compound interest is a simple reinforcing loop without a corresponding balancing loop, and this is why the compounding of money produces astounding results.

For an example of the otherworldly nature of compound interest over extended time periods, imagine a young man witnessing the birth of Jesus Christ. He sees the three wise men give gifts and decides to give them too, but he only earns a wage equivalent to one penny. Embarrassed by such a small amount, he deposits the penny into a no-fee investment account at 5 percent annual interest and then hands Mary the receipt. Each subsequent generation passes this receipt on to the next, and there are no further deposits or withdrawals. The original penny just keeps compounding at 5 percent interest annually. Now, let's imagine you are the closest surviving relative, so the "penny" gift is now yours. How much is your small investment worth as of 2020? Before guessing, let me emphasize the need to select an extremely high amount. Why? Because that single penny gift is now worth in excess of 32 million Earth-sized spheres of pure gold! That's right! If we could make an earth-sized sphere of gold, you would be owed 32 million spheres to pay you in full. And with every passing year, it becomes more unreal. Even though the math is correct, the concept is not correct because it does not account for the limiting factors that always occur in the real world. Just as cattle have natural growth limits, so too must compound interest be limited, or the metaphysical world will consume the physical one. This is why people should avoid placing themselves on the wrong side of compound interest and should instead treat it like cancer and eliminate it as soon as possible.

This extreme example indicates how compound interest mathematically loses touch with reality after extended periods of time. Let's review the math behind the $0.01 invested at a 5 percent compound interest rate per year since the birth of Christ:

| YEARS | AMOUNT IN DOLLARS |
|---|---|
| 15 | $0.02 — *It took about fifteen years for the penny to double.* |
| 30 | $0.04 |
| 70 | $0.30 |
| 150 | $15.07 |
| 200 | $172.92 |
| 250 | $1,983 |
| 378 | $1,022,245 — *In 378 years, the savings account has over one million dollars.* |
| 500 | Over $393 million |

# LEGITIMATE VERSUS ILLEGITIMATE BANKING

The dollar amounts are becoming so outrageous that we should probably convert them into tons of gold (1,000 kilograms per metric ton) and set the price of gold at $60,000 per kilogram:

| YEARS | METRIC TONS OF GOLD |
|---|---|
| 500 | 6.6 tons |
| 600 | 862 tons |
| 800 | Almost 15 billion tons |
| 1,000 | Almost 260 billion tons |
| 1,200 | Almost 4,500 trillion ton |
| 1,400 | Over 77 million trillion tons |
| 1,490 | Over 6 billion trillion metric tons |
| 1,525 | This is a gold sphere the size of the Earth |
| 1,800 | Almost 700,000 gold spheres the size of Earth |
| 2,000 | Over 12 billion gold spheres the size of Earth |
| 2,024 | Over 39 billion gold spheres the size of Earth |

*The gold is now heavier than earth* (at 1,490)

*5.5 times heavier than Earth* (at 1,525)

*The actual global supply of gold only fills a little more than three Olympic-sized swimming pools.*

The 2024 total dollar value of the original penny investment is now: $77,115,435,855,130,000,000,000,000,000,000,000,000,000.00 or over $77,000 trillion, trillion, trillion . . . .

This makes the actual total worldwide money today (under $100 trillion) seem hardly more than spitting in the penny-compounded ocean. As such, compound interest is no laughing matter. This is precisely why the Biblical Jubilee restored land that was sold back to its original owner every fifty years, limiting the ability of compound interest to no longer represent reality. Be-

97

fore the 18th century, national debts did not compound because, when the monarch passed away, the new king or queen was not responsible for his debts. This was a natural jubilee built into each nation-state. However, in our modern nations, debts do not reset. Hence, bankers have been compounding interest on national debts for over four hundred years! No wonder the bankers supported and promoted democracies against monarchies at the end of World War I. Woodrow Wilson declared that the reason America entered World War I was to "make the world safe for democracy," but that also means we made the world safe for infinitely compounded national debt interest. Compound interest is a legitimate profit for banks in the free market; however, that compound interest should not be charged for any nation or company beyond fifty years, and individuals should hesitate to go beyond fifteen years, because when compounded over any longer time period, the results become illusory, and thus the bankers profit illegitimately and exorbitantly.

The American national government, for instance, according to CNN, is shelling out $659 billion in interest payments in fiscal year 2023, which is up $184 billion, or 39 percent, from 2022, to service the national debt. Even more shocking is that the interest payments have doubled since just 2020! This is what happens when compound interest is allowed to accumulate since before the turn of the twentieth century, and it will only grow bigger as the total national debt continues to grow. CNN further reported:

> *Interest payments now rank fourth in spending, behind Social Security, Medicare, and defense, according to Marc Goldwein, senior policy director for the Committee for a Responsible Federal Budget. The government spent more on net interest than on Medicaid, veterans programs, and all spending on children in the last fiscal year. And if rates remain high, as expected, interest payments could overtake defense within a few years. This means more federal*

*tax revenue is going toward interest payments. The obligation ate up about 30 cents of every tax dollar in the first three quarters of fiscal 2023...*[4]

America's fastest growing expense item is compound interest, not only because the national debt has been exploding in recent years due to wild spending but also because it has been compounding for nearly one hundred and fifty years. America is becoming a credit risk. Alas, any national government carrying revolving debt beyond a fifty year period is robbing its future to pay for its past extravagances, as the following graphic comparing simple interest (interest paid annually) to compound interest (interest allowed to compound on top of itself) illustrates. In a simple interest loan, the amount of annual interest is unchanged, but as nations allow national debts to compound for hundreds of years, the "hockey stick" phenomena of interest upon interest kicks in and the debts become unmanageable.

# SIMPLE vs. COMPOUND INTEREST

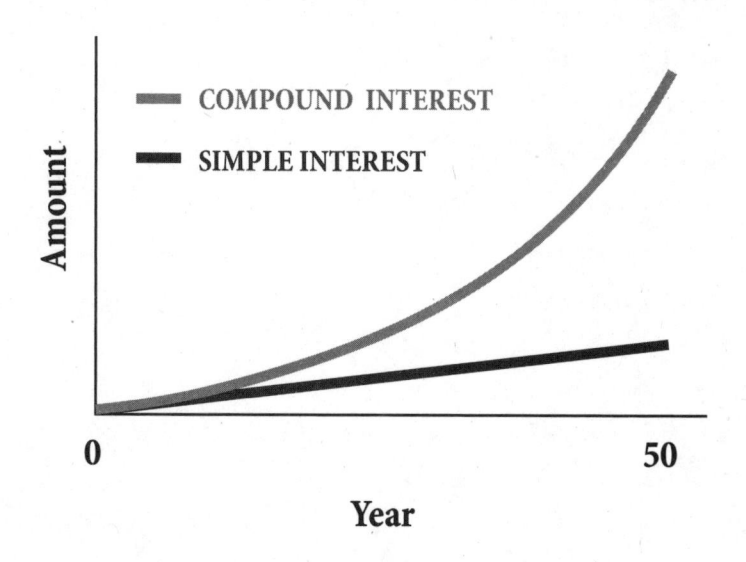

When the compound interest begins increasing annually more than the original annual simple interest amount (somewhere around year fifty), the repayment of national debts becomes practically impossible. This is exactly what the bankers count on, for they then receive compound interest on national debts indefinitely. The result is astronomical annual profits for bankers and an incalculable drain upon the world's production.

Now that we understand the difference between legitimate and illegitimate banking (lending at compound interest), we are ready to study fractional reserve banking itself, the bankers' first fraud, conjurer's illusion, and original sin all rolled into one. From this we will see how bankers obtained absolute power and astronomical profits.

*I have discovered the secret of the philosopher's stone: it is to make gold out of paper.*
—*Financier John Law*

# –5–

## Fractional (or Fictional) Reserve Banking
*You can have your cake and eat it too.*

Fractional reserve banking is deceptively simple yet incredibly difficult to detect. As we already discussed, it originated back when bankers accepted customer deposits in precious metal money and then committed fraud by creating more metaphysical titles for that money than they actually had. Because paper titles were safer and more convenient to carry around than physical money, paper notes began replacing physical coinage for making purchases. Naturally, once people trusted that the metaphysical banknotes were accepted as readily as the physical coins, depositors rarely requested the return of their physical coins since it was safer to leave them in bank vaults. In time, paper certificates (banknotes) became the preferred medium of exchange rather than physical coins. In other words, the people readily went along with the shift from physical money to symbolic money because it was convenient.

Modern money is occult-like, where banking high-priests bring to life magical money symbols for which people must labor. Interestingly, F.A. Hayek noticed the connection between FRB fraud and dark magic when he explained "activities that appear to add to available wealth 'out of nothing,' without physical recreation, and by merely rearranging what already exists, stink of sorcery..."[1] Such sorcery, however, leads to a mismatch between a bank's alleged assets and its liabilities. Depositors expect all their money to be available on-demand at any moment, which means the bank has a short-term liability to the customer. However, fractional reserve banks loan most of the customer's deposits to other people and, in so doing, claim the customer's money is now a long-term asset of the bank. This is the inherent fraud within the FRB system—the same money at the same time is both a short-term liability and a long-term asset. This, of course, is why it is a legal impossibility, and why this inherently insolvent system suffers from routine liquidity crises. This is also why the FRB scam is so profitable, for even though physical money and physical production are limited, the bankers' metaphysical note creation through these layers of lending is unlimited. The very term 'fractional reserve' is misleading. It should instead be "fictional reserve," as the money simply isn't there in the vault.

To be sure, physical assets being represented by metaphysical symbols is not in itself magic or fraud; however, *when metaphysical symbols increase beyond the physical asset they represent, fraud is being committed.* Fractional reserve banking pretends to have the right to create more metaphysical symbols than actual money in existence. Essentially the banks are performing monetary alchemy, which was the dream of every power-hungry monarch in the Middle Ages. Those original alchemists sought the mythical 'philosopher's stone' to turn base metals into gold, and they failed miserably. The bankers sought a new philosopher's stone that turned metaphysical symbols into something that people accepted as gold, and they succeeded fantastically. David Hawkes stated: "The implication is that alchemy did not disappear because it failed, but because it succeeded."[2]

Symbolic alchemy is simply the expansion of the symbols beyond the physical reality they are supposed to represent. To give an example, banknotes are to money what titles or deeds are to houses. They both represent physical assets metaphysically. To protect against housing alchemy, a title search is performed before the sale of a home to ensure the seller is the sole owner of the house. This limits alchemic scammers from creating and sell-

# FRACTIONAL (OR FICTIONAL) RESERVE BANKING

ing counterfeit house titles. After all, if a city has ten thousand houses, then it must have exactly ten thousand house titles, for if any more exist, then someone has committed fraud. Ironically, the alchemy that the housing market prevents as standard practice is permitted in the banking field as standard practice.

**Fractional Reserve Banking**

Fractional reserve banking is gambling. Rarely would all of a bank's depositors request the return of their money all at once; therefore, banks gamble and profit on the fact that it's an unlikely occurrence. The banks therefore profit from the funds that are supposed to be safe and secure in their vaults.

For example, imagine fifty people depositing $2,000 each into checking accounts at the local bank, which means the bank now has $100,000 in total deposits. The bank then lends out $50,000 to someone who uses it to purchase something. Now imagine the seller, the person the borrower purchased the item from, depositing that $50,000 into his checking account at the same bank. The bank claims its total deposits are now $150,000, but that $50,000 is actually being double counted. How can the bank owe the $50,000 to both the original depositors and the new depositor at the same time? Different people believe they are the full owners of the same money, which is a logical impossibility but a fraudulent reality. The bank only has $100,000 in actual deposits, and if all depositors were to withdraw their funds at the same time, the bank would be $50,000 short. Of course, in the instance where the borrower pays back the $50,000 plus interest, the bank will be ahead, but it will take years to be repaid in full, while the depositors could expect their money on demand at any moment. In effect, the FRB system operates like this: short-term customer deposits come in, and the bank uses these super secure short-term customer deposits to invest in riskier long-term assets and gambles that customers don't all want their funds back at the same time.

We have discussed this process of fractional reserve shenanigans so much that it might be helpful to stop for a moment and highlight how honest banking should operate. An honest bank would request from depositors the right to use their funds for a period of time in order to lend them to another party. This would 'lock up' the funds and prohibit them from being withdrawn while the borrower is using them. Importantly, this prevents the expansion of the money supply since every dollar is only used and counted once. The bank would have to pay interest to the original depositor to use his funds and then earn higher interest by lending them to the borrower for that longer time period. Interestingly, banks already perform this function, for this is how a Certificate of Deposit (CD) works, where the depositor agrees to commit the funds for a period of time to receive interest, and the funds are only available for withdrawal after that time period. It's not that the banking system doesn't know how to be honest; it's just that it's so much more profitable to be dishonest.

Economist Murray Rothbard stated the case against fractional reserve banking in no uncertain terms:

*I believe that fractional reserve banking is disastrous both for the morality and for the fundamental bases and institutions of the market economy...I am familiar with the many arguments for fractional reserve banking. There is the view that this is simply economical: The banks began with 100 percent reserves, but then they shrewdly and keenly saw that only a certain proportion of these demand liabilities were likely to be redeemed, so that it seemed safe either to lend out the gold for profit...The banks here take on the character of shrewd entrepreneurs. But so is an embezzler shrewd when he takes money out of the company till to invest in some ventures of his own. Like the banker, he sees an opportunity to earn a profit on someone else's assets. The embezzler knows, let us say, that the auditor will come on June 1 to inspect the accounts; and he fully intends to repay the "loan" before then. Let us assume that he does; is it really true that no one has been the loser and everyone has gained? I dispute this; a theft has occurred, and that theft should be prosecuted and not condoned. Let us note that the banking advocate assumes that something has gone wrong only if everyone should decide to redeem his property, only to find that it isn't there. But I maintain that the wrong—the theft—occurs at the time the embezzler takes the money, not at the later time when his "borrowing" happens to be discovered.*[3]

Interestingly, even in today's environment, banks are not allowed, without the consent of the owner, to access private safe deposit boxes to 'borrow' their contents. Why aren't the same rules applied to the money deposited in the banking system itself? In other words, leave my money in the vault so I can access it on demand, and if the bank wants to use it, they can request to do so for a specific time period at an interest that would entice me to agree. While there is nothing wrong with the legitimate banking function of loan-brokering, assuming both parties agree to the terms, the FRB cartel forces all deposits to be part of their lending operation, which again indicates FRB is not a free market.

**Fractional Reserve Boating**

The fractional reserve banking system is so universal today that few realize how scandalous it is. Perhaps the best way to highlight the foolishness of this fraud is to propose its practice within another business field. For instance, imagine a clever marina owner with two hundred dock slips and a boat repair shop located in sunny Florida. The owner was tired of standard 5 percent returns from the marina, and wanted to make ten to one hundred times the returns like the banking field does. After studying fractional reserve banking principles extensively, he shut down his marina to revamp it to include the practice of fractional reserve boating. Of course, he didn't publicly advertise the FRB concept but just put it into practice. First, he identified northern boaters as his target market and offered to not only dock their boat for free but actually pay them 2 percent of the value of their boat annually if the owner kept the boat at the marina year-round. In addition, the marina offered to fix major repairs at cost, and perform routine and cosmetic touch-ups free of charge. The northern boat owners could not believe it! They had formerly paid thousands of dollars per month in slip fees, but now instead they would be paid a small fee for the same result. And maintaining the boat would now be less than a third of the previous cost. Although too good to be true, the deal was too enticing for out-of-state boaters not to capitalize on, and the marina not only filled all the dock slips, but had hundreds of new customers on a waiting list.

The marina owner easily paid the 2 percent annual bonus for owners who kept boats in slips all year and easily handled the extra boat maintenance costs because he made use of his customers' assets (their boats) when they were not in Florida. The marina owner launched a fractional reserve boating scheme by creating nine counterfeit titles for every boat stored there. Then he walked people through the boats and sold the counterfeit titles, meaning he now had nine other people all believing they owned the same boat. Meanwhile, the marina still behaved as if each owner was the sole one, and the boat was apparently readily available whenever the owner wanted it. Occasionally, if two parties wanted the boat on the same date, the second party to the request was told that the boat would be undergoing free cosmetic work and was put off until it was available again.

# FRACTIONAL (OR FICTIONAL) RESERVE BANKING

With such a scheme, the marina owner sold two hundred boats nine more times each, and pocketed massive profits! No wonder he could afford to pay the 2 percent annual fee to ensure people's boats resided in his marina and therefore were involved in his scam all year long. The marina owner will naturally justify his con by claiming more people are enjoying boating privileges than ever before at a lower cost than ever before. He will be quick to point out that he has stimulated the boating economy by helping dormant assets become active ones, and all of these amazing results were achieved through the magic of fractional reserve boating!

FRB is undeniably brilliant, but it's also undeniably wrong. It thrives upon deception, and it steals real value while selling synthetic value. The marina owner can claim he benefited others, but the truth is he stole value from the people who truly owned the boats and the people who manufactured boats by substituting and selling counterfeit boats instead of the real thing.

Importantly, FRB is not partial ownership of an asset or the renting of an asset, both of which, with full disclosure under liberty and justice for all, would be perfectly legitimate. As I hope the boating example has shown, the FRB scam instead creates counterfeit titles and attempts to pass them off as true wealth, even though Say's Law illustrates that true wealth in society is the supply of actual marketable goods and services for sale. The fractional reserve boat charlatan did not increase the supply of real goods, only fraudulent titles. Amazingly, the banking system has run a similar scam since the late Middle Ages. Part of the reason they've gotten away with it is that money is much easier to hide than FRB in most other fields, because money is completely fungible (meaning one dollar is completely interchangeable with and indistinguishable from all other dollars), whereas boat owners would probably detect someone else was using their boat. Still, the silly boating example illustrates FRB for the serious fraud it truly is.

**Fractional Reserve Supporters**

There are many so-called experts who will wax eloquently in praise of FRB. To my mind, there are only two reasons why so many otherwise intelligent and informed economists and historians would support fractional reserve banking: 1) they haven't dug deep enough into FRB to understand its inherently fraudulent nature, or 2) they understand very clearly what it is but either benefit from, or are complicit in covering up the scam by purposeful convolution, obfuscation, and misdirection. Jack Weatherford, for instance, who is an otherwise solid monetary historian, marveled at the evident ability of FRB to manipulate the money supply. He described how a Renaissance noble's one hundred gold florins that used to sit idle, when expanded through FRB, mysteriously benefited multiple parties:

> *Even though only one hundred gold coins were involved, the miracle of banking deposits and loans had transformed them into many hundreds of florins that could be used by different individuals in different cities at the same time. This new banking money opened vast new commercial avenues for merchants, manufacturers, and investors. Everyone had more money: it was sheer magic.*[4]

I shake my head when monetary historians explain FRB using terms like "magic," "mystery," and "alchemy." After all, economic science is supposed to be rational, logical, and systematic. Although magic is one possible answer as to how numerous buyers hold identical titles to the same physical piece of gold all at the same time, fraud is the much more likely explanation. I wonder if Weatherford would defend our wayward boat seller in a court of law and invoke magic as his main defense?

# FRACTIONAL (OR FICTIONAL) RESERVE BANKING

Believe it or not, FRB was once argued in the courtroom in a case entitled Lawrence versus Morgan. The acting president of the First National Bank of Montgomery testified about banking practices in the landmark 1968 Credit River Case. Rarely are banking practices discussed in the courtroom, for they do not hold up well under the bright lights of legal inquiry, and even when cases do go to trial, banking witnesses usually give perfunctory testimonies about the specific details. In this particular case, however, the people caught a glimpse of how banking really works. In cross-examination, trial lawyer Jerome Daly asked the bank president, "If you were just opening up your bank and no one had yet made a deposit, and I came into your bank and wanted to take out a loan of $18,000, could you loan me that money?" When Morgan said, "Yes," Daly then asked, "Does this mean that you can create money out of thin air?" And the bank president said, "Yes, we can create money out of thin air."[5] This is under oath in a court of law, and the president of a bank flat-out admitted that his bank, and all banks, create mortgage debts by mere notations in their logbooks. The bank can create the credit out of thin air, even if it had never received a single penny in deposits. Morgan even admitted that he knew of no US law that gave his bank permission to do this, but simply stated that it was the standard banking practice.

This testimony bolstered the defendant's claim that since the banks produce money out of thin air, they had no lawful consideration for the note because the bank had parted with absolutely nothing of value to create the money in the first place! And since the buyer had paid on the house mortgage for years, he has much more lawful consideration than the bank, which merely created the money out of thin air. Nonetheless, the bank lawyers were demanding the physical house be given to them, even though they didn't build it, live in it, or pay anything to create the original loan. At this point, Justice Martin V. Mahoney was puzzled, for he had no idea that was how the modern FRB system operated. He thus concluded, "It sounds like fraud to me," and everybody in the courtroom nodded in agreement. The jury subsequently ruled unanimously for the defendant. This case should have opened the door to financial justice, but the case was thrown out on appeal because the bank claimed Mahoney had no jurisdiction, even though the bank had originally agreed to Mahoney's jurisdiction. The bankers, strikingly, didn't argue that they did not receive a fair trial, but only sought a different jurisdiction in order to get a ruling in their favor. The case went down the memory hole, but for those who desire financial justice, Bank President Morgan's shocking admissions should not be forgotten. Economist Murray Rothbard provided an even more direct testimony when he wrote: "It should be clear that modern fractional reserve banking (FRB) is a shell game, a Ponzi scheme, a fraud in which fake warehouse receipts are issued and circulate as equivalent to the cash supposedly represented by those receipts."[6]

This is not just a moral issue. FRB expands the total money supply, which has huge ramifications for the economy and individuals. For simplicity sake, let's consider a Renaissance bank with 10 percent reserves. That bank could theoretically expand 100 pounds of gold into 1,000 pounds of debt-money. The FRB system, in this example, has created 900 pounds of debt-money out of thin air. This means that a nation's FRB system practicing 10 percent reserve levels inflates the total money supply by $(1/.1 = 10)$ ten times. This is really bad news for everyone but the banks because, as Say's Law shows, the true wealth in society is in the supply of products and services that are exchanged for money. Therefore, when the FRB cartel expands the money supply ten times beyond the naturally physically limited precious metal money, it has effectively stolen $(9/10 = .90)$ 90 percent of the nation's wealth because it can use counterfeit money to buy

# FRACTIONAL (OR FICTIONAL) RESERVE BANKING

real goods and services. The following chart depicts just how much the money supply can expand when doing the exact same thing the Renaissance banks did, only on a larger scale.

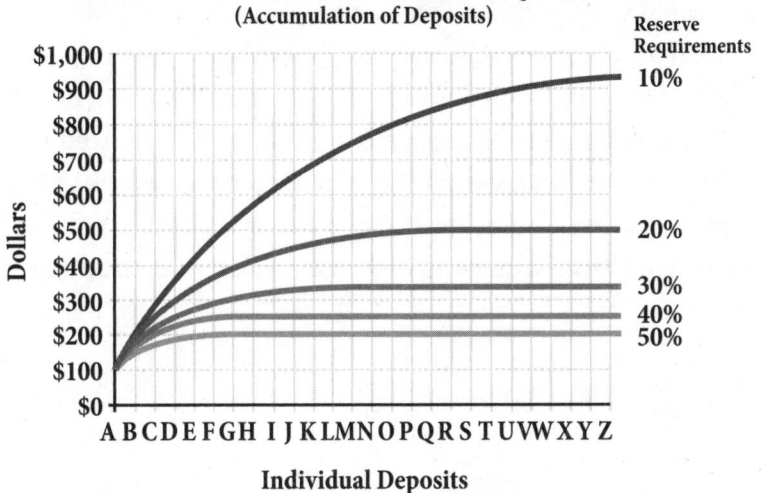

**THE EXPANSION OF $100 THROUGH FRACTIONAL RESERVE BANKING WITH VARYING RESERVE REQUIREMENTS**
(Accumulation of Deposits)

*Y-axis: Dollars ($0–$1,000); X-axis: Individual Deposits (A–Z)*

Reserve Requirements: 10%, 20%, 30%, 40%, 50%

The worst aspect of fractional reserve banking fraud, however, is that every monetary inflation is systematically followed by a monetary deflation, for FRB creates a debt-money supply that expands and contracts as part of its very nature. Although this inherent instability of debt-money has been pointed out by several economists, no one has described how the FRB system's architecture is the root cause of its inherent instability. To do this ourselves, we must remember that, although dynamic systems can be complicated, they consist of only two fundamental types of loops: reinforcing and balancing. Reinforcing loops occur when a change in the system serves as a signal for further change in the same direction. These loops lead to explosive exponential growth or decline, depending upon whether the loop is positive or negative reinforcing. Disastrously, the FRB system is a reinforcing loop that switches from positive expansion of the money supply to negative contraction when further FRB expansion is no longer possible, producing a destructive economic whiplash. The key point here is that positive and negative reinforcing loops inherent within its system architecture mean that FRB can expand and contract the money supply, but it can never provide a stable money supply. The Free Market Mechanism (FMM) and the free market economy, in contrast, are balancing loop systems, where a change in the system serves as a signal for change in the opposite direction as the goal-seeking system seeks to restore its own balance. The money supply, as defined by its systems architecture, is the set parameter in the free market system and must remain stable (this stability is why gold and silver are free market money).

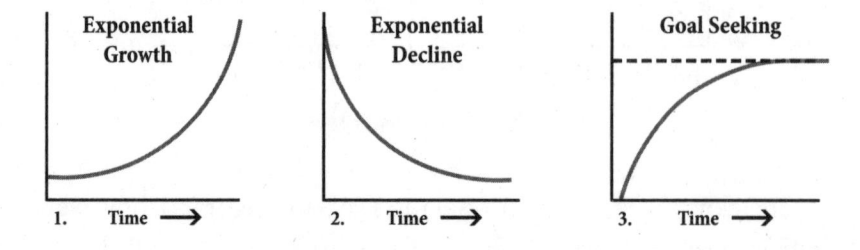

|  |  |  |
| --- | --- | --- |
| Exponential Growth | Exponential Decline | Goal Seeking |
| 1. Time → | 2. Time → | 3. Time → |

As we have said many times before, this is because money measures the natural variation between market demand and supply to arrive at the dynamic equilibrium price. Instead of providing a stable money supply, the FRB system through its positive and negative reinforcing loops, causes a wave-like oscillation in the money supply. This is due to the mathematical absurdity of total debts increasing faster than the total supply of actual money it is supposedly based upon.

Let's consider an example. When FRB lends $250,000 for a mortgage at 5% interest, the borrower owes $488,000 over the next thirty years, even though only $250,000 of FRB debt-money was created. Because no debt-money is created to pay for all that interest, an unnatural scarcity is created between the total debts

# FRACTIONAL (OR FICTIONAL) RESERVE BANKING

and total money supply. Even though the borrower owes $250,000 in principal and another $233,000 in interest, only $250,000 of total debt-money was ever created. This forces the borrower to compete with other borrowers in a progressively scarcer money supply (just like musical chairs, it has built in systemic scarcity that is unnatural) to raise enough funds to service his debts.

To describe how positive and negative reinforcing loops work in a system, imagine a slinky attached to the ceiling of the space shuttle in a no gravity environment. If one of the astronauts were to pull the slinky down to expand the spring and then release it, the system would form a simple harmonic motion (SHM) where the spring expands from its base and contracts back to its base again. Without friction, this SHM would move the block up and down forever as an oscillating wave. This describes the FRB system wonderfully, for it expands (inflation of the money supply) and contracts (deflation of the money supply) like a spring. Because of the inherent imbalance between total debt-money supply and total debts, the FRB system either expands or contracts, but it can never be stable. This is the systemic cause of the inherent instability within the FRB architecture.

Let's dig a little deeper into why this is. Once FRB fraud is practiced, every month additional FRB loans must be procured to ensure enough new debt-money is created to service the old FRB loans. This continues every month until the gap between the total debt-money and total debts is so large that not enough new FRB loans can be created for the borrowers to service their loans (as our example of the mortgage above demonstrates). As soon as this happens, the most marginal (the least solvent) borrowers begin defaulting, meaning they stop paying and lose the claim to the asset that was financed. Instantly, the money implied in their loan agreement evaporates. The bank confiscates the asset and usually sells it off on the cheap to try and recover at least some of the principle. The difference between the contracted amount the borrower owed (including total predicted interest) and the fire sale price of the liquidated asset is the amount of money that disappeared from the money supply. Naturally, every default applies additional stress to the inherently insolvent FRB fraud, which makes the FRB system lend even less money the following month and even more borrowers default. This is why FRB is systematically either a positive reinforcing loop, where every FRB loan leads to the need for even more FRB loans (like a game of musical chairs), or a negative reinforcing loop, where the first round of FRB defaults leads (when the music stops in the game of musical chairs) to progressively more FRB defaults. In this scenario, the money supply greatly expanded during the FRB inflation and then greatly contracted during the FRB deflation.

Picture now the spring expanding during the FRB inflation and then contracting during the FRB deflation in a simple harmonic motion. Since such oscillation is a mathematical phenomenon and there is no friction in this numerical system, the process repeats indefinitely so long as the FRB fraud is practiced. In other words, the FRB system expands the money supply like the expanding spring, but with each monetary expansion, it becomes progressively more difficult to keep the money spring expanding, and eventually the tension is too much and things have to snap back in the other direction. And, as you are probably imagining, the "snapping back" is almost always more sudden and violent than the gradual tensioning of the slinky spring in the first place. This is exactly what it feels like in the economy when things go bad.

# FRACTIONAL (OR FICTIONAL) RESERVE BANKING

## SIMPLE HARMONIC MOTION

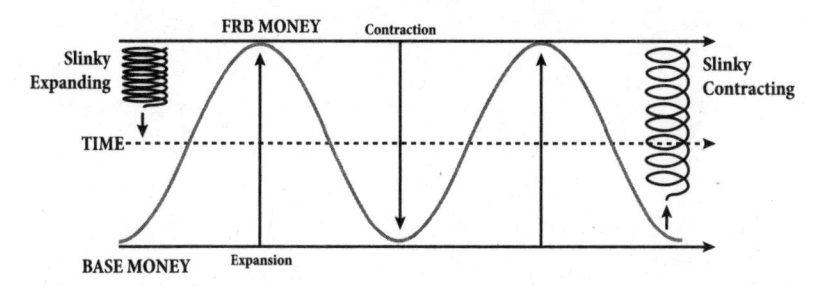

Knowing that monetary stability is the most important function of money in the free market, to select FRB debt-money to run the economy instead, which produces inflationary and deflationary oscillating money supply waves, is the height of insanity. But such a damaging financial mechanism has generated disproportionate wealth for a disproportionate few for a long time now, and that's why it remains unaddressed. The fact that this causes disruption and pain for the many does not seem to bother the few, as elites can always be relied upon to find academic justifications for their profits and power. Normally, such explanations fall into the 'it's for their own good' category (refer to the 'it's like magic' exclamations of academicians cited above). Indeed, there are endless academic and structural curtains to hide the wizards pulling the levers while keeping the people mesmerized by the magic of the FRB Oz. In such a way, the banking system has gained control over most of the economy. At this point one might wonder, "How did we get here?"

*Taking a bribe, letting yourself be bought off, accepting flattery in exchange for some sort of loyalty, is sabotage. Refusing to confront an issue because if you keep quiet, you'll get a promotion or be made an elder or keep your job corrupts you down deep.*
—John Eldredge

# -6-

## Medicis and Fuggers Develop the Private Money Playbook
*The borrower is slave to the lender.*

Fractional reserve banking is an increasingly destructive force. As author David Hawkes explained, "The more abstract and self-referential money grows, the less reference it bears to the physical world or to any objective reality, and the more energetic, voracious, and destructive it becomes."[1] Once FRB is permitted, fraudulent money symbols create unlimited opportunities for corruption and control. Proverbs 22:7 states, "The rich rules over the poor, and the borrower is slave to the lender." A verse written three thousand years ago predicted our modern enslavement of borrowers to bankers. Alas, the unlimited ability to create money symbols has naturally given the bankers an unlimited power to corrupt.

Indeed, the early Italian bankers that fueled the Renaissance undermined the traditional code of ethics in the West. Instead of acknowledging the danger of man's inherently sinful nature, which leads to corruption, crime, and war to oppress others, the Renaissance, as expressed by its spokesman Niccolo Machiavelli, celebrated man's quests for unlimited power. Jesus's Golden Rule, "Do unto others what you would have them do unto you," was replaced with the Power Rule, "Do whatever you have the power to do." Writer Bradley Birzer explained:

*From Socrates forward, one may trace a line of ethics that demanded "do no harm." From Socrates to the Stoics to Cicero to Augustine to Aquinas to Dante. The West had acknowledged sin, but had done much to limit its capacity to grow. Machiavelli—through just a few works—gave justification to the growing impetus of the post-medieval world to embrace power at the expense of sacrifice and love. In more ways than one, Machiavelli served as the direct counter to Aquinas, who had argued forcefully time and again that the only good leader was one who would sacrifice himself for his people as had Christ...Making no apology for admiring both Mohammad for his violence and Pope Alexander VI for his cruelty, Machiavelli openly embraced the use of power and utility over the restraint and charity of love and dignity. The effective ruler, in an almost perfect contrast to the teachings of St. Thomas Aquinas, utilizes good as well as evil when working toward a greater good. Machiavelli calculated how much force to bring to bear by, slyly redefining "prudence."*[2]

Machiavelli, in other words, provided the intellectual framework for bankers' divorce of power from ethics. Instead of moral absolutes guiding power, absolute power now guided morality. One could even say Machiavelli was the creator of the worldview depicted in The Matrix movie because he shamelessly promoted that those in power should exploit the gap between perception and reality. He wrote, "For the great majority of mankind are satisfied with appearances, as though they were realities and are often more influenced by the things that seem than by those that are."[3] Power was no longer restrained by ethical considerations, having become autonomous from God's laws. And since the ends now justified the means, FRB money was the fraudulent means for bankers to gain the ends of absolute power and profits.

Now that we understand how the FRB fraud has helped bankers achieve control conceptually, let's study how they achieved it

## MEDICIS AND FUGGERS

in actuality. Two Renaissance banking families, the Medicis and Fuggers, turned theory into practice and used the FRB fraud to achieve power and influence over the rulers of Europe. While both families began as humble servants to church and state rulers, in time they became the power behind both church and state. The Medicis and Fuggers exchanged loans for favors, and as borrowers became increasingly desperate as the size of their loans increased, so too did the size of the favors requested (or demanded). These stories are not shared to denigrate church and state but merely to illustrate the corrupting influence that unlimited money can have on every human institution. As Lord Acton said, "Power corrupts, and absolute power corrupts absolutely." As regards our journey into the Financial Matrix, we might best modify this to "money corrupts, and limitless money corrupts absolutely."

The Medicis, followed by the Fuggers, ruled the banking world in the 15th and 16th centuries. Five successive generations of Medici bankers and several generations of Fuggers controlled the destinies of popes, rulers, and armies alike. Although today the Medici are remembered more for their patronage of the arts during the Renaissance, and the Fuggers for their Fuggerei housing project, these vanity displays were merely the public relations side of their highly profitable banking ventures. Just how profitable the FRB fraud was for these families is noted by their biographers, as Christopher Hibbert explained that the Medici were the "most profitable family business in the whole of Europe,"[4] and Greg Steinmetz stated that "a German banker named Jacob Fugger became the richest man in history."[5] The Medicis and Fuggers generated profits ten to twenty times higher than conventional businesses by unleashing the fractional reserve banking (FRB) fraud upon Christendom.

Both banking families profited greatly through serving the Roman Catholic Church, which received tithe revenue from nearly every city, kingdom, and ken in Christendom. Indeed, it was this money deposited into the Medici and Fugger banks that supplied the monetary base for the FRB loans. Ironically, despite the church's condemnation of usury interest, no medieval organization contributed more to the growth of banking than the Roman Catholic Church, whose monthly deposits were invaluable for the growth of the Medici and Fuggers. According to their own accounts, whereas traditional merchant trade businesses generated profits of around 5 percent, Medici and Fugger FRB loans produced annual returns of around 50 percent! And this rate of profit was recorded in their public books, the ones they showed to the tax authorities, not the private books, where they hid even more exorbitant profits. Thus, if they admitted to 50 percent profits when traditional enterprises at the time were making 5 percent, it makes you wonder about the true magnitude of their profits. The Medicis and Fuggers, although impressive business people, when engaged in their traditional businesses made normal levels of profits, but in the banking field, their FRB fraud made them look brilliant. Their returns regularly dwarfed those of their competitors because of their close affiliation with and flow of funds from the official church. In fact, the first generation Medici bankers averaged around 1,900 florins profit annually, at a time when a prosperous gentleman could live comfortably on 200 florins a year, and skilled workers supported entire families on less than 100 florins annually. Fugger banks were even more impressive, with over 50% returns on investments for decades, and this return is after the Fuggers made their capital withdrawals to support their lavish lifestyles.

The bankers secured profits and power through corrupting the church, state, and societal leaders. For example, they made a killing working with the popes, who were always in need of more money. The unscrupulous bankers served the popes by reviving simony, the selling of church offices. The bankers were the matchmakers who connected potential buyers to the pope, who was the seller. Although simony was unlawful, it nonetheless became widely practiced because it benefited all three parties. The pope gained extra money, the buyer gained a new office, and the bankers gained new loans from the borrower to pay the pope. Of course, the buyers knew they could repay the loans from the monthly proceeds of the new office they had just purchased. Prospective bishops, cardinals, and popes wanted to be first in line when offices became available and thus began serving bankers more than they served God. And since the bankers prequalified the potential buyers, the banker families became highly influential in the papal hierarchy. Is it any wonder that two Medici later became popes? The loans were repaid promptly because delinquent borrowers were threatened with excommunication by the popes. Of course, since excommunication would separate the borrower from his new church office and its monthly revenues, the threat of losing monthly income normally helped the delinquent "repent" and resume loan repayments.

Cosimo de Medici, in fact, grew so wealthy that his biographer Vespasiano noted that Cosimo "accumulated quite a bit on his conscience, as most men do who govern states and want to be ahead of the rest"[6] Cosimo asked Pope Eugenius, one of his clients, how he could curry favor with God to "have mercy on him and preserve him in the enjoyment of his temporal goods." Eugenius encouraged Cosimo to invest ten thousand florins to restore the San Marco monastery. This was the first of many more devotional art investments the Medici made to renovate churches. Naturally, in return for his extravagant donations, Cosimo was granted a papal bull absolving him of all his sins. Cosimo had these words engraved in stone in his special double-sized monk's cell, which he commissioned for himself at the convent of San Marco: "Never shall I be able to give God enough to set him down in my books as a debtor."[7] Perhaps nothing else indicates how the banker Cosimo interacted with others more than this statement. He saw life, even eternal life, transactionally. Cosimo evidently believed only God was powerful enough to not be swayed by his banking money. Indeed, the Medicis and Fuggers learned that each loan given to borrowers carried with it an unspoken expectation that the borrower was on the line, not only monetarily but also psychologically, to serve the bankers.

Tim Parks described how money not only affected society, but because the bankers created money out of thin air, they could affect society on a previously unimaginable scale:

*With money, you can change your social position, you can have women and go to heaven. This is the contradiction behind so much mental activity in the West. We love money and what we imagine it can do and buy; and at the same time we are haunted by a fear as old as Achilles: surely there must be some value that is beyond buying and selling, something beyond the art of exchange. Oh, but not something, please, that tells us that money is altogether evil, that the plague that took away my child is God's punishment for my financial transactions. Such is the divided consciousness of the banker in the fourteenth and fifteenth centuries, such the contradiction that over the years will encourage the cultivation of less disturbing and morally demanding non-monetary values—in philosophy, aesthetics, and love.*[8]

The Medicis also paved the way for bankers to gain political power by exploiting the gap between perception and reality, which in Florentine politics was euphemistically referred to as "the secret things of our town." Despite having a lottery system every two months to select the nine person ruling council called the Signoria, which was created to share power between the various political factions in Florence, the Medicis corrupted and controlled the entire process. Indeed, for over sixty years, with six lotteries per year, the Medicis successfully achieved a majority of Signoria members in their faction. Although the law of averages cannot account for this amazing run, the strategic use of Medici money certainly can, as the bankers not only ensured the right names were placed in the bag but also that the right person drew the names from it. The Medicis mastered the fine art of predictable election results over the "free" Florentine elections by using political corruption, lessons that future bankers have not forgotten. Thus, Florence had the best government Medici money could buy. The early Medicis, however, did not flaunt their elective powers, but instead celebrated Florentine's tradition of liberty to make sure the people's perceptions were not disturbed by the new reality. Cosimo brilliantly humbled himself to Florentine perceptions while ruling in reality, as Machiavelli described, "He mixed power with grace. He covered it over with decency."[9] Another Cosimo associate, Vespasiano da Bisticci, added, "And whenever he wished to achieve anything, to avoid envy, he gave the impression, as far as was possible, that it was they who had suggested the thing, not he."[10] Even though the celebrated Florentine republic was, in reality, a footstool for Medici power, Cosimo understood that absolute power is maintained by sustaining people's false perceptions of shared power. Alas, every fraud must have its facade.

In time, the people became aware of the gap between perception and reality when foreign ambassadors no longer lobbied at the Palazzo della Signoria (the Florence Town Hall), but instead visited the Medici palace. The Milanese ambassador went even further by moving into the Medici household. Lorenzo the Magnificent, the fourth generation Medici banking titan, removed all pretense and decided to rule publicly. This proved a mistake, for without the gap between the perception of freedom and the Medici reality, the consent of the people was gradually lost. As a result, opponents of Medici rule gathered strength, and after

Lorenzo's death, the family's reign was doomed. The Fuggers and all future bankers learned the lesson from this, namely, that control over state power is more secure when it remains secret and therefore does not ruffle the people's illusions.

The banker families also acquired economic monopolies through monetary corruption. For instance, Pope Paul II partnered with the Medicis in 1466 to monopolize the sale of alum throughout Europe, even though monopolies were illegal. Florence had a thriving wool trade business, and alum was an essential part of preparing the wool to be dyed. The Church and Medici monopolists publicly justified the profits, claiming they would support a new crusade against the Turks, but this again points to the gap between the noble motives communicated to the public as contrasted with the ignoble motives of the plunderers' reality. Fugger created an even bigger monopoly through his control over copper. He owned two big copper mines and negotiated a monopoly agreement where copper from each could only be sold in certain areas. This increased the prices and profits for Fugger, but when the agreements accidentally became public, the Germans were outraged. The German Reichstag attacked Fugger for his practices, and when enough of the assembly supported the measure, the imperial advocate started proceedings against Jacob for violating Germany's anti-monopoly laws, and the local town's government piled on by proceeding along the same lines.

Although Fugger was perturbed, he never panicked. He mobilized his lawyers and political operatives to attack those who attacked him. Fugger also requested Emperor Charles V write to the chief advocate directly, asking him to end all prosecution, and finally Fugger requested Archduke Ferdinand to quash the local court proceedings. These actions ended the attack against him, but Fugger was still not satisfied. He further directed Charles V to issue another decree, this time prepared by Fugger's imperial lobbyists, declaring that mining contracts granting monopoly

## MEDICIS AND FUGGERS

rights to merchants would no longer be considered a violation of the Reichstag decrees. Finally, the clearly riled Fugger insisted the Emperor issue a final decree to whitewash his 1515 and 1520 monopoly contracts, declaring that they did not involve "criminal enhancement of prices." There are a few historical examples that better illustrate how bankers use state influence to protect their business practices and reputations from state prosecution.

Jacob Fugger, despite being the financier who, more than any other individual, developed the Financial Matrix's playbook and became the richest and most powerful man of his age in the process, is practically unknown today. This is because Jacob deftly exercised his power behind the scenes and used the FRB fraud to gradually shift power and profits from the monarchs to the bankers. The Fuggers gained aristocratic titles, noble marriages, landed estates, and massive profits to go along with the mining monopolies they shrewdly built in the 1400s. This was achieved by lending to everyone who was anyone, including the monarchs Henry VIII of England, Charles V of Spain, and, of course, the Fuggers' meal ticket—the German Emperor Maximilian I. Jacob took Maximilian I to the cleaners, stripping the emperor, whom economist Richard Ehrenberg claimed was "the worst manager of all the Hapsburgs"[11] of nearly all his physical assets. Maximilian I was driven, prideful, and impractical. Considered the "last knight of Europe," the idealistic emperor was progressively impoverished by Fugger because his reach was routinely beyond his grasp. This led to a series of financial predicaments from which only Fugger could extricate him. Of course, every bailout led to an increasingly special deal for Fugger. The symbiotic relationship between banker and monarch flowed physical assets, pecuniary profits, and immense influence to Jacob, while flowing debt, stress, and eventual poverty to Maximilian and his royal offspring. Although Fugger loans provided perceptions of the royal Hapsburgs basking in wealth, glory, and prestige, the reality was far different. Jacob pillaged Maximilian I, gaining monopolies, tax abatements, land grants, and anything else he desired, while his client became debt dependent. Sure, Maximilian I gained state power and control in his territories, but only because Fugger used centralized state power to protect the bank's interests.

As Emperor Maximilian I realized he was sinking further and further into debt, he attempted to use his newly gained state powers to force Fugger and the other bankers to invest in bonds for yet another war. Fugger was incensed that the emperor would seek to use force against the bankers. Even though force and fraud were the cardinal virtues of his FRB fraud and mining monopoly, he was shocked when Maximilian I proposed to force the bankers to serve his empire. In 1508, as a result, Fugger paradoxically represented himself as a defender of free markets and ethical business practices, despite knowingly practicing the FRB fraud and mining monopolies to build his business empire. Jacob's growing arrogance is already apparent in his communication with the emperor, as author Greg Steinmetz described:

*Fugger started with what he said was obvious. Companies like his benefitted every level of society, producing jobs and wealth for all. Business could only work its magic if the government left it alone. If politicians threw up roadblocks and killed the profit motive, business had no chance. Merchants and bankers were good citizens, he argued. They treated each other and their customers fairly. Sure, self-interest propelled them. But they knew better than to cheat customers. Reputation was everything and the need for credibility checked the urge to lie, gouge and steal. Hinting at the allure of tax havens (the Swiss border was only sixty miles away), he declared that other countries show businessmen more respect. He blasted those who condemned commerce and enterprise. They failed to understand that "it is for the common good that honour-*

*able, brave and honest companies are in the realm. For it is not disreputable but rather it is wonderful jewel that such companies are in the kingdom"*[12]

By 1515, the disparity between Fugger and Habsburg lifestyles could no longer be hidden. At the Congress of Vienna, where Fugger was surrounded by his magnificently attired family and rich bank agents dispensed invaluable gifts to favored nobles to gain influence, another scene was unfolding in the royal chambers. The Emperor Maximilian, believed to be one of the most powerful and richest monarchs in Christendom, was greeting guests in his resplendent attire, draped with an opulent robe radiating with priceless jewels. Although the crowd was awed by the Hapsburg's theatrics, the reality was much less dazzling, for Maximilian was broke and didn't possess any jewelry because he had surrendered it to the Fuggers as collateral toward one of his many loans. The invaluable jewels worn by Maximilian I belonged to the Fuggers and were provided to the emperor for the night so he could keep up appearances. Whereas Fugger became one of the wealthiest men in history, Maximilian died impoverished, embarrassed, and embittered. Fugger got power and profits while Maximillian got poverty and pain. The Fuggers sustained the perception of monarchical power for Maximillian while achieving actual power for themselves.

One of Fugger's last services on Emperor Maximilian I's behalf was helping the monarch's grandson, King Charles of Spain, become the next Holy Roman Emperor. The deplorable election process involved immense bribery due to the bidding war between the rulers of Spain and France. For instance, King Francis of France offered one elector a rich French wife with a large dowry, but Fugger quickly countered with the granddaughter of Maximilian (the sister of King Charles) and 300,000 Rhenish gulden. Maximilian had commissioned Fugger to carry out all arrangements, but when the Emperor died, the brash Charles notified Fugger of another banker who would complete the services at a lower price. Needless to say, Fugger was furious. The imperious banker told Charles that if his services were no longer needed by the Hapsburgs, then he would consider supporting King Francis's bid instead. Fugger was playing chess compared to the monarchs' checkers, for he slyly bribed the electors a second time, promising to pay them even more funds if they insisted their money be paid by the Fuggers and no other banks. When King Charles's ministers reported back the electors' new demands, he realized Fugger had outfoxed him. Fugger understood that bribes are only as good as the ability to pay, and with the record breaking amounts of bribery involved, Fugger's reputation and secondary bribes ensured he was the logical choice to pay the electors to ensure King Charles' election. The humbled Charles reluctantly submitted, Fugger completed the arrangement, and the new Holy Roman Emperor became Fugger's loyal client.

Fugger understood that the ability to create money out of thin air gave the bankers power over the rulers, who were constantly in need of that money, but he was wise enough to keep the people and the rulers, believing the kingdom was sovereign over its policies. Nevertheless, if the public State Power ever encroached upon the private Financial Power, Fugger knew how to tweak the wayward ruler's nose. One glaring example of this is a missive he wrote to Charles regarding a delinquent loan. Here is Fugger's full letter:

*His Most Serene, Ail-Powerful Roman Emperor, and most Gracious Lord!*

*Your Royal Majesty is undoubtedly well aware of the extent to which I and my nephews have always been inclined to serve the House of Austria and, in all submissiveness, to promote its wel-*

*fare and its rise. For that reason, we cooperated with the former Emperor Maximilian, Your Imperial Majesty's forefather, and, in loyal subjection to His Majesty, to secure the Imperial Crown for Your Imperial Majesty, pledged ourselves to several princes, who placed their confidence and trust in me as perhaps in no one else. We also, when Your Imperial Majesty's undertaking, furnished a considerable sum of money, which was secured not from me and my nephews alone but from some of my good friends at heavy cost, so that the excellent nobles achieved success to the great honor and well-being of Your Imperial Majesty.*

*It is also well known that Your Majesty without me might not have acquired the Imperial Crown, as I can attest with the written statement of all the delegates of Your Imperial Majesty. And in all this, I have looked not to my own profit. For if I had withdrawn my support from the House of Austria and transferred it to France, I should have won large profit and much money, which were at that time offered to me. But what disadvantage would have risen thereby for the House of Austria, Your Imperial Majesty, with your deep comprehension, may well conceive.*

*Taking all this into consideration, my respectful request to Your Imperial Majesty is that you will graciously recognize my faithful, humble service, dedicated to the greater well-being of Your Imperial Majesty, and that you will order that the money which I have paid out, together with the interest upon it, shall be reckoned up and paid without further delay. In order to deserve that from Your Imperial Majesty, I pledge myself to be faithful in all humility, and I hereby commend myself as faithful at all times to Your Imperial Majesty.*

*Your Imperial Majesty's most humble servant,*
*Jacob Fugger*[13]

Despite language that seems flowery and verbose to our modern ears, this was a direct and boldly stinging rebuke. And it was hurled at a sovereign so powerful that, according to author Greg Steinmetz, "When the pope defied Charles, he sacked Rome. When Francis fought him, he captured the king," and an imperial councilor claimed Charles was "...himself a living law and above all other law. His Majesty is as God on earth."[4] The emperor clearly got the message, though. For even if he was the "living law," he was not above the laws of economics. Since Charles needed Fugger loans to fund his imperialistic ventures, he not only paid the debt but also wrote a letter to the Augsburg assembly demanding they terminate prosecution against Fugger for his monopolistic practices. The most powerful monarch in the world, in other words, meekly acquiesced at Fugger's rebuke. This is one of the most revealing episodes in the long history of power politics, clearly exposing the difference between perceived State Power and real Financial Power.

Interestingly, due to the hidden nature of banking practices, few realized that Fugger was instrumental in the events triggering the Reformation. It all started when an archbishop of two towns decided he wanted a third one. The corrupt bargain that was struck surpassed any previous case of simony, for the dataria (the church's sacred bureau) informed the bishop in question that for an additional 10,000 gulden bribe on top of the normal amount of fifteen or twenty thousand, they would approve the sale. Naturally, the bishop saw Fugger for the loan but also requested the banker work with the Papacy to help raise revenue to pay for the loan. Fugger was up for the challenge and developed a creative income stream by combining two immoral acts (simony and indulgences) to pay for Fugger's loan and Rome's new St. Peter's Church. Fugger partnered with Pope Leo, who granted a plenary indulgence for the bishop. Although this indulgence was ostensibly for the building of St. Peter's Church, the proceeds would in reality be split fifty-fifty between the Pope and the bishop. Fugger's scheme was ingenious: the pope got his bribe, the bishop got his third archbishopric, and Fugger secured loan payments through the revenue from the sale of indulgences.

This turns our modern stomachs, to be sure, but such chicanery was rampant and often largely undetected. The trouble arose in this case, however, when news of this dirty deal leaked and reached none other than the now famous Martin Luther. The indignant Augustinian monk exposed and castigated all parties involved, including the pope and archbishop, who "sent Fugger's cutpurses throughout the land" to collect money allegedly for sacred reasons, but in reality to pay Fugger loans. Although the roles of Pope Leo X, Luther, and indulgence salesman Tetzel are widely known by Reformation scholars, few realize how Fugger's immoral money scheme was the spark that set the Luther flame ablaze.

Now that we have learned what fractional reserve banking is and how the fraud has allowed bankers to corrupt state institutions and even the Catholic Church in order to achieve power within society, it's now time to look into how the FRB fraud causes disastrous Business Cycles.

*I think there is universal agreement within the economics profession that the decline—the sharp decline in the quantity of money played a very major role in producing the Great Depression.*
—Milton Friedman

# –7–

## Business Cycles
*What goes up must come down.*

Business Cycles, those cyclical periods of economic booms and busts, have confounded economists and historians for generations. According to David Fischer and James McPherson, in fact, the economics profession is no closer to identifying the root cause of Business Cycles today than it was three hundred years ago:

*They have produced a large literature, and much of it is intelligent, deeply informed, and highly inventive. But nobody has been able to find an explanation that most other scholars accept. Economists seek to understand this event in terms of theoretical propositions that take the form of "if x...then y..." Even when they share the same neoclassical frame, as most do, their explanations of this puzzling event have been very different. Monetarists of the Chicago School (Friedman, Schwartz, et al.) have concluded that monetary policy had been too tight. Others, of the Austrian School (Hayek), believed that monetary policy was too easy. Many economists at the time attributed the Crash to the growth of excess capacity in American industry. Others followed Schumpeter in thinking that the root of the problem was underconsumption. Keynes believed that the cause was a contraction of investment. Kindleberger thought it was a decline in foreign trade. Eichengreen suggested that it was the "golden fetters" of the bullion standard. Galbraith preferred to think in terms of institutional dysfunction. Others have argued for "diminished expectations" from the impending Smoot-Hawley tariff or other sources. Many economists have combined two or more of these theoretical propositions within a single neoclassical model, but none has been able to put the pieces together in a way that is thought to be generally satisfactory.*[1]

Fischer and McPherson correctly summarize how various economic schools attempt to explain the 'boom and bust business cycle' by lifting up one or another of the many economic phenomena that occur during the wild swings in the economy. However, when studying any system, cause and effect cannot be described in a simplistic, linear fashion. This is partly due to the fact that linear thinking cannot always make sense of systemic issues, as we discussed before. But it is also often because the effect might occur months after the cause, as Peter Senge explained,

*"Underlying all of the above problems is a fundamental characteristic of complex human systems: cause and effect are not close in time and space...There is a fundamental mismatch between the nature of reality in complex systems and our predominant ways of thinking about the reality. The first step in correcting that mismatch is to let go of the notion that cause and effect are close in time and space."*[2]

After studying all the economic phenomena to be accounted for as well as the fractional reserve banking system's architecture, I humbly submit that fractional reserve banking (FRB) is not only an insidious monetary fraud, as we've covered in detail to this point, but is also the underlying source of the Business Cycle. It is the simple harmonic motion within the FRB inflation and deflation of the money supply that causes the corresponding simple harmonic motion within the boom and bust periods of the economy. Truth be told, without consistent protection from the state, the FRB system's inherent insolvent nature would have collapsed the banking system during many previous bust periods. The boom periods profit the FRB system greatly, while the bust periods lead to state rescues. This is a classic case of 'privatizing the gains while socializing the losses.' Speaking of losses, the economy suffers during recessions and depressions when consumers, according to an IMF article, "stop spending as much as they used to; business production declines, leading firms to lay off workers and stop investing in new capacity."[3] The contraction of the FRB money supply shrinks the entire economy because the lower money supply causes consumers, who now have access to less money, to stop spending as much.

In fractional reserve banking, the total amount of bank deposits and larger total amount of loans over and above those deposits can be hidden during inflation periods, when everything is going great and savers are depositing their money, but are quickly revealed during bust periods, when money starts to be withdrawn and loans default. As economist Frank Graham noted, "The attempt of banks to realize the lending cash, or merely the multiplied claims to cash, and still to represent that cash is available on demand is even more preposterous than... eating one's cake and counting on it for future consumption."[4] The Great Depression exposed all the world to FRB's inherently imbalanced nature when nearly one-half of the banks failed, and the remaining banks would also have gone under without government intervention.

Interestingly, in the 1930s R.G. Hawtrey had already detected that the banking system's debt-money was deficient when he described "the inherent instability of credit."[5] However, instead of recognizing that this instability of bank credit was caused by the fraudulent systemic nature of FRB itself, most economists simply assume FRB is part-and-parcel of the free market economy and look right past it, therefore seeking to ameliorate its imbalance by further monetary interventions. Sound familiar? One external manipulation leads to problems that elites rush to fix with even further manipulations.

The blindness of experts is explained by Professor Hugh Rockoff, "Milton Friedman and Anna J. Schwartz believed that Laissez-Faire [the unhampered free market] was the best general rule for guiding economic policy. But when it came to banking, they advocated government intervention designed to mitigate the 'inherent instability' of fractional reserve banking."[6] When two of the top free market economists, who are strong defenders of economic liberty in every economic field, all of a sudden do an about-face and carve out an inconsistent and completely unnecessary exception for money and banking, we must pause and take notice. After all, they correctly identified that FRB is not balanced like the rest of the market, but instead of eliminating the root cause of this instability (FRB itself) to restore the free market, they shifted the burden and compounded the issue by recommending even more government interventions. This culminated in these allegedly Laissez-Faire proponents going so far as to propose a legalized banking cartel with levels of planning and control of which any Communist would be proud.

Instead of giving banks the special deal of the century, perhaps a better plan would be to eliminate the FRB system entirely. After all, customers are best served when entrepreneurs compete with one another in a free market, not when the state gives bankers centralized control over the money supply to procure monopolistic profits. This would restore consistent free market principles in every field. By removing the inherently unstable FRB fraud, we would also rid ourselves of the imbalanced economy that results from the Business Cycle, killing two predatory birds with the proverbial one stone. Thus, there would be no need for a central bank, just as there is no need for a central organizer in every other economic area. The result would be a completely free market that would restore liberty and justice for all.

Economist Hugh Rockoff stated the case clearly:

*The straightforward way of eliminating the inherent instability caused by fractional reserve banking is to simply eliminate fractional reserve banking. Make it a law that all deposits or privately issued bank notes must be backed dollar for dollar by reserves. Although it might sound implausible on first hearing—how would banks make any money?—100% reserves is a feasible system. Banks would have to charge for the service of warehousing cash and providing other services. And any loans or investments they made would have to be financed by issuing stock or long-term bonds. But it could be done, and bank panics would be impossible because any demand from depositors for cash could be met.*[7]

Rockoff correctly concluded that if FRB is producing the negative result and if combining this negative FRB system into the positive economic system is producing a negative economic system, then the fastest, most efficient, and only logical solution is to eliminate the negative intervention causing the problem in the first place. Unfortunately Rockoff's proposal was not seriously considered. Instead, monetary interventions more compliant with Financial Matrix hegemony have only gained momentum. The FRB fraud is the goose that lays the golden eggs, and because everyone is addicted to the yokes, it's highly doubtful the money system will reform itself. Hence, any proposal to end the FRB special deal is quickly shot down. The party, you see, must go on.

While the inherent instability of FRB credit has been noted, to my knowledge, no one has tracked it back to the underlying imbalance within its very architecture. Recall that the free market system and the FRB system behave differently because they are built upon different feedback mechanisms (those reinforcing and balancing loops we discussed before). The free market system is a balancing feedback loop where supply and demand meet at the dynamic market price. The money supply within the free market must remain stable in order to properly measure demand and supply so the dynamic equilibrium price can be arrived at. The only way a balanced system becomes imbalanced is when a set parameter within it is manipulated. This is exactly what is being done with FRB. It throws the money supply back and forth between positive reinforcing loop inflation and negative reinforcing loop deflation. As a result, the only factor that is supposed to remain fairly stable, the money supply itself, becomes more unstable than the supply and demand it is supposed to be measuring! This leads to false price signals being communicated to entrepreneurs, who then make inaccurate production decisions that discombobulate the entire economy.

Because the FRB money supply is an oscillating wave and money is used in nearly every transaction in the modern economy, when the money supply oscillates up and down, so too does the economy. In other words, when FRB fraud is practiced, the unnaturally unbalanced and unstable money supply is injected into the naturally balanced and self-regulating economy, which results in an unbalanced and unstable economy. Business Cycles are not separate and unrelated events. They can be traced back directly to the systemic wave-like motion inherent within the FRB fraud.

Let's dig into why expansion and contraction of the money supply causes booms and busts. Entrepreneurs rely upon economic signals to make production decisions, but FRB causes the money supply to cycle between expansion and contraction, which sends false signals to producers. Things are fine for a while during expansion, as entrepreneurs invest to meet demand. But entrepreneurial failures begin when the oscillation cycle flips. Now production predictions are confronted with the new reality of the money contraction phase. All of the previous predictions based upon the money supply expansion are suddenly revealed to be overly optimistic. Naturally, there will always be some entrepreneurs who make bad production decisions, but when nearly all entrepreneurs find themselves in the same boat, it is evidence of a systemic issue. Murray Rothbard described this as a "cluster of errors" and noted that there were three common features that must be accounted for to validate any theory that seeks to explain the existence of Business Cycles: 1) How do we explain the "curious phenomenon of the crisis that almost all entrepreneurs suffer sudden losses?" 2) How do we explain the well-known fact that "capital-goods industries fluctuate more widely than consumer-goods industries?" and finally, 3) Why does the boom period always have an "increase in the quantity of money" and the bust period "generally though not universally" have a "fall in the money supply?"[8] Let's quickly consider how FRB clearly satisfies all three of Rothbard's Business Cycle stipulations.

In their works, Mises, Hayek, and Rothbard, among other top economists of the "Austrian school' of thought, correctly described how the balanced economic system becomes imbalanced by monetary inflation. That's all well and good, but we must go further by taking stock of the various types of inflation and their underlying architectures in order to truly identify the root cause of monetary instability. In short, all inflations are not created equal. For instance, debasement of coins is a simple positive reinforcing loop wherein the money supply is progressively inflated upward, which means there is no deflationary cycle in debasement's architecture. Although debasement still harms the economy, the money supply progressively expands but does not contract because the systems architecture of debasement is only a positive reinforcement loop.

In contrast, because fractional reserve banking creates more total debt than it does debt-money, that imbalance causes FRB's money supply architecture to be an imbalanced interconnected series of positive and negative reinforcing loops, as discussed in Chapter Five. Therefore, the FRB money supply follows a simple harmonic motion of monetary inflation and deflation cycles. Due to its systemic nature, the FRB money supply can either expand or contract, but it can never stabilize.

Let's consider why FRB produces an inherently unstable economy. A free market economy is ideally a closed feedback loop system that constantly adjusts to find the price where supply and demand for every item are balanced. Then along comes FRB's monetary intervention, which distorts the previously harmonious economy, just as adjusting the blood pressure of a patient would immediately affect every vital organ. Indeed, one of the main reasons gold and silver were the free market's natural choice was their stability, because precious metals are scarce and difficult to mine. By contrast, stability is the very feature FRB money cannot provide. Absurdly, the most stable of moneys (precious metal gold and silver) has been usurped by the most unstable of moneys (FRB debt-money). Alas, the wave-like inflation/deflation oscillations inherent within the FRB money supply are naturally transferred into the economy as wave-like boom/bust oscillations that are referred to as Business Cycles. Business Cycles, in short, are not inherent within an unhampered free market system, but are inherent within the fraudulent FRB money supply.

## 1. FRB Money Supply Accounts for Entrepreneurs' Cluster of Errors

Thus, FRB not only accounts for why entrepreneurs make a "cluster of errors," but also when such errors occur—namely, at the point when FRB monetary expansion reverses to contraction. The cluster of errors can be understood by returning to the Free Market Mechanism which shows how entrepreneurs respond to the altered economic environment. Now confronted with a money supply that is deflating, whereas previously it was inflating, entrepreneurs are suddenly faced with shrinking demand. On the supply side, things are not impacted as greatly or as quickly as on the demand side because money (capital) is just one of the factors entrepreneurs use to produce goods and services. Hence, when FRB contracts the total money supply, demand drops immediately, but supply does not drop at first because money only impacts future supply decisions, not the current supply. So one side, demand, leads the other side, supply, and creates a confusing imbalance that catches entrepreneurs unaware and leads to Rothbard's cluster of errors.

Because the total money supply has dropped, the FMM dynamic float, as a result, moves to the right. This causes the equilibrium price for practically every product and service in the economy to lower simultaneously. This dislocation across the economy causes inventories to pile up as entrepreneurs are hesitant to admit they misread the demand signals, so they do not lower prices or production immediately. Nonetheless, the dynamic price will continue to lower as the money supply continues to contract, with the result that there are not enough buyers at the original prices. This is why inventory accumulates throughout the economy. The delay between the immediate reduction in the demand signal and the gradual reduction in the supply signal leads to imbalances. This occurs across the entire economy, as the money supply is like the water in a pool—to lower it in one corner is to lower it everywhere. In consequence, recessions are periods of stagnation caused by an oversupply of goods priced at previously inflated levels.

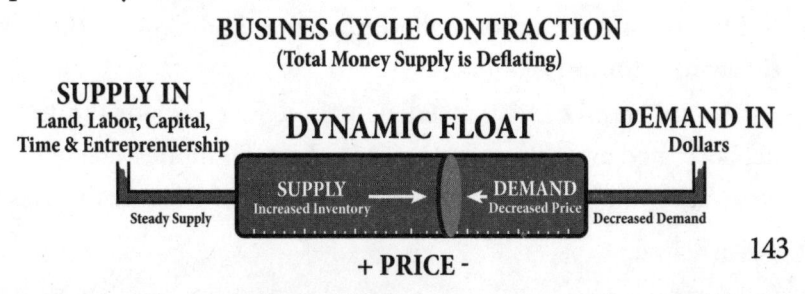

**BUSINES CYCLE CONTRACTION**
(Total Money Supply is Deflating)

| SUPPLY IN
Land, Labor, Capital,
Time & Entreprenuership | **DYNAMIC FLOAT** | DEMAND IN
Dollars |
|---|---|---|
| Steady Supply | SUPPLY
Increased Inventory → ← DEMAND
Decreased Price | Decreased Demand |

+ PRICE -

143

## 2. FRB Money Supply Accounts for Capital Goods Fluctuating More than Consumer Goods

The duration of the bust cycle is dependent upon how far the money supply is allowed to contract and how quickly the prices and wages recalibrate to the new normal. This recalibration process begins when entrepreneurs adjust production decisions based upon the new reality. The result is that most of the production choices that appeared logical under a steadily expanding money supply are now revealed as grossly optimistic under a contracting one. This leads entrepreneurs to eventually cut prices, lay off employees, and conserve cash by reducing the supply of consumer goods (products and services for end consumers). This means that practically all future orders for capital goods (physical equipment used to produce consumer goods) will be canceled, as there is no need to purchase equipment to increase the supply of consumer goods that aren't selling. What follows is that entrepreneurs in all industries, who are focused on reducing costs during the downturn respond by laying off employees and slashing capital goods orders. After all, they have a desperate need to conserve cash. Thus, like a traffic jam that began with just a few cars briefly slowing, the cars racing up behind must jam on their brakes, and the ones behind are completely stopped. Similarly, while consumer goods sales may slow down during a monetary contraction, capital goods investments screech to a halt. This clearly shows that money-supply expansion and contraction fulfill Rothbard's second condition for proving a theory of the Business Cycle.

## 3. FRB Itself Accounts for the Expansion and Contraction of the Money Supply

The inherently imbalanced nature of FRB, where the total debts created are always higher than the total money created, is what accounts for Rothbard's third feature of Business Cycles:

the money supply's inflation and deflation periods. FRB does not provide enough total debt money to pay off the debts it creates. New debt money must constantly be created (positive reinforcing loop expansion of the spring we talked about earlier) during the boom stage. More FRB loans, however, create an even bigger gap between total debt-money and total debts (stretching the spring ever tighter), so even more FRB loans are needed this month than last month. This positive reinforcing cycle continues until the banks can no longer create enough new FRB loans to service the preposterous gap between total money supply and total debts. When this occurs, the FRB system begins to deconstruct (a negative reinforcing loop as the spring begins to contract), with the least solvent borrowers defaulting first, followed by bankers becoming more conservative, which leads to the next round of defaults (the spring racing back to its base), and the money supply returns to a more "normal" previous level. The only thing that can prevent this contraction is intervention by the state, which is always a further injection of money expansion (pulling harder on the spring to keep it expanding). This keeps the expansion going, to be sure, but at the cost of an even bigger contraction down the road.

As we said, there is simply not enough total money available for all borrowers to pay their debts. This is why FRB is systematic fraud. The interest owed on the debts was never created, and so it is logically impossible for the people to pay off their total debts when not enough money is available to do so. The following chart indicates just how large the gap is between total debts and total debt-money supply. Shockingly, America's total debts are now over three times larger than the total money supply available, with total debt over $50 trillion, but a total money supply of only around $15 trillion. What's crazy is that with every passing month, the gap between the two gets even bigger! This is becoming increasingly unsustainable, and we're ultimately heading toward the mother-of-all negative reinforcing loop contractions. This is the fruit of our modern FRB debt-money system.

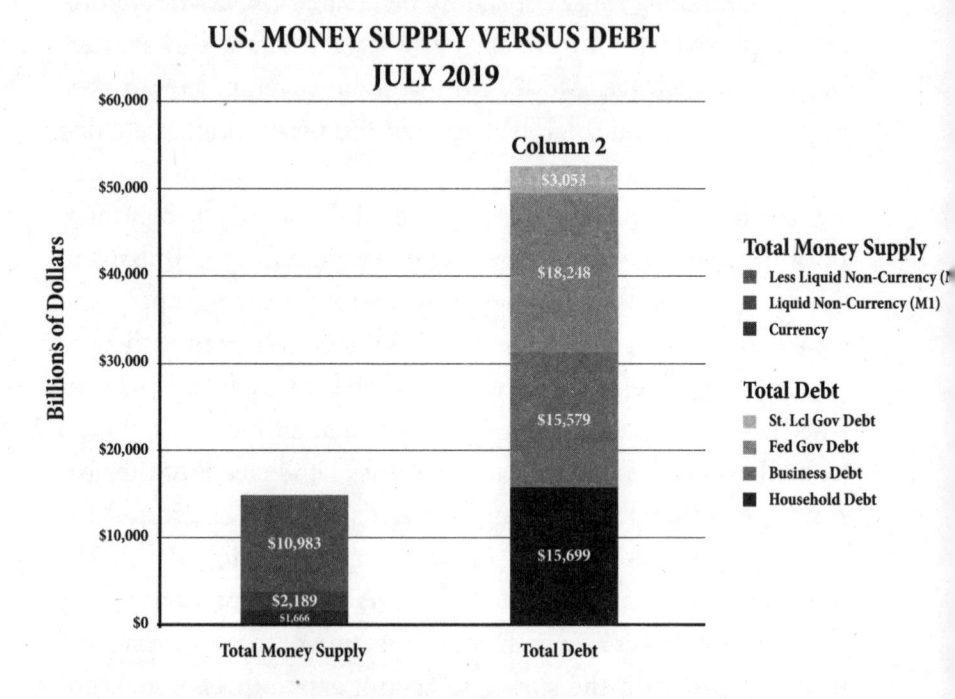

**U.S. MONEY SUPPLY VERSUS DEBT JULY 2019**

| Category | Total Money Supply | Total Debt |
|---|---|---|
| Currency | $1,666 | |
| Liquid Non-Currency (M1) | $2,189 | |
| Less Liquid Non-Currency (M) | $10,983 | |
| Household Debt | | $15,699 |
| Business Debt | | $15,579 |
| Fed Gov Debt | | $18,248 |
| St. Lcl Gov Debt | | $3,053 |

With total debts three times higher than the total money supply, if every bank demanded full repayment of every loan at the same time, the money supply would disappear entirely into the hands of the bankers, but two-thirds of total debts would still remain unpaid.

Thus, the FMM has successfully demonstrated how FRB's fraudulent money supply fully accounts for the three features described by Rothbard in theory and practice. First, the system delay between the immediate drop in demand and slower drop in supply causes the cluster of entrepreneurial errors, leading to the realization that predictions made during the boom are no longer valid during the bust. Second, the reason capital goods are the hardest hit area during the contraction phase is because entrepreneurs recognize there is no need for capital-goods to help them produce even more consumer goods when they are having trouble selling the supply they already have. In a recession, the money contraction causes almost all businesses to experience inventory gluts simultaneously, which leads the capital-goods future orders to be slashed as the consumer-goods businesses seek to conserve cash. Finally, the FRB's inherent inflationary and deflationary oscillations account for the increasing money supply during the boom, and a slowing of the increase, and eventually a decrease in the money supply during the bust.

According to the National Bureau of Economic Research, since 1854 the United States economy has experienced thirty-four business cycles, twelve of which have occurred since World War II.[9] Something very telling can be seen when comparing the theoretical models predicted by FRB's systems architecture to the historical results generated by FRB debt-money, for the predicted wave-like oscillations in the FRB money supply were experienced in reality. Even more revealing, however, is when we overlay the historical wave-like oscillations in the money supply over the historical wave-like oscillations in the economy, and we discover that we have a direct match. In other words, when the rate of the money supply increases slows down, the waning money supply growth (just like the FMM predicts) also slows down the growth of the entire economy. The next graphic displays the direct correlation between the monetary increase slowdowns and the beginning of each new U.S. recession or depression. This confirms that the FRB's imbalanced systems architecture that causes the wavelike oscillation of the money supply is the systemic root cause of the Business Cycle.

**UNITED STATES: M2 GROWTH, YEAR ON YEAR**

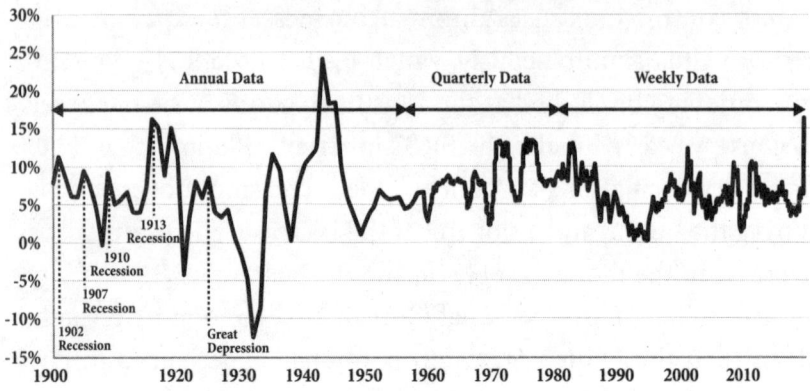

Source: Oscar Jorda, Moritz Schularick, and Alan M. Taylor 2017, Macrofinancial history and the new business cycles facts, Bloomberg

Now that we've shown how the FMM is justified in laying the blame for Business Cycles at the feet of FRB, let's consider just how difficult it has been to live with Business Cycles in our economy. The particular reason for this is that they invite government interference in the economy because, as people feel the sting of a contracting money supply, the cry goes out that "somebody should do something!" As governments specialize in interfering anyway, they rarely hesitate to start turning knobs and pulling levers.

Without government or bank interference, when booms turn to busts, the recalibration process of demand, supply, and prices to the deflating money supply, though painful, can occur fairly quickly, usually within twelve to eighteen months. However, when governments intervene to deaden the pain and keep the party going, spending billions, if not trillions, of dollars in doing so, these interventions into the free market do not allow the economy to rebalance itself. This is what happened during the decade-long Great Depression, the most damaging Business Cycle in American history. Presidents Hoover and Roosevelt unleashed so many collectivist, convoluted, and contradictory economic interventions during the Great Depression that it is difficult to detect any underlying strategy besides action for action's sake, even if the said actions were nonsensical. The Free Market Mechanism makes it clear that nearly every one of these actions was counterproductive at best and destructive at worst. These "New Dealers" interfered with all four aspects of the free market (money, supply, demand, and price) to sustain inflated prices and wages. They did this through governmental coercion—forcing businesses to obey the state, not the market. Economist Hans Sennholz captured the insanity of the Federal government's interventions during that period:

*President Hoover called together the nation's industrial leaders and pledged them to adopt his program to maintain wage rates and expand construction. He sent a telegram to all the governors, urging cooperative expansion of all public-works programs. He expanded federal public works and granted subsidies to ship construction. And for the benefit of the suffering farmers, a host of federal agencies embarked upon price-stabilization policies that generated ever larger crops and surpluses, which in turn depressed product prices even further. Economic conditions went from bad to worse...In this dark hour of human want and suffering, the federal government struck a final blow. The Revenue Act of 1932 doubled the income tax, the sharpest increase in the federal tax burden in American history.*

*However, when Franklin Delano Roosevelt assumed the presidency, he, too, fought the economy all the way...Instead of clearing away the prosperity barriers erected by his predecessor, he built new ones of his own. He struck in every known way at the integrity of the US dollar through quantitative increases and qualitative deterioration. He seized the people's gold holdings and subsequently devalued the dollar by 40 percent. With some third of industrial workers unemployed, President Roosevelt embarked upon sweep-*

*ing industrial reorganization...This was a naive attempt at "increasing purchasing power" by increasing payrolls. But the immense increase in business costs through shorter hours and higher wage rates [implemented by his legislation] worked naturally as an anti-revival measure. Nor did President Roosevelt ignore the disaster that had befallen American agriculture. He attacked the problem by passage of the Farm Relief and Inflation Act, popularly known as the First Agricultural Adjustment Act. The objective was to raise farm income by cutting the acreages planted or destroying the crops in the field, paying the farmers not to plant anything, and organizing marketing agreements to improve distribution. The program soon covered not only cotton, but also all basic cereal and meat production as well as principal cash crops. The expenses of the program were to be covered by a new "processing tax" levied on an already depressed industry...Again, economic production, which had flurried briefly before the deadlines, sharply turned downward.*[10]

In a nutshell, the federal government doubled taxes so that they could pay producers to lower supply and thus lower society's wealth. This indescribably foolish effort to sustain inflated prices occurred while the money supply itself was contracting, which predictably caused massive market distortions. And when all of these market interventions failed, the government borrowed billions of dollars to, among other things, hire people to dig holes one week and fill them in the next, in an absurd attempt to stimulate the economy. The New Dealers had plenty of zeal but little knowledge, and we are still paying taxes to service the compound interest on the national debts accrued from their economic follies way back then. Disastrously, the only thing they actually achieved was transforming an eighteen month recession into a ten year Great Depression.

As all of this shows and the Great Depression certainly brings starkly to light, it is madness to build the world economy upon an FRB money supply, which is the most unstable and imbalanced of all monies. But since the Financial Matrix makes trillions of dollars in profits and has achieved absolute power directly because of such a fraudulent system, we can expect the folly to continue. As we've said before and as we'll summarize for this section, the FRB system has wreaked havoc upon the global economy because it is wholly incapable of providing the one thing the free market money system needs—stability. Terminating fractional reserve banking would return profits and power to the people, help limit the corruption and control within the economy, and permanently end the Business Cycle. However, because the banking system was not interested in ending the highly lucrative FRB fraud, they maneuvered to construct an even bigger intervention—a systematic, powerful advocate to protect and propagate it. This is the main reason why central banks were created. The Empire had now recruited its Darth Vader.

*A system of capitalism presumes sound money, not fiat money manipulated by a central bank. Capitalism cherishes voluntary contracts and interest rates that are determined by savings, not credit creation by a central bank.*
—Congressman Ron Paul

# –8–

## Central Banks and the Gold Standard
*All that glitters is not gold.*

Fractional reserve banking is a house of cards that cannot long survive on its own in a free market, as Economist Murray Rothbard remarked, "Fractional reserve banks are sitting ducks and are always subject to contraction. When the banks' state of inherent bankruptcy is discovered, for example, people will tend to cash in their deposits, and the contractionary, deflationary pressure could be severe."[1] While FRB damages everything in the economy, financiers were quick to realize that during busts it was most punishing to the banks themselves. The early Italian bankers reacted to this by seeking protection in numbers. The idea was to combine their fractional reserves in the hopes that a broader network would be able to withstand the violent downturns caused by FRB's inherent illiquidity. In so doing, the Italian bankers believed they could mitigate downside risk while reaping upside rewards. Their plan failed because the most conservative banks found themselves risking their reserves to rescue the least conservative ones. This is a classic example of moral hazard, where bad actors lack incentive to guard against risk because they are assured others will come to their aid.

Eventually, fractional reserve bankers learned to partner with national governments. In this marriage of convenience, bankers offer loans to help the state increase its power against other nations and over its own people, and in turn the state offers the FRB cartel protection against collapse from its inherent insolvency. To be sure, this partnership didn't end the banking system's moral hazard, but it did shift it from the bankers to the state, and the state has bailed out the FRB cartel ever since. After all, what nation can afford to let its banks, money, and economy collapse? Accordingly, governments routinely violate the liberty and justice of their people in order to save the banks that are "too big to fail." Banks learned this long ago, as Murray Rothbard explained:

*Specie (gold or silver) payments were suspended from August 1814 to February 1817. For two and a half years, banks could expand while issuing what was in effect fiat paper and bank deposits. From then on, every time there was a banking crisis brought on by inflationary expansion and demands for redemption in specie, state and federal governments looked the other way and permitted general suspension of specie payments while bank operations continued to flourish. It became clear to the banks that in a general crisis they would not be required to meet the ordinary obligations of contract law or of respect for property rights, so their inflationary expansion was permanently encouraged by this massive failure of government to fulfill its obligation to enforce contracts and defend the rights of property.*[2]

## The Creation of Central Banks to Benefit Both Bankers and the State

The FRB system, unwilling to give up the immense profits earned from lending to the state but also unwilling to risk bankruptcy when states defaulted, conceived of a more proactive solution that benefited both parties. The solution was found after things came to a head in 1672, when King Charles II borrowed loads of money from the English FRB cartel (including many London goldsmiths who went into banking) to maintain his extravagant lifestyle. When he finally realized just how indebted he had become, he reasoned that because he was king, he

## CENTRAL BANKS AND THE GOLD STANDARD

could simply refuse to pay back the loans. As a result, most of the London goldsmith bankers collapsed, and any fortunate enough to have survived were not interested in any further loans to the monarch. This downside risk is what drove the FRB cartel to create a central bank and what drove the new sovereign William III to grant it to bankers, as the Bank of England Museum Officer, Alice Beagley, described:

*William III was desperately trying to raise funds for wars against France. He went to the remaining goldsmiths to see if any of them would fund him. They all said no, so William had to come up with a new way of raising the money. The King discussed a number of ideas from the government, wealthy merchants, and noblemen... William Paterson, a Scottish merchant, suggested that members of the public could lend...to the government...People who signed up to this scheme effectively became shareholders in a new joint-stock company. That means it was owned by the public and the government. The company was called The Governor and the Company of the Bank of England. People invested in it by purchasing 'bank stock' and the government paid them 8% interest. It was a good deal for the government as goldsmiths charged lending rates of more than twice that amount! And if that wasn't enough to tempt people to invest, the other selling point of this new 'National Bank' was that investors could be reassured that any money stored within our walls was safe from royal hands—what's not to like?!*[3]

The FRB cartel, in other words, insisted the state create a new type of bank, a central bank, to protect against the downside risks of FRB insolvency and also against monarchs defaulting on their loans. In return, the central bank and FRB cartel would flow fraudulent money to the state rulers so they could fund their wars. This is a clear win for the banks and the sovereigns, but a clear loss for the people who would suffer from price inflation resulting from the growing money supply.

The central bank would be the "lender of last resort," who would proactively inject funds into banks confronting liquidity issues before they were forced to close their doors. The FRB cartel, in other words, had coerced the state into creating a second intervention into the free market to support the volatility of their first intervention (namely, fractional reserve banking itself). The central bank would be owned and operated privately (the financiers still want the profits, of course), and the national monarchs or state rulers would sponsor these centralized (and socialist) banking measures because they desperately needed the funds to run their growing governmental bureaucracies and fight their wars.

The central bank money system is the antithesis of a free market, but the bankers were not looking for a free market; they were looking for secure profits without risk at the public's expense, and that is exactly what they obtained. The defaults of King Charles II, in effect, caused the FRB cartel to insist all future loans be backed by a central bank designed to protect the banks, fund the monarch, and ensure the king could not default on his loans. Catching on quickly, in the 17th and 18th centuries, the FRB cartels from every nation insisted their rulers create central banks of their own to perform similar functions, and the free markets gradually died as debt money replaced its free market rival (the sound, un-inflatable precious metal money of gold and silver).

The international network of central banks directing the FRB network in each country is what I earlier referred to as the Financial Power. Although such Financial Power is privately owned and operated (in order to profit), the central banks are also government sponsored so as to be able to enforce central bank regulations and policies. For the bankers, it's the best of both worlds. The incredible result is that supposedly free nations worldwide granted to the Financial Powers-that-be Karl Marx's Fifth Plank of his *Communist Manifesto*, "Centralization of credit in the banks of the State, by means of a national bank with state capital and an exclusive monopoly."[4] If the free market was seriously wounded by FRB, then it was given a Marxian execution with the creation of central banks. As Congressman Ron Paul observed, "The essence of socialist economics is government allocation of resources either by seizing direct control of the 'means of production' or by setting the prices businesses can charge. Federal Reserve manipulation of interest rates is an attempt to set the price of money."[5] Instead of banks competing in the free market like every other business must, the Financial Power was permitted to create a centralized socialist cartel through which the supply and price of money are dictated by banking potentates who are "too big to fail." This insidious coup essentially renders the rest of us "too small to succeed."

**Systems Thinking: Shifting the Burden**

Today central banks claim they minimize inflation and eliminate Business Cycles, but historical data shows that neither of these claims holds water. In fact, central banks, in systems language, have merely shifted the burden to the people, doing nothing to address FRB's fundamental instability, which causes Business Cycles in the first place. In systems thinking this is described as a "fix that fails" because, in their desire to resolve the built-in illiquidity of the FRB system while still getting its profits, they did a second intervention that didn't come anywhere near addressing the root cause. A classic example of shifting the burden is to consume pain pills to relieve chronic pain rather than visit a doctor to address the underlying issue. Sure, pain pills may temporarily dull the symptoms, but the underlying problem remains unaddressed, and worse, it is always a risk one could become addicted to pain medication. "Shifting the burden" interventions, in short, cause more problems than they solve, which is exactly what resulted from the creation of central banks.

This is bad news for the people as the Nobel Prize-winning economist F. A. Hayek emphasized, "The history of government managed money has, except for a few short happy periods, been one of incessant fraud and deception."[6] Such incessant fraud and deception led to this: central banks, although claiming to be on a gold standard, created fractional reserve loans of paper notes on top of gold reserves and then allowed the FRB cartel to pyramid again on top of those notes with further loans, which greatly expanded the money supply. Central banks, with a 10 percent fractional reserve ratio, can expand their notes above their gold reserves ten times (1/.1 = 10), and then the FRB network takes these central bank notes and, with a 10 percent reserve ratio, again expands the central bank notes another ten times (1/.1 = 10). In other words, the central banks pyramided on top of the gold supply, and the FRB cartel pyramided on top of the central bank pyramid, so that the total money supply increased one hundred times (10 x 10) from its base amount. As this math shows, national central banks were created to benefit the FRB cartels, not the people.

**Central Banks in America**

It is little wonder that in 1787, the Financial Powers supported the ratification of the U.S. Constitution because they were then allowed to establish a money monopoly in America like that which had previously been established in England. As Murray Rothbard explained, their aim was:

*To reimpose in the new United States a system of mercantilism and big government similar to that in Great Britain, against which the colonists had rebelled. The object was to have a strong central government, particularly a strong president or king as chief executive, built up by high taxes and heavy public debt. The strong government was to impose high tariffs to subsidize domestic manufacturers, develop a big navy to open up and subsidize foreign markets for American exports, and launch a massive system of internal public works. In short, the United States was to have a British system without Great Britain.*[7]

Once the Constitution was ratified, the Financial Powers pushed through their central bank and FRB cartel. Nonetheless, in the 1830s, President Andrew Jackson nearly stopped them by vetoing the renewal of America's central bank. Jackson's 'Bank War' was the high-water mark for the free market economy. Afterwards, it was progressively downhill. As Franklin Roosevelt noted, "The real truth of the matter is, as you and I know, that a financial element in the large centers has owned the government ever since the days of Andrew Jackson."[8] Although not realized at the time, free market money was on its last legs. By studying the Bank War, we can see how Financial Power corrupts and controls the government. Interestingly, although President Andrew Jackson was considered a country bumpkin by Financial Power forces, he surrounded himself with perhaps the most impressive group of free market advisors in American history. For instance, Amos Kendall, one of Jackson's closest confidantes, described the inherent danger of banking powers to the people's freedom in a campaign speech:

*"In all civilized as well as barbarous countries,"* he declared, *"a few rich and intelligent men have built up Nobility Systems; by which under some name and by some contrivance, the few are enabled to live upon the labor of the many."* These ruling classes, he said, have had many names—kings, lords, priests, fundholders, but all *"are founded on deception, and maintained by power. The people are persuaded to permit their introduction, under the*

*plea of public good and public necessity. As soon as they are firmly established, they turn upon the people, tax and control them by their influence of monopolies, the declamation of priestcraft and government-craft, and in the last resort, by military force."* Was America immune from this universal pattern? "The United States," said Kendall ominously, "have their young Nobility System. *Its head is the Bank of the United States; its right arm, a protecting Tariff and Manufacturing Monopolies; its left, growing State debts and States incorporations.*"[9]

Nicholas Biddle, the president of the Second National Bank (the central bank) at the time, ignored the warning signs from the campaign, but shortly after Jackson's election, he learned that Jackson was upset because the Bank's branch officers were using its funds to gain political influence. Biddle declared the charges "entirely groundless," but in November 1829, Biddle foolishly suggested the Bank assume the final small amount of national debt remaining so the President could use the paid off national debt in his re-election campaign. Of course, Biddle also requested the Bank be rechartered as his quid-pro-quo. Jackson was offended by Biddle's backroom dealings, considering this nothing more than camouflaged corruption to bribe him into supporting the Bank. Jackson's suspicions regarding the Bank were now confirmed.

Jackson declared war in his presidential address, "Both the constitutionality and the expediency of the law creating this bank are well questioned by a large portion of our fellow citizens, and it must be admitted by all that it has failed in the great end of establishing an uniform and sound currency." Biddle was still overconfident, however. Writing about Jackson's address, he stated, "They should be treated as the honest though erroneous notions of one who intends well."[10] Even so, Biddle strengthened the Bank's political support by offering perks and privileges to anyone in Congress who would support the Bank's recharter, including Henry Clay and Daniel Webster, both senatorial demi-gods, who promised to lead the process.

Although the Bank bill was approved by both houses of Congress, Jackson vetoed the bill without equivocation. In his veto message, he wrote:

> *It is to be regretted that the rich and powerful too often bend the acts of government to their selfish purposes. Distinctions in society will always exist under every just government. Equality of talents, of education, or of wealth can not be produced by human institutions. In the full enjoyment of the gifts of Heaven and the fruits of superior industry, economy, and virtue, every man is equally entitled to protection by law; but when the laws undertake to add to these natural and just advantages artificial distinctions, to grant titles, gratuities, and exclusive privileges, to make the rich richer and the potent more powerful, the humble members of society—the farmers, mechanics, and laborers—who have neither the time nor the means of securing like favors to themselves, have a right to complain of the injustice of their Government.*[11]

Biddle then pulled out all the political stops. He purchased newspaper columns across the country for propaganda pieces refuting Jackson's veto message. He told one editor, "If you will cause the articles I have indicated and others which I may prepare to be inserted in the newspaper in question, I will at once pay to you one thousand dollars,"[12] (over $150,000 today).

Daniel Webster, who opposed the Bank on constitutional grounds when it was originally chartered, now curiously supported its renewal. Perhaps Webster's conversion can be explained by a letter he sent to Biddle: "I believe my retainer has not been renewed or refreshed as usual. If it be wished that my relation to the Bank should be continued, it may be best to send me the usual retainers."[13] Biddle provided members of Congress loans, retainers, and outright gifts to help him break Jackson's veto. Jackson responded by withdrawing the United States Treasury deposits (the government's tax revenues) from the Bank, which severely limited the funds Biddle then had to buy support.

Biddle was aghast, proclaiming to Webster, "They will not dare to remove them. If the deposits are withdrawn, it will be a declaration of war which cannot be recalled."[14] In response, Biddle launched a blistering loan foreclosure policy that created a nationwide panic. The loans were not in arrears, but Biddle demanded full repayment from borrowers throughout the nation anyway in order to damage the economy. He wrote:

> *My own view of the matter is simply this...The [instigators] of this last assault on the Bank regret and are alarmed by it. But the ties of party allegiance can only be broken by the actual conviction of existing distress in the community. Nothing but the evidence of suffering abroad [in the various states] will produce any effect in Congress...**This worthy President thinks that because he has scalped Indians and imprisoned judges, he is to have his way with the Bank. He is mistaken** [emphasis added].*[15]

Biddle's capricious actions confirmed the danger of having an unelected and unconstitutional power over the nation's money supply. Jackson explained, "The Bank has by degrees obtained almost entire dominion over the circulating medium, and with it, power to increase or diminish the price of property and to levy taxes on the people in the shape of premiums and interest to an amount only limited by the quantity of paper currency it is enabled to issue."[16] Biddle even bragged about his power to corrupt the political system: "In half an hour, I can remove all the constitutional scruples in the District of Columbia: Half a dozen presidencies (of bank branches), a dozen cashierships, fifty clerk-

## CENTRAL BANKS AND THE GOLD STANDARD

ships, a hundred directorships, to worthy friends who have no character and no money."[17]

The Financial Power believes everyone has a price, and Biddle believed he would discover Jackson's, writing, "My own course is decided, all other banks and all other merchants may break, but the Bank of the United States shall not break."[18] Jackson, however, was a soldier who had endangered his life routinely for the things he believed in, and explained to Martin Van Buren, "The Bank is trying to kill me. But I will kill it."[19] Biddle and his lack of character were formidable, but Jackson's resolve was unbreakable. By the end of his second term, President Jackson had defeated the central bank, ensured the FRB network competed against one another in the free market, and paid off the national debt. Near the end of his final term, Jackson was able to make the incredible boast, "We have no emergencies that make banks necessary to aid the wants of the treasury; we have no load of national debt to provide for, and we have on actual deposit a large surplus."[20]

Unfortunately, Jackson's veto delayed Financial Power's money takeover, but it did not stop it. Alas, Jackson would not be President forever, and the bankers knew that America's limited free market money would only survive as long as their limited and debt-free government did. Therefore, when America's Civil War started just two decades later, the demand for unlimited money to fund war measures led to the abandonment of free market money once again. Expensive wars are almost always the harbingers of unlimited fraudulent money. As one modern autocrat recently quipped, "Never waste a good crisis."[21]

Historically, there have been only three approaches to money and banking: 1) Free Markets 2) Financial Power, or 3) State Power. And once America discarded free market money, the only question was which type of fraudulent money would monopolize the money supply. Would it be the private Financial Power fraudulent money system, where private banks create debt-

163

money to loan to governments? Or would it be the public State Power fraudulent money system, where the state creates its own debt-free fiat money by governmental decree? At first America during the Civil War avoided going into Financial Power debt and instead used State Power fiat money, called Greenbacks, to fund the early years of the Civil War. Even historians committed to the ways of Financial Power admit this:

> *In 1863, the United States was entering its third year of violent and costly fighting. Originally expected to be a short skirmish, the Civil War quickly developed into a full-blown military and industrial endeavor. The conflict required significant government spending, and despite large tax increases, the federal budget went from a surplus of $5.6 million before the war to a deficit of $423 million by 1862... The Legal Tender Act of 1862 also authorized $150 million in non-interest-bearing notes in denominations as small as $5 that later became known as "greenbacks." Although not convertible into gold or silver, greenbacks could be used to pay taxes and purchase the bonds authorized by the act. They therefore represented the first real paper money ever issued by the United States government.*[22]

This State Power step didn't stand on its own for long. In 1863 and 1864, Congress passed the National Banking Acts, which returned centralized control over the American FRB cartel to the private Financial Power. Although President Lincoln's government had proven that public State Power fraudulent money (greenbacks) could fund the war without debt or compound interest, it had suddenly reversed course and gave the private Financial Power centralized control over the money supply. Not only did this overturn President Jackson's hard fought central bank victory, but it also ended the use of State Power's debt-free greenback money.

## CENTRAL BANKS AND THE GOLD STANDARD

Why did America reestablish private Financial Power debt-money and the national debts, when the greenbacks were funding the war without debt? Author Doris Goodwin Kearns provides a clue by describing how investment banker Jay Cooke cultivated and then corrupted Treasury Secretary Salmon Chase:

*The sense of injustice Chase felt in having to bear the burdens of public life lured him into a questionable relationship with a wealthy Philadelphia banker, Jay Cooke, who had granted a lucrative contract from the Treasury Department for the sale of government bonds. Perceiving both Chase's financial strain and his aggrieved pride, Cooke began to send valuable gifts to Chase household, including an elegant open carriage for Kate [widower Chase's daughter] and a set of bookcases for the parlor. As the relationship warmed, Chase borrowed money from Cooke, and eventually, Cooke took it upon himself to set up his own investment account for Chase. "I will take great pains to lay aside occasionally some choice "tidbits" managing the investments for you and not bothering your head with them." If all went well, Cooke hoped, the profit earned would make up "the deficiency" between Chase's salary and his expenses, "for it is a shame that you should go 'behind hand' working as you do."*[23]

As we learned from the example of the Medici and Fugger families, war and corruption are how fractional reserve bankers gain control over the money system, and Jay Cooke apparently had learned or discerned the lesson well. With Salmon Chase in his back pocket, along with many influential senators and representatives, the Financial Power regained its centralized control over the FRB money supply, prohibited any further creation of greenbacks, and even ensured greenbacks would eventually be withdrawn from circulation. Author Ron Paul explained:

> *Chiefly responsible for passing the National Banking Act of 1863 was Ohio investment banker Jay Cooke, who gained a government-granted monopoly on public debt underwriting. His success in the bond business gained him enormous influence with the Republican administrations during the Civil War and after, and especially with Salmon Chase, secretary of the Treasury...and Senator John Sherman...Together they were able to push through Congress and past the public the National Banking Acts, all of which would benefit banking tremendously. Fractional reserve banking was guaranteed by the government....*[24]

Ideological whitewashings are almost always used to grease the change of power from one regime or philosophy to another. Shortly after the end of the Civil War, the Financial Power sought to maintain its centralized control over the American FRB money supply and keep the State Power's fiat money (greenbacks) at bay by aligning itself with the gold standard. This gave it the 'moral high ground' in public opinion because people readily understood that having a money tied to gold was more secure than having a money not tied to anything. This publicity coup would give the Financial Power a leg-up in the grudge match soon to erupt between State Power money and Financial Power money. But to understand just how the chessboard for this battle was arranged, let's take a quick look at the operation of the gold standard.

### The Classical Gold Standard

The classical gold standard fixed the value of a nation's currency (money) in terms of a specified amount of gold. All participating national currencies were freely convertible into gold at their own fixed price, with no restrictions on the import or export of gold. Although each central bank could inflate its own money supply nationally, each currency was internationally valued in

## CENTRAL BANKS AND THE GOLD STANDARD

terms of gold. Gold was the common denominator against which every currency was measured. This meant the exchange rates between participating currencies could also be calculated in terms of gold, which made international trade between participating nations much simpler. The classical gold standard began in the 1870s and ended at the outbreak of World War I in 1914.

The gold standard community required each country to convert its banknotes to gold upon request (or demand, as in "demand notes"). This international market discipline ensured each nation's central bank did not inflate its FRB notes beyond other gold standard central banks. After all, if a central bank inflated its national money supply beyond its rivals, the inflated prices within the nation would cause other nations to buy less goods from that nation, but the citizens of the inflating nation would have more money to buy goods from other nations. This double-whammy market effect caused a gap in the international balance of trade payments between nations. And under the gold standard, the gap was settled in gold. Nations with a balance of payments surplus received gold inflows, while those with deficits experienced gold outflows. Naturally, gold outflows reduced a nation's central bank reserves, which limited its ability to pyramid FRB on top of a now lower gold reserve base. Consequently, balance of payments deficits experienced not only an outflow of gold, but also a reduction in the FRB money supply, which caused domestic prices to decline. The lower prices would inevitably raise the nation's competitiveness (same products at a lower price) compared to its rivals, and the self-correcting nature of the international gold standard would close the balance of payments gap. Of course, the reverse is also true for countries with a balance of payments surplus. This is what David Hume identified as the international "price-specie flow mechanism," the market's natural ability to self-correct as it pertains to international trade.[25]

Not surprisingly, central banks did not want to lose their gold, which disciplined them into not over-inflating compared to rival countries' central banks. Paradoxically, the classical gold standard allowed central banks to run an FRB cartel within their borders, thereby profiting from inflating the money supply one hundred times its gold base, while simultaneously running a decentralized pseudo-free market banking structure internationally. In other words, the classical gold standard was at-one-and-the-same-time a centralized pseudo-socialist FRB cartel money nationally and a decentralized pseudo-free market gold standard money internationally. In consequence, the classical gold standard was a brilliant halfway house designed to profit the private central bank FRB cartel nationally while using the gold standard's credibility internationally to hammer State Power money, as we will explain.

Of course, the truth is that each nation's central banks mostly just expanded the FRB money supply even further and largely in sync together, thus increasing the size of the wave-like oscillations inherent within FRB's system. This only compounded the size of the Business Cycles. As economist Richard Cooper observed:

*Price stability was not attained, either in the short run or in the long run, either during the period of the gold standard proper or over a longer period during which gold held dominant influence. In fact, in the United States, short-run variations in wholesale prices were higher during the prewar gold standard period than from 1949 to 1979...However, the gold standard did not assure price stability in the long run either. Price "stability" in the sense of a return to earlier levels of prices was obtained over longer periods only by judicious choice of the years for comparison. If one chooses 1822, 1856, 1877, late 1915, and 1931, for instance, the*

## CENTRAL BANKS AND THE GOLD STANDARD

*U.S. wholesale price level indeed appears unchanged. But between these dates, there were great swells and troughs.*[26]

The classical gold standard, in other words, did not resolve FRB wave-like oscillations. The truth is that central banks and the gold standard were never intended to create sound money. Instead it created fool's gold, and those who controlled the fool's gold controlled the fools. The gold standard, combined with central banks, was cleverly used to centralize the money supply of every nation, while using the supposed soundness of the gold standard to pummel State Power in what could best be called "The Money War." To this, we will now turn.

*If Congress has the right under the Constitution to issue paper money, it was given them to use themselves, not to be delegated to individuals or corporations.*
—*Andrew Jackson*

# –9–

## The Money War: Financial Power Versus State Power
*What happens when an unstoppable force
meets an immovable object?*

For over three hundred years, Financial Power and State Power battled over who would control the money supply, but it wasn't until the implementation of the classical gold standard (CGS) that private international FRB money finally surged ahead of public national fiat money. The strategy employed by Financial Power was as devious as it was brilliant. Despite both fraudulent systems expanding the money supply against the actual gold reserves, Financial Power shamelessly waved the gold standard flag to represent itself as the sound money choice. It did this while castigating State Power fiat money as fraudulent because it was created by government decree and not pegged to the gold standard. The Civil War killed off free market money, leaving just the two contenders for who would control the world's money supply, and the gold standard was the whitewashing international Financial Power needed to finally finish off its national State Power rivals.

Curiously, of the three types of money (free market, State Power fiat, and Financial Power FRB), the Financial Power FRB money is by far the worst for the economy and the people. This is because it is debt-money loaned to the government and the people at compound interest, as we described before. Sadly, the worst of the three options won out, and we've been paying the price for this victory ever since. Just how this came about, however, is a telling example of how devious Financial Power can be.

Although the classical gold standard (CGS) was used by Financial Power to hide its monetary fraud, the truth is that the CGS itself greatly strengthened centralized control over the money supply, as economist Ryan McMaken aptly described:

*The classical gold standard was key in solidifying state control over national monetary systems... It is not enough to wax nostalgic about the classical gold standard and seek a return to nothing more than gold-backed national currencies. Rather, the very idea of national currencies must be abandoned altogether, while embracing true currency competition and private commodity money.*[1]

Indeed, any time a centralized system is mixed with the free market, even if it has some sound money virtues as did the gold standard, the centralized aspect allows the controllers to gain a stepping stone for even further centralization. Like cancer, centralization only grows. As economist Marc Flandreau noted, "the emergence of the Gold Standard really paved the way for the nationalization of money. This may explain why the Gold Standard was, with respect to the history of western capitalism, such a brief experiment, bound soon to give way to managed currency."[2] So something "virtuous" was used as the front man for something insidious moving in behind.

Author Eric Helleiner explained:

*Moving onto the gold standard was often seen as the key monetary reform that could lead to a more unified and homogeneous monetary order controlled by the state...Although economic liberals saw the gold standard in primarily economic and internationalist terms, nationalists saw it in a more domestic and political*

# THE MONEY WAR: FINANCIAL POWER VERSUS STATE POWER

*manner as **useful for their goals of strengthening state power** [emphasis added].*[3]

The Financial Power, in other words, used the classical gold standard to ingeniously accomplish its two main objectives: 1) centralize each nation's FRB money supply under its central bank supervision, and 2) wave the free market conservative money flag as a public relations coup in order to defeat its State Power opponent. This is why F.A. Hayek was lukewarm when discussing the classical gold standard: "I still believe that, so long as the management of money is in the hands of government, the gold standard with all its imperfections is the only tolerably safe system. But we certainly can do better than that, though not through government". Just as Frankenstein was part man and part monster, Hayek understood the classical gold standard was part free market but mostly socialist, which led him to conclude, "If we want free enterprise and a market economy to survive, we have no choice but to replace the governmental currency monopoly and national currency systems by free competition between private banks of issue."[4]

Of course, neither Financial Power nor State Power wanted a return of free market principles to the money and banking system. In fact, the real history of the modern age is a series of economic, political, and military battles we might aptly call 'The Money War.' This three-hundred-year conflict was a Battle Royale between Financial Power and State Power to see who could secure a fraudulent money monopoly over the nations of the world. The State Power consisted of powerful rulers who challenged the Financial Power's private money monopoly by creating a State Power public monopoly instead. State Power advocates asked: why borrow debt-money from private bankers (and owe principal and interest) when we, the state, can simply create money out of thin air by government mandate and not owe anyone anything? Their logic was solid.

Since both frauds constitute private property theft by inflating the money supply, the question is: which system is the lesser of the two evils? The Financial Power central bank system originally claimed to be backed by gold but used FRB to inflate the money supply one hundred times or more. By contrast, State Power was more forthcoming with its fraud and just created money symbols by government mandate without any tenuous connection to gold. In both cases, governments wanted access to money beyond their tax revenues. On one side, if the state created money without private banker debts, the people would pay less taxes because the government would not have debts and so wouldn't have to pay interest on those debts. On the other side, Financial Power created its debt-money through FRB fraud, which means not only would its borrowers (in this case, the national governments) have to pay principal and interest, but the economy would also be battered by Business Cycle swings. Alas, if we must choose between the two frauds, then the State Power fraud is unquestionably less costly to the people and less destructive to the money supply than the Financial Power fraud.

In the end, private Financial Power triumphed over public State Power, and we are left with a global economy enslaved to the worst possible money system. How could this happen? The Financial Power orchestrated a united global force and fraud strategy to defeat its State Power opponent. It began with this: private bankers purchased political support to secure government power (as Medici, Fugger, and Biddle did). Thus, the force of law became a tool to ensure the central bank's monetary policies. Private banker money had one huge advantage over its public money rival. Since the banks created the fraudulent money privately, they could use this money to buy political support and thereby capture state power for their own ends. By contrast, pub-

# THE MONEY WAR: FINANCIAL POWER
# VERSUS STATE POWER

lic State Power created money directly for government use, and any offer to pay people to support it would be to embezzle government funds. Alas, even though Financial Power is by far the most costly and damaging money model for the people, it is by far the most profitable and lucrative model for the bankers and their loyal political lieutenants.

While Financial Power schemed up a *global* money network through its control over the central banks in each nation, State Power was limited to a *national* money network because its law enforcement ended at its national boundaries. Even with its global reach, and private money to purchase government influence, the Financial Power still struggled to squash State Power. After all, every new powerful state leader would question why the national government should pay billions to private bankers for borrowed funds when the money could be created themselves without debt. This was why the Money War continued for three hundred years, since "force" was mainly on Financial Power's side, but the "facts" were mainly on the State Power's side.

It was this stand-off that prompted Financial Power's insidious alteration of people's perceptions by cloaking its machinations in the drapery of the gold standard. Since free market money had long since been defeated, Financial Power seduced the remaining free market advocates by gold-coating its FRB fraud. They exploited the gap between the *reality* of their centralized socialist money system and the *perception* of the gold standard's sound money, in order to erect their money monopoly. State Power was defenseless against gold standard criticism because it boldly proclaimed, with startling tone-deafness, the state's right to create fiat money by governmental decree. Now the Financial Powers had a winning dual strategy. The first part consisted of buying political favors in order to control government forces and get laws passed. The second involved gaining public support by masquerading as the free market money alternative. Despite the reality of Financial Power increasing the money supply more than State Power even proposed to do in theory, by falling for the false free market money propaganda, the people themselves were duped into forging the chains that enslaved them.

Interestingly, while both frauds inflate the money supply, one through FRB debt-money and the other through sovereign fiat money, their underlying architectures are vastly different. Whereas State Power money is a simple positive reinforcing loop (similar to the older approach of debasing coins) in which the money supply expands as new money is created, Financial Power money is created by FRB and contains positive *and* negative reinforcing loops. As we covered before, these create a simple harmonic motion, or the wave-like monetary oscillations that cause the Business Cycle. Neither system can expand the money supply without inflation, but State Power money, unlike its Financial Power rival, does not suffer from deflation because it is not built upon FRB debts, or the inherent imbalance between total debts and the total debt-money supply. In short, State Power money inflation may be compared to being run over by a van. But the absurdity of Financial Power money (the one running the world economy today) is that the van not only runs over you but reverses to run over you again and then again and again without end.

The unethical Financial Power plan for money is the height of madness when viewed systemically because it is both highly ineffective *and* inefficient, and even worse, unstable. But the profits are simply too astronomical for Financial Power to relent. This is what made State Power such a viable threat because it proposed a less damaging unethical money. Make no mistake, it is still fraud, but it does not suffer from the same inherent systemic issues the Financial Power's version does. Thus the private Financial Power, to ensure the continuation of private profits at public expense, declared unremitting warfare upon the public

# THE MONEY WAR: FINANCIAL POWER VERSUS STATE POWER

State Power money until their foe was vanquished. Needless to say, there were many minds who questioned the rationale of nations indebting themselves to private international bankers, including none other than Thomas Edison, who was shocked when he learned about the Financial Power fraud and declared:

*If the Nation can issue a dollar bond, it can issue a dollar bill. The element that makes the bond good makes the bill good also. The difference between the bond and the bill is that the bond lets the money broker collect twice the amount of the bond and an additional 20 percent. Whereas the currency, the honest sort provided by the Constitution pays nobody but those who contribute in some useful way.* **It is absurd to say our Country can issue bonds and cannot issue currency. Both are promises to pay, but one fattens the usurer and the other helps the People** [emphasis added].[5]

Now that we have described the two contenders, Financial Power and State Power, let's review their three-hundred year Money War history. While the full story may never be known, by studying the various biographies, histories, and monetary philosophies, enough evidence can be found to put the puzzle pieces together. What emerges is a shocking new view of world history that, once seen, can never be 'unseen.' The hidden Money War forces directing national government policies explain the paradoxical actions of state rulers that A.K. Chesterton observed, "The main mark of modern governments is that we do not know who governs, de facto any more than de jure. We see the politician and not his backer; still less the backer of the backer; or, what is most important of all, the banker of the backer."[6]

Private Financial Power practiced every deceptive, deceitful, and dishonorable technique imaginable to carve out victory in the Money War. The gap between perception and reality, as a result of these duplicitous methods, has led many heroes to be believed villains and many villains to be believed heroes. History, after all, is written by the victors. Over the next several chapters, we will learn how international Financial Power quashed national State Power every time its monetary opponent reared its head in this global, multi-generational Money War. Although Financial Power eventually won, this outcome was by no means guaranteed.

We have studied how Financial Power was formed with national central banks and the FRB cartel structure. Now, let's take a look at how its State Power opponent was created and how it proposed to monopolize the national money supply.

**State Power**

In one sense, the public State Power was the logical choice to run the money monopoly in each nation because the state is by definition the monopoly of force in each nation. However, in another sense, the private Financial Power had hundreds of years of experience in money and banking, made immense profits, and had influential connections in each nation-state, which would make it difficult for public State Power to take over their monopoly. The only thing certain was that the fraudulent alliance between the state and banking system was falling apart. With every passing year, it became increasingly evident that private bankers benefited even more than did the public rulers by their control over the money monopoly. Recall that in the early days of the partnership, monarchs were the acknowledged senior partners, and the upstart bankers served their monetary needs in exchange for the protection monarchs could provide. Back then, if the monarch defaulted, the bankers had little recourse. By the nineteenth and twentieth centuries, however, those days were long gone. The international central bankers were by then so aligned and powerful that, for all practical purposes, the servants now appeared to be the masters. Instead of the national rulers

# THE MONEY WAR: FINANCIAL POWER VERSUS STATE POWER

(monarchs or ministers) directing private bankers, international central bankers were directing nation states. The borrowers had truly become slaves to the lenders.

This turn of events increased the stakes of the Money War as the public State Power sought to regain control over the money monopoly and put the private Financial Power back in its subservient role. Any time a particular state achieved success using State Power money, Financial Power would pounce upon the offending nation using its international monetary network to threaten repercussions. Usually, just the threat of a military or economic war was enough to cause the boldest ruler to flinch and cease from his State Power money plan. At other times, however, costly military interventions were required, where Financial Power funded allied nations to bring the State Power opponent to heel. The money monopoly could not have two masters; either State Power or Financial Power would have to achieve complete victory. There would be no negotiated settlement, for, like oil and water, the two monetary frauds could not mix.

Like a game of whack-a-mole, each time State Power forces attempted to regain control over its own nation's money monopoly, the international Financial Power would fund military and economic interventions to hammer the resisting nation. Practically every generation had a bold and ambitious ruler who recognized the benefits of using State Power money and thus sought to push through State Power money reforms. Soon, however, he realized that Financial Power did not permit nations to be sovereign over their own money supply, and if he persisted in his quest for State Power money, he would suffer the consequences. There was no compromise. Either the State Power ruler submitted or he would be punished by Financial Power alliances until defeated. The same pattern of economic, political, and military conflicts continued for generations until the Financial Powers finally completely defeated State Power just after the end of WWII.

### State Power Fiat Money

Interestingly, State Power money was originally derived from wooden tally sticks in Medieval England back in the 12th century. Made of hazel or boxwood, these sticks were used by the government's tax collectors to track tax payments into the Royal Treasury. The knight chamberlain would cut a tally stick representing the amount paid, with different sized notches cut into the stick to record the various denominations. Payment details (the name of the tax collector and the total sum) would be inscribed on the side. The tally stick would then be split lengthways down the middle; one half (the stock) would be kept by the tax collector, while the other half (the foil) would be kept by the government. Soon, these tallies were used as interest-free IOUs (promises to pay) that were fully transferable and acceptable as a means to pay taxes. The tally, in other words, became State Power fiat money, which substituted for and extended the reach of the government's coined money. These tallies allowed the king to create fiat money without the need to borrow money or pay interest. Tally sticks, in effect, became the first fiat money in the West because, although they began by recording the king's debt, they soon were created without reference to any debt and were used by the government as money to make purchases. These were used in England for over four hundred years, but when William and Mary claimed the English throne, they brought Financial Power with them, and after setting up the Bank of England (the English central bank), the tally sticks were burned.

State Power money, however, reappeared again rather quickly, for in less than fifty years, colonial Americans developed a debt-free fiat paper money of their own. The population of the colonies was exploding, and their thriving agricultural production led to significant land wealth, but precious metal money was scarce. Of course, they could borrow money from English banks, but that proved expensive, especially for people without enough precious metal money to service their debts. This is what led the colonies to avoid borrowing from the English bankers and instead make their own colonial paper money. Economists Farley Grubb, in a short essay on Ben Franklin, described how the colonies were introduced to both monetary frauds:

*There are two distinct epochs of paper money in America. The first began in 1690 and ended with the adoption of the U.S. Constitution in 1789. In this first epoch the legislatures of the various colonies (later states) directly issued their own paper money—called bills of credit—to pay for their own governments' expenses and as mortgage loans to their citizens, who pledged their lands as collateral. This paper money* [State Power] *became useful as a circulating medium of exchange for facilitating private trade within the colony/state issuing it. By legal statute and precedent, people could always use their paper money to pay the taxes and mortgage payments owed to the government that had issued that specific paper money, which, in turn, gave that money a local "currency." There could be as many different paper monies as there were separate colonies and states. At the 1787 Constitutional Convention, the Founding Fathers took the power to directly issue paper money away from both state and national legislatures. This set the stage for the second epoch of paper money in America, namely, the ascendance of government-chartered and regulated, but privately run bank-based* [Financial Power] *system of issuing paper money, an epoch we are still in today.*[7]

Twenty-three-year-old Ben Franklin was an up-and-coming printer who had both private and public reasons for supporting paper money. After hearing all the traditional arguments that money must be backed by gold or silver and acknowledging that paper money inflation was a danger if too many notes were printed, he still believed his colony had addressed both concerns.

By 1723, Pennsylvania was connecting its paper money to land ownership. If you owned land, and wanted to convert some of it to paper money, then you could borrow against the value of your property. The state created the money, charged a low fee to the borrower, and thus the state raised money without taxation, and the borrower and economy now had the benefit of a circulating money supply. Franklin imagined such paper money as "coined land," which, having the backing of land, protected the money's value. After all, the money wasn't printed out of thin air, but was related to the value of actual land, and if too many notes circulated, the bills would lose exchange value compared to silver or gold, which would cause the landowners to buy the bills to pay their mortgages. In contrast, if too few bills were on the market, then more people would mortgage their lands to acquire more of them. Franklin wanted to end the Bank of England's money monopoly in the colonies, and although earlier colonies had overprinted bills and suffered inflation by not backing them with real value, Pennsylvania did not because they were pegged to the value of land, as described.

In 1763, the Bank of England asked Franklin why the American colonies had such prosperity, and he answered, "That is simple. In the Colonies we issue our own money. It is called Colonial Scrip. We issue it in proper proportion to the demands of trade and industry to make the products pass easily from the producers to the consumers. In this manner, creating for ourselves our own paper money, we control its purchasing power, and we have no interest to pay no one."[8] Of course, the colony's money threatened the Financial Power's profits, and the King shortly afterward issued the 1764 Currency Act, which prohibited the colonies from issuing paper money as "legal tender." The Financial Power, in other words, used government force to quash its State Power competitor. The colonies suffered because the only way to obtain money was through bank loans or trade, but the English

# THE MONEY WAR: FINANCIAL POWER VERSUS STATE POWER

restricted the colonies' ability to trade with the other nations. The result was a perpetual trade imbalance with England, who provided the colonies with more products than the colonies could provide in return, with the difference made up in precious metal money. After the Currency Act was enacted, Franklin summarized its dire consequences, "In one year, the conditions were so reversed that the era of prosperity ended and a depression set in, to such an extent that the streets of the Colonies were filled with unemployed."[9] Even in the backwoods colonies, the Financial Power kept a firm grip on its money monopoly through the application of government force. And as usual, this outside meddling caused a drop in the colonies' money supply, which led to the pain and suffering of yet another Business Cycle.

A decade later, the colonists were on the verge of rebellion, and in 1775, the Second Continental Congress authorized State Power bills of credit to fund the Revolutionary War. War is one of the most costly of government endeavors, and without the ability to tax, the Continental Congress could only print more money. Between excessive Continental issues and rampant British counterfeiting designed to destroy its value, the Continental's purchasing power suffered greatly. By 1781, the exchange value of Continental notes had fallen to one-hundredth of their nominal value and would later fall to 1000 to 1.[10] Although the depreciated Continental gave rise to the phrase 'not worth a Continental' (meaning an utterly worthless object), historians admit that the Revolutionary War could not have been won without it, especially when we consider Congress had no other independent source of funding.

In the Money War, Financial Power concentrated on two main strategies in every conflict: gaining public support for its private money on one hand, and debasing the public State Power money through counterfeiting its notes on the other. In fact, in the 1750s Ben Franklin recognized the danger counterfeiters posed to State

Power money, and according to *Science News*, "Franklin and his associates thwarted counterfeiters to help early American paper currency succeed, including by adding a reflective mineral to bills."[11] In the War of Independence, counterfeiting was a weapon of war. In January of 1776, the English created counterfeit Continentals aboard the Royal Navy's *HMS Phoenix*, which was moored in colonial territory and an easy base from which to spread the fake bills. This was accomplished when the British captured Philadelphia and seized one of the official Continental printing presses, which they then used to produce countless copies of Continentals to flood the market. The Financial Power sought not only to destroy State Power money but also its reputation. Many historians believe there were as many counterfeit Continentals in circulation as originals. One telling piece of evidence: British Intelligence had hired John Blair and David Farnsworth of New Hampshire to circulate fake bills throughout the colonies. The men, who were known British sympathizers, were arrested in Connecticut in 1778 with over ten thousand dollars (a lot of money in those days) in counterfeit Continentals.[12]

Even with the counterfeiting assault upon the Continental, it was still fundamental to the American victory. Unfortunately, after the war America missed several international debt payments to Financial Power lenders, so almost immediately Alexander Hamilton called for a new Constitutional Convention to ensure America paid Financial Power its money. The convention viewed the depreciated Continental Currency as a complete failure, despite knowing how counterfeiting was an essential aspect of the English war strategy. By creating State Power money without debt or interest, the Continental Congress had defeated the English Empire, the world's greatest super power, without coercive taxation of the states. However, the only apparent monetary lesson the participants in the Constitutional Convention learned was that State Power money is always bad, and Financial Power

# THE MONEY WAR: FINANCIAL POWER
## VERSUS STATE POWER

money (the one that ensures debt and compound interest for all) is always good.

In fact, one of Hamilton's first acts was to borrow money from the bankers to pay the full value of the "worthless" Continentals. In other words, even though Continentals were state fiat money, Financial Power insisted they be considered debt notes that must be gathered and redeemed at full value. Unsurprisingly, Financial Power had purchased most of the Continentals ahead of time for pennies-on-the-dollar because they knew Hamilton would redeem them (as they had directed him to do so). As a result, at its inception the new American government borrowed money from Financial Power and then absurdly gave most of the money back to the lenders to buy worthless Continentals, then incurred compound interest on the new debt.

The Founders rightfully believed gold and silver coins were the primary money, for Article 1 of the Constitution specified that Congress, not the States, "shall have the power…To coin Money, regulate the Value thereof, and of foreign Coin, and fix the Standard of Weights and Measures." However, even though it prohibited State Power paper by warning that, "No State shall… coin Money; emit Bills of Credit; make any Thing but gold and silver Coin a Tender in Payment of Debts," in no part of the Constitution did it prohibit the creation of paper banknote debts. Thus, even though the Constitution appeared to be against paper money, in reality, one of the first acts approved by President Washington was America's first central bank. In other words, the Constitution wasn't against Financial Power paper money (lent out with principal and interest), but only against State Power paper money (created without debt and interest). Hamilton made certain the Constitution prohibited the states from creating State Power money while enabling and encouraging banks (Financial Power) to generate FRB paper money loans using America's new central banknotes as its reserves. It is difficult to imagine a more supportive advocate for Financial Power interest than Alexander Hamilton. Everywhere we look, his agenda benefited Financial Power over State Power.

If paper money was bad, then why didn't the framers outlaw both monetary frauds? Tellingly, Alexander Hamilton and his minions instead believed it was safe for banks to issue unregulated amounts of FRB debts (with principal and interest expenses), but not for State Power governments to issue and regulate paper notes (without debt or interest). So fraudulent money is good so long as it profits the banks and impoverishes the people, but it's unacceptable otherwise. This illogical rationale from so many of the founders makes no sense until we recognize that Financial Power was directing the strategy for their own benefit, not America's. Hamilton argued: "A national debt, if it is not excessive, will be to us a national blessing...The wisdom of the Government will be shown in never trusting itself with the use of so seducing and dangerous an expedient as issuing its own money."[13] In other words, even though State Power money would provide a revenue for debt-free governments without taxation (just as Ben Franklin described), Hamilton decided all fraudulent money must be created as debts so that all governments, businesses, and people owed the bankers principal and interest. Apparently Hamilton wanted Americans to ignore the resulting pain from 72 percent inflation over the next three years and instead consider it a blessing.[14] Hamilton did not terminate monetary fraud, but as an agent for and promoter of Financial Power, he terminated State Power fraud. As a result, America freed itself from England's Financial Power only to enslave itself again. This Money War reveals the true causes and results of the American Revolution. In 1787, Financial Power partnered with American founders to create a central government strong enough to enforce its monetary policies, which the geographically distant English government could not. The Founders created a Constitu-

## THE MONEY WAR: FINANCIAL POWER
## VERSUS STATE POWER

tion to support Financial Power money fraud, sponsored a central bank and FRB cartel to protect it, and shut down the State Power fraud, the only viable competitor, and one that, incidentally, had helped America win its freedom. Alexander Hamilton, to be sure, did not throw away his shot to put the newly minted United States on a path to endless indebtedness.

*War does not determine who is right - only who is left.*
*—Bertrand Russell*

# –10–

## Financial Power Wins the Money War
*If you can't beat them, join them.*

We have just seen how the Money War in the fledgling United States was mostly won by the Financial Powers. Europe would undergo a similar conflict. King Louis XIV, the 'Sun King,' bankrupted France in a series of wars against the Dutch, English, and their allies. Many subsequent attempts were made to rejuvenate France's dismal financial situation, including John Law's fractional reserve national bank fiasco, but a straight line can be drawn from steadily declining finances to King Louis XVI's guillotining at the beginning of the French Revolution. By 1793, the nation was woefully indebted to private bankers while also at war with its enemies. The French government, familiar with Ben Franklin's Pennsylvania plan, created the *assignat*, a paper note backed by the value of Church properties shamefully stolen by the revolutionaries. The original idea was to create notes returnable for Church lands, but due to the insatiable demand for money during the war, the assignat was soon converted into non-redeemable fiat money. The total assignats in circulation doubled to 5 billion by August of 1793 and then 8 billion by June of 1794. The assignat collapsed from 31 percent of its face value in August 1794 to 24 percent in November, 17 percent in February, and by April of 1795 to only 8 percent. By 1796 the French revolutionaries had issued 45.5 billion francs, and the assignat was worthless.[1] In addition to all the money printing by the government, French money further suffered from counterfeit assignats. This was not only because they were easy to fake, but also because it was a war strategy designed to damage the French money supply, precisely as the British had done to American Continentals during the American Revolution. Although foreign opponents started the counterfeiting, printers in France soon joined the party. Some counterfeits were easily detectable, but many were practically indistinguishable from government issues.[2] Financial Power opponents in England, Germany, and Switzerland not only corrupted the political leadership of revolutionary France but, in so doing, also corrupted the State Power money system that funded France's power to resist.

No state can endure without consistent funding, which is why Napoleon Bonaparte, when he rose through the revolutionary chaos to become First Consul of France in late 1799, immediately addressed monetary policy. In 1800, the audacious Napoleon, as the public leader of France, moved into the private Financial Power's domain by birthing his own central bank. Napoleon was the central bank's first shareholder, and his friends and relatives also received pride of place among subscribers, connecting the wealth of France to the health of its central bank.[3] He also introduced a currency of set value and gave the bank special privileges to serve national interests. Napoleon's assault on the bankers was unlike any previous State Power challenge. After all, he wasn't merely replacing private Financial Power money with public State Power money; he was effectively saying that the best way to beat the private central bankers was for state rulers to become the private central bankers. Napoleon used his public power to undergird his private bank, in essence comingling State and Financial Powers into one mega power led by the First Consul himself. Napoleon was a military genius who quickly grasped an opponent's weakness and was bold enough to exploit it. He recognized that the Financial Power relied upon governments to protect and preserve their private central banks and FRB cartel.

# FINANCIAL POWER WINS THE MONEY WAR

Thus, Napoleon reasoned that since he had become the power behind the state, and had gathered great wealth through war plunder, why not create the central bank himself, fund it both privately and publicly, and then run the FRB cartel in France for the empire's benefit instead of for international Financial Power? Napoleon had observed, "When a government is dependent upon bankers for money, they and not the leaders of the government control the situation, since the hand that gives is above the hand that takes. Money has no motherland; financiers are without patriotism and without decency; their sole object is gain."[4]

The Financial Power recognized they were in a no-holds-barred battle to the death. For the next fourteen years, with a few temporary respites, Napoleon's national monetary vision battled with Financial Power's international monetary vision to determine whose money monopoly would survive. Napoleon's ownership of the central bank sought to make bankers serve state interests. If Napoleon's empire needed funding, his central bank created the banknotes for his military needs. Henry Dundas, British Secretary at War at the time, said, "All wars are a contention of purse,"[5] and the Financial Power prepared for this contention in 1797 by ensuring the English government (at war with France almost constantly during the reign of Napoleon) permitted the private central bank to create unlimited banknotes without the need for gold convertibility. In other words, the English central bank could create an unlimited supply of banknotes used to fund the Napoleonic wars without the danger of insolvency since the notes were not redeemable in gold. Nothing could have emphasized more just how serious Financial Power took the Napoleonic threat, and this policy was continued until Napoleon was finally defeated and his monetary threat fully destroyed.

The British served the Financial Power wonderfully from the beginning of the French Revolution until after Napoleon's final defeat. During those years, Financial Power underwrote seven war coalitions against Napoleon, which cost Britain dearly. The national debt tripled as the British paid subsidies to thirty different allies and supplied immense amounts of war materials produced at British factories. Ultimately, it was Financial Power's practically unlimited funding of other nations' militaries that ensured Napoleon's defeat. British spymaster William Wickham described money's essential role in buying coalition support when he observed, "In a word, money you must give them; for without money, they cannot possibly go on, and without them we can do nothing."[6]

When Napoleon's central bank created money, it was legal tender only in France and for her allies. The monetary and physical resources Napoleon could access were no match for the resources the international Financial Power could access worldwide, with the predictable result that Financial Power slowly strangled Napoleon's empire. Nonetheless, a clear advantage in money and manpower did not immediately matter against Napoleon, who applied brilliant leadership and military acumen to crush the first five coalitions aligned against him. Even the sixth, despite exposing the limits of his resources, was not fully victorious. But during the seventh coalition, Financial Power armed forces were too much for even Napoleon, and he was finally vanquished. Financial Power expediently suspended gold convertibility for the duration of the Napoleonic wars, and even with such unlimited funds, it still nearly lost. This was due not only to Napoleon's military prowess but also to his shrewd and effective blockade of English goods, preventing them from entering Europe. In the end, however, Financial Power won by funding Admiral Horatio Nelson's sea mastery, Duke Wellington's land mastery, and the feeding, equipping, and transporting of the many allied armies arrayed against Napoleon, who was eventually overwhelmed.

As the dust settled, Financial Power reigned supreme in Europe for the next several generations. The Money War, however,

## FINANCIAL POWER WINS THE MONEY WAR

returned to America during Jackson's Bank War, as we discussed earlier. Because Jackson had killed America's central bank, during the American Civil War (1861–1865), President Abraham Lincoln could not run to the national central bank to receive war loans. As a result, he lacked the necessary funds to raise an army to quell the Southern rebellion. This led Lincoln to New York to negotiate loans from the Financial Power bankers connected to Europe's central banks. Needless to say, he was shocked to discover that the bankers would only lend him money at rates between 24 and 36 percent interest. Infuriated, he categorically refused the loans. Later, when he discussed the matter with a Chicago friend, Colonel Dick Taylor suggested a State Power money solution, "Just get Congress to pass a bill authorizing the printing of full legal tender treasury notes, and pay your soldiers with them, and go ahead and win your war with them also." And this is exactly what Lincoln did. Whereas Financial Power intended to punish Americans for eliminating their central bank by charging high interest rates, Lincoln responded by creating State Power fiat money created without debt or interest. Between 1862 and 1863, the North issued $450 million of debt-free money called 'Greenbacks.' The name came from the green color ink on the back of the notes. Lincoln called the Greenbacks "the greatest blessing the American people have ever had." Once again, State Power fiat money had worked in an emergency.[7]

While Greenbacks may have been a blessing to the people because they were created without banker debt or interest, Financial Power was furious, as they then had to deal with yet another State Power threat from America. Abraham Lincoln was a commonsense lawyer who won many legal cases by identifying and highlighting key distinctions. He clearly recognized the differences in cost between private Financial Power debt money and State Power debt-free money. This is why Lincoln firmly supported State Power money, as his actions and this statement confirmed:

*The Government should create, issue, and circulate all the currency and credits needed to satisfy the spending power of the Government and the buying power of consumers. By the adoption of these principles, the taxpayers will be saved immense sums of interest. Money will cease to be master and become the servant of humanity.*[8]

By late 1863, Financial Power had recruited many new congressmen by funding their elections, lobbied senators from key states to support its measures, and finally threatened that Lincoln and his cabinet would be ruined if they continued with their Greenback money plan. Not surprisingly, Congress suddenly reversed its course and revoked the Greenback Law, enacting a National Banking Act instead that served the Financial Power interests. This Act demanded that Greenbacks be retired from circulation when they returned to the Treasury in tax payments. Lincoln knew the benefits of the Greenbacks, but his most urgent objective was to save the Union, and he bowed to political necessity. Of course, he knew that after the South was defeated, he would then have time to defeat the Financial Power. As Lincoln himself allegedly declared, "I have two great enemies, the Southern army in front of me and the bankers in the rear. And of the two, the bankers are my greatest foe."[9] Tragically, we will never know what Lincoln intended to do, for he was assassinated shortly after the Civil War ended. And when he died, America's best opportunity since Andrew Jackson to terminate Financial Power's money monopoly died with him. The bullet in the back of Lincoln's head was also a dagger in State Power's heart. The sad, deflationary post-war era saw Greenbacks quietly with-

# FINANCIAL POWER WINS THE MONEY WAR

drawn from circulation as America joined the Financial Power's gold standard debt-system in 1879.

Economist Richard Cooper said, "Gold has been used as a store of value and as a means of payment since ancient times, but the international gold standard properly dates only from the 1870s,"[10] a date, not coincidentally, immediately following America's Civil War. Financial Power central bankers rallied to the gold standard because they needed an effective method of denigrating the Greenbacks. Modern terminology might brand it "gold-washing," the act of using one thing (in this case, gold) to legitimize some nefarious other. The gold standard was essentially weaponized to alter society's perception about State Power money, the money that had effectively helped win the war and avoided massive interest and debt burdens that would have been enacted if the Financial Power had had its way. The ruse of 'branding itself' with the gold standard worked wonderfully well for the Financial Power. Other nations noted what Lincoln had done with the Greenbacks, and even though Greenbacks only paid for a portion of the war, Lincoln had proven State Power money could function precisely as its advocates predicted. Financial Power was then on the defensive, facing the biggest threat to its profits and power since Napoleon. Hence, Financial Power private central bankers promoted the gold standard, not because they had suddenly found sound-money religion, but because it was a brilliant way to paint itself as conservative and its State Power rival as radical.

Even though the Bank of England shamelessly suspended gold convertibility for the duration of the Napoleonic Wars (nothing could be more radical than that), it still had the temerity to portray itself as the safer money choice because its money supply was connected to a gold base. The Financial Power discredited both the North and South State Power fiat monetary experiments, despite their results in funding the Civil War without debt or compound interest. While the Financial Power might not have had the best facts, it did have the best funding. This was effectively utilized to write propaganda pieces on the value of 'conservative' money, even though the truth of the matter was that their schemes always expanded the money supply by massive multiples upward. Their consistent and relentless marketing campaign altered society's perceptions of Financial Power money compared to its State Power challenger. As a result, any country's rulers proposing State Power money would not only lose the consent of the people but also the Financial Power money and media support necessary to sustain political power. This made sure that the nations of the world towed the line and would not follow Lincoln's example.

In the ongoing Money War, with State Power money mortally wounded, the year 1913 witnessed a massive victory for Financial Power. The Federal Reserve (a central bank in all but name), was created in the United States. This entity would direct, enforce, uphold, and in every way protect America's FRB money cartel. The creation of the Federal Reserve (often called "the Fed") tilted the scales of the Money War because America, due to its power and wealth, was the vital battleground in the struggle. Whoever controlled America's money could control the world's. Financial Power applied two main strategies to secure control over American money, and it is almost impossible to overstate the importance of each. The first was the Federal Reserve Act. The second was the Income Tax Act. Both occurred in that same year of 1913, which was not a coincidence. The Federal Reserve was designed to provide an "elastic currency," or the ability to inflate the money supply to prevent future monetary disorders. In reality, however, the purpose was for the central bank to serve Financial Power by directing and protecting the FRB cartel. The Sixteenth Amendment (the Income Tax Act) gave Congress the "power to lay and collect taxes on incomes, from whatever source

# FINANCIAL POWER WINS THE MONEY WAR

derived, without apportionment among the several States, and without regard to any census or enumeration." Again, this was a step so radical that one wonders if the founders were rolling over in their graves. After all, they had essentially gone to war against the largest empire in the world at the time over some tiny taxes and a 2 percent tax on tea. Taxing one's very income? That could easily become confiscatory. Therefore, the Financial Power knew it had to move slowly, reminiscent of the frog in the ever-heating water from an earlier chapter. So from 1913 to 1915, few people paid any income tax at all, and the top income tax rate was set at only 7 percent on annual incomes above $500,000 (which would be nearly $50 million today). The refrain was the now familiar, "Don't worry. It's tiny, and it only affects the rich!" Predictably, however, when America entered World War I and had its first 'emergency' since the creation of the Fed a mere few years before, the top tax rate jumped tenfold to 73%! And even though the top rate was later lowered to 24 percent under President Coolidge, the government had conditioned the people to accept the Financial Power's money monopoly, national debt, and the income tax to service those debts.[11] This was a grand slam homerun for the Financial Power. And, once Financial Power gained hegemony over the United States, America's foreign policy radically changed to serve its new master in its effort to win the Money War around the globe.

Financial Power's next move internationally was to break the monarchs, the intermarried and interconnected kings and queens of Europe, who threatened Financial Power's absolute control over their nations. Thus, only seven months after obtaining a monopoly over America's money, the First World War broke out, a war that would kill more people and cost more money than any in previous world history. Financial Power had three main objectives for this conflict and it achieved them all. First, it received the greatest wealth transfer from society to bankers ever achieved up to that time by lending money to both sides of the conflict; the Allied Powers on one side and the Central Powers on the other. There was no wrong or right side for the bankers, only profits from both. The only principles Financial Power is interested in are those they can charge interest on. How this was accomplished is very telling. Financial Power secured the right for its central banks to create fiat money (the same type of money State Power had previously used during the French Revolution and American Civil War), but since they were private bankers, they then loaned this counterfeit money to the belligerents to be paid back with compound interest. In other words, the warring nations were so desperate for money that they surrendered to private Financial Power central bankers the right to create unlimited amounts of money out of thin air (which the governments could have done themselves for free) and then loan it back to them for a price. The precedent achieved by the private Financial Power in World War I laid the groundwork for the coming Financial Matrix—the all-encompassing, unassailable global money monopoly that we will explore in more depth in the coming pages.

Finally, Financial Power replaced monarchical governments with democracies because they were easier to control. Whereas powerful monarchs could thwart the will of Financial Power, democratic leaders, who need money and media support, cannot. WWI was a stunning victory for Financial Power. Monarchy as a system of government was essentially deposed, and the original senior partner in the state/bank partnerships that had normalized the FRB fraud was now banished from the scene. In fact, President Woodrow Wilson said America entered the world to "make the world safe for democracy," but a more accurate slogan would have been "make the world safe for Financial Power monetary fraud." At the end of WWI, practically every monarchy was replaced by democracies, republics, or socialist govern-

## FINANCIAL POWER WINS THE MONEY WAR

ments. In the main, there were four long-standing monarchical ruling dynasties destroyed in the war: the German Kaiser, the Austro-Hungarian King, the Ottoman Sultan, and the Romanov Czar. These empires were broken up into smaller democratic and socialist regimes obedient, of course, to Financial Power central banks. Democratic candidates and communist dictators alike both require the support of those who control the money and media. Since Financial Power owned most of each, no one could be elected or assume party leadership without Financial Power's approval. Finally, since national debts would no longer be owed by a monarch but by governments themselves, they would carry forward regardless of which particular minister or president was in charge. This is why many nations are even today still paying for debts incurred during World War I. Ultimately, the First World War eliminated Financial Power's main rival for control of the nations (monarchs), and set the precedent that in a pinch, private bankers would be allowed to globally create counterfeit money with debt and compound interest attached.

Financial Power was closing in on a total victory in the Money War, threatening to completely remove its State Power competitor. However, the immense money manipulations during and after the First World War led to the Great Depression, the world's largest Business Cycle up to that time. Financial Power's FRB system was compounding on top of global central banks' debt-based fiat money to create a massive inflationary/deflationary boom/bust cycle. The Great Depression confirmed that central banks cannot end Business Cycles, but that they can turn an eighteen month downturn into a decade-long decline. Because America's political leaders lacked even the most basic systemic economic understanding, Presidents Herbert Hoover and Franklin Delano Roosevelt (FDR) spent billions violating practically every free market principle in existence. Their actions call to mind the black-and-white movie image of chimpanzees loose in a restaurant kitchen, throwing flour and slinging pasta around to supposedly cook a gourmet meal. In fact, FDR and his advisers went even further than frenzied lever-pulling and knob-twisting, for they not only intervened in the free market, but when their foolish machinations failed, they then blamed the free market system for the resulting calamities. Thus, they shifted the burden even further, rewarding Financial Power with greater control over the money and banking system, and this with the full support and urging of the U.S. political leaders. Even though fractional reserve banking behaved exactly as systems theory predicted, with repeated expansions and contractions leading to the simple harmonic wave-like motions in both the money supply and the economy, FDR never seriously considered eliminating the FRB root cause. Despite the slinky-like oscillations being evident in practically every graphic describing business cycles, as this Business Insider graphic displaying the peaks and troughs indicates, FRB and the simple harmonic motions it creates were protected by the American government.

## BUSINESS CYCLE PHASES

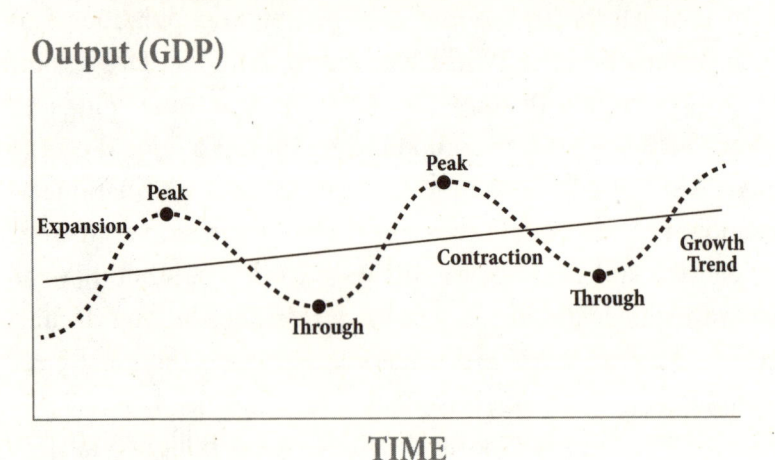

**Output (GDP)**

Expansion • Peak • Through • Peak • Contraction • Through • Growth Trend

**TIME**

Source: Business Insider

In fact, FDR strengthened the FRB cartel by eliminating the gold standard nationally, which allowed the Financial Power to inflate and profit from America's money supply without limits. And all this was done while ignoring the underlying systemic FRB issue.

Perhaps the greatest long-term damage the Great Depression did was destroy people's belief in the free market system, even though it was interventions *into* the free market that caused the problems in the first place. It was like throwing sand into a perfectly running manufacturing machine and then blaming the resulting friction and malfunction on the machine itself. Unfortunately, few Americans understood that the money supply was monopolized by a centralized socialist FRB cartel that was anything but a free market. The truth of the fraud was obscured by its complexity, hidden by propaganda, and protected by duped politicians. But if the cause was invisible, the pain was plain to see. In fact, it was downright brutal. From 1929–1933, production at the nation's factories, mines, and utilities fell by over 50 percent. The real (adjusted for inflation and deflation) disposable incomes for Americans dropped by 28 percent. Stock market prices collapsed to one-tenth their pre-crash inflated heights, and the number of unemployed Americans increased eight times over from 1.6 million in 1929 to 12.8 million in 1933. Nearly one out of four American workers were unemployed at the height of the Great Depression. FDR and the 'New Dealers' created willy-nilly a Frankensteinian economic monster that was part socialist, part fascist, and no part free market.[12] A bewildering flurry of counterproductive and conflicting government programs were created, which was bad enough, but worse, most are still in operation today. As President Ronald Reagan would quip decades later, "There is nothing so permanent as a temporary government program." And yet, none of the New Deal interventions actually helped America out of its deflationary morass.

It wasn't until the mega-inflationary measures taken heading into World War II that the out-of-control FRB contraction period was brought to heel. To this day, there are still defenders, and even worshippers, of the befuddling array of contradictory programs and policies enacted during the New Deal period. Author Henry Hazlitt explained the underlying issue, "The art of economics consists in looking not merely at the immediate but at the longer effects of any act or policy; it consists in tracing the consequences of that policy not merely for one group but for all groups."[13] In other words, without understanding systems, and the ramifications of any move made within a system, any intervention into the economy may appear to alleviate some immediate issue temporarily but will almost assuredly lead to even worse long-term consequences.

Incredibly, State Power had not been completely killed off by World War I. There was one last and mighty gasp from the fascist economic systems that emerged in Italy and Germany at the beginning of the Second World War. When people hear the word "fascism" they immediately think of ugly, racist political regimes, but for our purposes we need to understand their underlying economic ideas, which gave them the ability to enforce their deplorable social policies in the first place. Fascists sought to eliminate the autonomy of private large-scale businesses and relegate them to serve the national ends. This put Financial Power, an international entity that was the largest and most profitable private business in the world, directly in the crosshairs of all its true believers. Fascism was pro-capitalist in the sense that it supported private, property rights and a market economy, but only as long as the business leaders remembered that the state comes before the individual. The essence of fascism, in other words, was that the state should be the master, not the servant, of the people. Fascism was a centralized system that converted large private businesses into public entities serving the needs of the state. These policies conflicted with the goals of the private Financial Power central bank FRB cartel. If allowed to stand, they would threaten to eliminate the private profits Financial Power had been making at the public's expense. In fact, fascist policies desired, like Napoleon before them, to convert private Financial Power into a public State Power FRB system that served the state instead of private bankers.

In the early 1930s, the German economy was flattened with huge war reparations they'd been punished with for their part in starting the First World War. This was added to a poisonous brew that included little foreign investment and minimal foreign lending. The same FRB monetary contraction that caused the Great Depression had stalled German capital investments, which led to unemployment and significant decreases in the country's production. Without understanding that the FRB was the source of these painful expansion and contraction cycles, the fascist policies did the next best thing to reverse the monetary contraction. They formed a limited liability company called Metallurgische Forschungsgesellschaft (MEFO) to issue "Mefo" bills of exchange, bonds issued at 4 percent interest (similar to how the continentals and assignats were first issued), convertible into Reichsmark upon demand. Mefo bills were initially intended to last for six months, but with the provision for indefinite ninety day extensions. These indefinite extensions effectively caused Mefo bills to circulate as State Power fiat money and the German money supply quickly reinflated without debt or interest being paid. This should now sound familiar to the reader. State Power fiat money reinflated the money supply without increasing debt. This created a virtuous cycle of increased capital investments, which led to increased employment and thus increased productivity. Millions of unemployed people began working again. The turnaround was dramatic, and the boom in government work soon flowed over into a boom in private business. At the same time, other countries were in the doldrums of the Great Depression, the German economy was operating at full capacity with an annual growth rate of 7 percent. Between January 1933 and July 1935, German employment had increased by nearly 50 percent. By 1938, nearly 40 percent of the German money supply was State Power Mefo Reichsmarks, and the destitute German government, which previously could not afford to borrow from the Financial Power, was now the strongest economy in Europe.[14]

Nothing draws the connection between a Business Cycle bust period with a contraction of the FRB money supply as clearly as the German Mefo miracle. Germany merely created its own State Power money to counter the monetary contraction caused by Financial Power money. And, since Mefo Reichsmarks were created without debt or compound interest, they did not bring a further drag on the economy but instead helped it to quickly revive. Of course, the best way to eliminate monetary contractions would be to remove FRB completely, cutting the cancer out at its root. The result would be a stable money supply. Instead, what the Mefo State Power money did was confront the FRB contraction (which was an intervention itself) with yet another intervention, which flowed enough new debt-free money back into the economy to get it moving again. The reason Financial Power was unable to get the American economy to do likewise was because they were using FRB *debt* money, which (as explained in the Business Cycle chapter) only exacerbated the gap between the total FRB money supply and total overall debts. While the Financial Power nations were mired in the decade long Great Depression, Germany (the same nation that was flattened in World War I, suffered through hyperinflation in the 1920's, and had initially suffered economically during the Great Depression) was now the world's fastest growing economy. And all of this was because it restored the money supply with debt-free money.

# FINANCIAL POWER WINS THE MONEY WAR

Needless to say, this fascist State Power monetary success infuriated Financial Power. State Power had not only pulled itself up off the mat but was surprising and embarrassing other national economies by throwing impressive economic punches. If this monetary threat were not addressed, other economically depressed nations would certainly follow the fascist example. Financial Power had to keep this challenger from going another round, and it raced across the ring to annihilate the State Power money once and for all. The bankers' very economic existence was threatened if State Power money was allowed to survive. Thus, Financial Power was driven to defeat State Power unconditionally and irrevocably by destroying the very governments that dared oppose its money monopoly.

The Second World War became the culminating act in the Money War. In 1943 President Roosevelt and Prime Minister Churchill issued an extraordinary announcement stating that the only way for the world to return to peace was through the unconditional surrender of the Fascist State Powers. Roosevelt clearly articulated that such an unconditional surrender did not mean the destruction of the contending nations' *populations* but *did* require the destruction of their *governments*. (Remember that these were the very institutions that dared to create State Power money to rebuild their economies and fight the war.) Roosevelt further stated that the goal was "the destruction of the philosophies in those countries which are based on conquest and the subjugation of other people."[15] There is definite irony in statements such as this coming from the Allied leaders, as the United States and United Kingdom were the two largest practitioners of imperialism in the modern age, arguably 'subjugating' more people in diverse areas than anyone else around the globe. By the 18th century, it was said that the sun never set on the English Empire, and after the First World War, American imperialism surpassed the English. So when the two leading imperialists issued an "unconditional surrender" ultimatum for the Axis governments with the stated purpose of protecting *against* imperialism, something didn't quite ring true. However, when viewed through the Money War lens, the "unconditional surrender" can be seen as a strategic masterstroke by Financial Power to permanently knock out its State Power monetary opponent. Although millions more people would lose their lives, billions more in debt would be accumulated, and incalculable levels of pain and suffering would be experienced worldwide to achieve unconditional surrender, what Financial Power desired is what it accomplished—the complete and final destruction of all State Power money governments. With total victory in its sight, Financial Power began working on an even more centralized global money system that would generate even more profits and power for itself while closing the door on any potential revival of its State Power foe.

*The powers of financial capitalism had another far-reaching aim, nothing less than to create a world system of financial control in private hands able to dominate the political system of each country and the economy of the world as a whole.*
—Professor Carrol Quigley

# –11–

## The Rise of the Financial Matrix
*Money doesn't grow on trees.*

In July of 1944, despite State Power being nearly a year away from its "unconditional surrender," Financial Power was determined the dead-man-walking would never be reborn again. This led to 730 global delegates from forty-four nations gathering in New Hampshire to hammer out what would come to be called the Bretton Woods agreement. While their publicly stated objectives were to construct an efficient foreign exchange system, prevent competitive devaluations of currencies, and promote international economic growth, the actual result was a centralized global monetary regime. Bretton Woods created two new financial institutions, the International Monetary Fund (IMF) and the World Bank.[1] These would further centralize control over each nation's private global central bank cartels. While this certainly increased Financial Power profits, the more important reason was to prevent rogue national leaders from restoring State Power money, as had occurred historically again and again. In short, Bretton Woods buried State Power money, and its centralized nature prohibited anyone from digging it up.

Remember the misguided Keynesian school of economic thought we discussed in Chapter Two? Bretton Woods expanded Keynesian fallacies, for just as they claimed Business Cycles could be eliminated by additional government spending, they now claimed international trade imbalances could be adjusted by additional central bank inflation. Bretton Woods arranged things so that nations would peg their individual currencies to the U.S. dollar, and then each central bank could, from there, inflate without shame. Critically, this meant they were no longer restrained internationally by the gold standard's price-specie flow mechanism (one in which they all had to be effectively pegged to a gold standard). What had once been at least a partly free market system (although one that had large socialist features) now became almost entirely socialist. The only remaining vestige of a free market feature was that fact that all the international currencies were now pegged to the US dollar, which itself was pegged to a $35 gold ounce. For a while, the Bretton Woods agreement appeared to be the Keynesian dream of 'something for nothing.' Murray Rothbard explained how in reality it globally plundered the people through inflation in order to fund America's power politics:

> *The Fed could inflate with impunity, for it was confident that, in contrast with the classical gold standard, dollars piling up abroad would stay in foreign hands, to be used as reserves for inflationary pyramiding by foreign central banks. In that way, the U.S. inflation could be lessened by being "exported" to foreign countries. Keynesian economists in the United States arrogantly declared that we need not worry about dollar balances piling up abroad, since there was no chance of foreigners cashing them in for gold; they were stuck with the resulting inflation, and the U.S. authorities could treat the international fate of the dollar with "benign neglect."* [2]

In other words, Bretton Woods was not seeking a stable money supply to bless the people of the world. Rather, its threefold objectives were to bury State Power money once and for all, increase national debts in order to expand profits, and maximize global power. Even though currencies were still weakly linked to gold through their tether to the US dollar, Bretton Woods greatly increased the world's money supply by adding yet another level to the money pyramid. The first level of the money pyramid was now the FRB Federal Reserve, which increased dollars upon its gold reserves by ten times. This money was then lent to the national central banks, who used the dollars as the base to FRB increase their own national currencies another ten times. Finally, the national currencies were loaned to the FRB commercial bank cartels in each nation that increased the money another ten times. In sum, Bretton Woods increased the global money supply one thousand times (10x10x10 = 1,000) more than the gold reserve levels at the Federal Reserve!

Every time governments centralize and regulate the economy, the world turns one more notch away from the consistent discipline of the free market, like a ratchet that locks in place and cannot be reversed. What is lost are the millions of infinitesimal communications of customer desires to suppliers and manufacturers, all naturally and automatically regulated by the FMM price action we discussed in Chapter Two. What replaces it is the inconsistent discipline of bureaucrats and bureaucracies that instead communicate the desires of those in power. In short, a free market serves consumers, while centralized control serves elites. Bretton Woods, in effect, ended the last vestige of market discipline in the global monetary economy. When it decoupled each national currency from gold, the balance of payments system (the Price-Specie Flow Mechanism that punished overinflating central banks with loss of national gold reserves from the subsequent trade imbalances) was also disconnected, and the inflationary games began in earnest. Each country's central bank now inflated their money supply on top of dollar reserves, and the centralized socialist system trusted the wisdom of monetary bureaucrats over free market discipline. The global free market was now a distant memory because money was nearly wholly centralized and socialist.

Recall how poorly the Soviet Union's centralized economy operated, with bureaucrats making all the major market decisions. This economic system was so woefully inept that millions of Soviet citizens starved to death. Nevertheless, Financial Power after Bretton Woods began operating the global monetary system on a similar socialist economic framework. Cleverly, they were not so foolish as to attempt to run the entire economy on a socialist model and therefore left some free market features in place where the people could compete. But Bretton Woods still produced a socialist nirvana for Financial Power, one in which they receive all the profits and power on the one hand while passing losses and blame to the national governments on the other. Just as we would not expect world-class athletes to be able to compete and win with poisoned blood flowing through their bodies, neither can we expect the free market to function properly with centralized socialist money in circulation. The Bretton Woods Soviet-style command-and-control money system may have indeed buried State Power, but the price paid for Financial Power's victory by the people was a disastrously ineffective global money system that compounds inflation and debt.

The twentieth-century history of monetary policy can be summed up in four fatal centralized interventions into the free market economy: 1) expansion of FRB; 2) expansion of central banks; 3) Bretton Woods centralized monetary socialism; and finally, 4) the 1971 Fiat Money Standard that ended the final link to gold convertibility. Economically, these four interventions were complete failures, but every "failure" advanced Financial Power control over the state, culminating in the last intervention that created the all-encompassing worldwide Financial Matrix.

We have discussed the first three interventions, which are merely prologues to the fourth and final intervention, one that was stunning in scope—a worldwide fiat money standard, pegged to absolutely nothing, created by the Federal Reserve, with all the world's currencies pegged to it. As you'll recall, Financial Power originally branded itself with a connection to the gold standard in order to smash its State Power competitor, who, for their part, had proposed to run a fiat money standard tied to nothing but without debt or compound interest. And as we saw, the ruse worked. Now, hypocritically, Financial Power proposed to adopt a privately controlled fiat money system tied to nothing *but with* debt and compound interest. In other words, despite criticizing fiat money for centuries so that they could defeat State Power money, once Financial Power achieved its victory, it added State Power fraud principles (fiat money tied to nothing) on top of the original Financial Power fraud (FRB money) to create the most insidious financial system imaginable. One that combines both types of money frauds, but does so *privately* so the international banking elites can obtain unlimited profits and power, which effectively enslaves people, companies, and nations with debt.

An observation to be made here is precisely how Financial Power implemented this strategy. They couldn't simply rush to implement their global private Fiat Money Standard immediately following World War II. The frog would likely have leapt out of the pan. After all, Financial Power had been attacking State Power money for several hundred years for daring to suggest a fiat money standard (without national debts), so to propose the same thing (but *with* national debts) right after defeating the State Power Fascists opponents was too audacious even for them. Further, Bretton Woods was unlikely to be approved without Financial Power leveraging the credibility of the gold standard. This is why they took a half-step towards the Fiat Money Standard by decoupling all national currencies from gold, but tying them all to the American dollar, which was still nominally pegged to gold.

Financial Power brilliantly used something called Hegelian Dialectics (which merges thesis and antithesis into a new synthesis) to drive the world into its Fiat Money Standard. On one side,

Financial Power promoted capitalism, the economic *thesis*. On the other side, it promoted communism, the economic *antithesis*. The *synthesis* of these two competing forces would become an international Financial Matrix over all the money, banking, and military-industrial complexes of each country. All that was needed to accomplish this was another major crisis, and for that the Cold War fit the bill perfectly. The Cold War (featuring a massive arms race and spy-laden shadow conflict of inherent mistrust), led to trillions of dollars of debt for both capitalist and communist nations, all of which was borrowed from the Financial Power. And the more debts each nation accrued, the more subservient they became to their global money overlords.

Professor Carrol Quigley spelled out the monolithic Financial Matrix plan:

*The apex of the system was to be the Bank for International Settlements...a private bank owned and controlled by the world's central banks, which were themselves private corporations. Each central bank...sought to dominate its government by its ability to control Treasury loans, to manipulate foreign exchanges, to influence the level of economic activity in the country, and to influence co-operative politicians by subsequent economic rewards in the business world.*[3]

Financial Power had achieved the replacement of physically limited commodity money with metaphysically unlimited money symbols, and had shrewdly and gradually manipulated the nations in order to achieve total global financial control. Financial Power, in so doing, had morphed into the Financial Matrix. And it did this courtesy of the American president, who famously claimed, "I am not a crook."

## The End of the World's Gold Standard

Bretton Woods may have been a windfall for Financial Power, but it had put U.S. President Richard Nixon between a rock and a hard place. Financial Power had given America a punchbowl of easy money, and it couldn't help but become inebriated, indebting itself like never before. What was worse, foreign nations were increasingly embittered, believing Bretton Woods to have caused global citizens to subsidize American interests. The French, in fact, called the Bretton Woods agreement "America's exorbitant privilege." Economist Barry Eichengreen noted, "It costs only a few cents for the Bureau of Engraving and Printing to produce a $100 bill, but other countries had to pony up $100 of actual goods in order to obtain one."[4] The French were correct about the "exorbitant privilege," but incorrect as to who was benefiting, for America and the other nations *both* were deluged in debts created by the private Federal Reserve working on behalf of Financial Power. It was private Financial Power that got the profits. Nonetheless, French President Charles de Gaulle demanded the dollars the French government held be redeemed for gold, as stipulated in the Bretton Woods agreement. This demand was soon followed by others from West Germany and Switzerland. The process was for the requesting nation to deliver the dollars and for the Federal Reserve to swap them for the equivalent amount in gold from its vaults. Trouble was, the Federal Reserve had created so many dollars to lend to the spend-thirsty US government, which had then spread into the economy and around the world, that the Federal Reserve did not have anywhere near the gold reserves required. The proverbial gig was up. Either the Federal Reserve would have to stop issuing further loans to America, a country that couldn't stop its spending addiction if its life depended upon it, or somehow the promises of gold convertibility inherent in the Bretton Woods agreement would have to be revoked. What resulted was an executive action taken by

President Nixon to "close the gold window" *temporarily* to stop allowing international convertibility of foreign-held US dollars into gold. Notice that Nixon said this was a temporary measure, a promise nobody believed at the time and one that, of course, remains in effect to this day, over half a century later. The Ronald Reagan quote we used in the last chapter bears repeating again: "Nothing is so permanent as a temporary government program." Outmaneuvered, Nixon ended gold convertibility and gave Financial Power what it truly wanted and had been scheming for all along this long, dark history—a global Fiat Money Standard tied to absolutely nothing and entirely under their own control. This would be the greatest and most lucrative special deal governments ever gave to bankers in the entirety of world history.

Systems guru Peter Senge explained the dilemma Nixon was in, although he wasn't speaking directly about this event:

> *A Third World nation, unable to face difficult choices in limiting government expenditures in line with its tax revenues, finds itself generating deficits that are financed through printing money and inflation. Over time, inflation becomes a way of life, more and more government assistance is needed, and chronic deficits become accepted as inevitable.*[5]

Nixon, however, didn't just print his own money (like Lincoln did with Greenbacks) to fund American government deficits. Worse, he effectively gave printing rights to the private Federal Reserve, who would then loan that newly created money to the US government with interest. This created trillions in debt for Americans and trillions in profits for the Financial Matrix. Nixon surrendered to the Federal Reserve, the Financial Power's central bank of central banks, because America couldn't help but behave like Senge's Third World dictator. But with the Bretton Woods agreement in place, this resulted in the inflation of the

# THE RISE OF THE FINANCIAL MATRIX

entire world's money supply. Even more disastrously, it did so through loans to the nations of the world, all bearing compound interest. In other words, because the private Financial Matrix fiat money is loaned to the nations as debt, unlike State Power fiat created without debt or interest, the world is now completely enslaved by the Financial Matrix, which is frolicking in profits, while the world drowns in debt.

With the last meager tether to the gold standard completely severed, the governments of the world couldn't stop themselves from inflating their money supply to fund their overspending habits. And every increase in their currency, because it came through debt with interest, gave correspondingly more control to their master, the Financial Matrix. This created a new form of global imperialism directed by the Financial Matrix. As economist Ludwig von Mises had warned, "Just as the sound money policy of gold standard advocates went hand in hand with liberalism, free trade, capitalism, and peace, so is inflationism part and parcel of imperialism, militarism, protectionism, statism, and socialism."[6] The monster, so to speak, was out of the cage.

Today the Financial Matrix controls the world, with North Korea the only major nation not in its central bank cartel. Indeed, over 99.9 percent of the world's population is in an economy where the money supply is created by the Financial Matrix's central bank system of control. Despite sound money (a stable money supply) being the essential ingredient for a free market, the Financial Matrix has monopolized the world's economy with a highly unstable money supply. The Financial Matrix today is open about its fraudulent money making powers, as Jerome Powell, the Federal Reserve Chairman, plainly explained: "We print it digitally. So as a central bank, we have the ability to create money digitally. And we do that by buying Treasury Bills or bonds or other government guaranteed securities. And that actually increases the money supply. We also print actual currency, and we distribute that through the Federal Reserve banks."[7]

In the last twenty-five years, the Financial Matrix has used this unlimited money making power to forcefully integrate every nation that resisted its call to create a central bank. For instance, in 2001, the United States invaded Afghanistan, and by 2003, a modern central bank, Da Afghanistan Bank, was established by presidential decree. When the United States invaded Iraq in 2003, not surprisingly, by early 2004, the Central Bank of Iraq was established to manage the Iraqi currency and integrate Iraq into the Financial Matrix. Finally, in 2011, the United States bombed Libya into submission, and even before Muammar Gaddafi was overthrown, the U.S. aided the rebels in establishing a new Central Bank of Libya, along with a new national oil company.[8]

The Financial Matrix system we live under today is the worst of all monetary worlds. As we've discussed, inherent in FRB's architecture are predictable expansions and contractions. But contractions are no longer allowed. Instead, the Federal Reserve dutifully counterfeits unlimited amounts of fiat money to protect the banking system. It effectively prevents the spring from contracting back to its base position. This is why the money supply (the graphic displayed on the cover of this book) that followed the limited gold supply for thousands of years has now expanded millions of times over. It is why nations, companies, and people are awash in debt, and why monetary inflation is the new global reality. The graphic below reveals how the Consumer Price Index (the prices paid by consumers for goods and services) exploded along with the money supply after Nixon disconnected the dollar from gold. Before 1971, routine periods of FRB deflation lowered prices for consumers, but now the Federal Reserve creates fiat dollars to replace any FRB deflation of the money supply (as displayed in the top section of the chart). Thus, FRB inflation is followed by fiat inflation that reinflates the money supply whenever FRB deflation begins. This has caused the Consumer Price Index to skyrocket upward as consumers pay higher prices to cover Financial Matrix sins (as shown by the bottom section of the chart).

## MONETARY REGIMES & PRICE INFLATION
(Price Deflation Was Common Before the Fed Was Established)

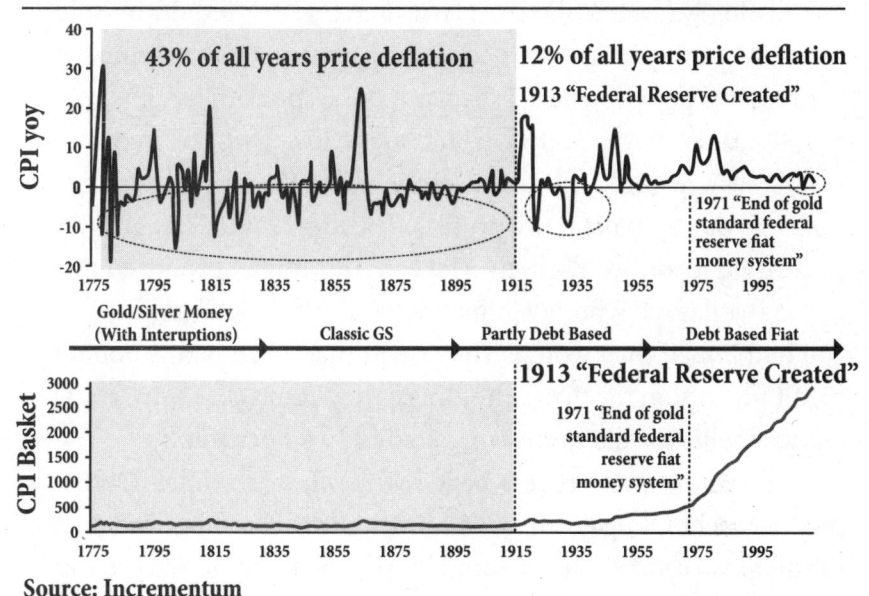

[Chart showing CPI yoy and CPI Basket from 1775 to 1995, with annotations:
- 43% of all years price deflation
- 12% of all years price deflation
- 1913 "Federal Reserve Created"
- 1971 "End of gold standard federal reserve fiat money system"
- Timeline: Gold/Silver Money (With Interruptions) → Classic GS → Partly Debt Based → Debt Based Fiat]

Source: Incrementum

### The Money Supply Slinky Grows Again - Collateralized Debt Obligations

Absurdly, the ability of the Financial Matrix to multiply the world's money supply and profit from doing so was given yet another new mechanism of amplification. This occurred even though the Federal Reserve could legally create unlimited amounts of fiat dollars, the other nations' central banks could recklessly expand their currencies on top of dollars, and the FRB lending institutions could expand another ten times on top of those. In the 1990s a new scheme was developed that would be layered on top of the three just described and generate astronomical profits for FRB cartel institutions. Originally, the FRB system required banks to keep on-hand a minimum of 10 percent of the amount of money they had loaned out. This was thought sufficient to protect against possible defaults, meaning, if several of the loans went bad, banks' overall money-on-hand (called capital requirements or reserves) would be high enough to still service withdrawals. The banks, however, instead of mitigating risk in this way, concocted a plan whereby "risk" could be sold to a third party. If regulators could be persuaded that this moved the risk "off books" where it became the responsibility of someone else, then perhaps they would allow lower reserve requirements, which would allow the banks to lend even more money (and, of course, make more profits). The idea worked beautifully. According to author Bethany McLean, JP Morgan proposed this to the regulators, who "eventually saw things exactly as JP Morgan had hoped they would. They ruled that when banks bought credit protection for their…holdings, they could cut their capital requirements for the underlying credits by 80 percent."[9]

The complicated process began with what are called Collateralized Debt Obligations (CDOs). These are special purpose financial instruments that essentially take a bunch of bank loans, say home mortgages, for instance, and stack them together in one bond that could be sold to investors. This stack of loans all have payments and interest due on a monthly basis, and that income is why an investor would be interested in purchasing it in the first place. Those monthly cash flows, but also the risk of those loans defaulting, now belong to the new owner of the CDO. The banks that originally made the loans are out of the deal, having made their profits up front. (Incidentally, because the value of this new product is *derived* from the value of the underlying loans making up the bond, these and other types of financial instruments are classified as "derivatives.")

When the regulators agreed that these (and other) shenanigans constituted reduced risk for the banks, the FRB cartel banks were ecstatic because they could now lower reserve requirements by 80 percent. This meant the original 10 percent FRB reserves were now reduced to 2 percent, and the FRB system expanded the money supply *an additional five times*, from the former ten-time FRB increase (1/.1 = 10) to a fifty-times increase (1/.02 = 50) over the central bank's notes held in reserve. While these CDOs radically increased bank profits, they were anything but risk mitigations. Warren Buffet's 2002 Berkshire Hathaway chairman's letter stated: "We view them [CDOs] as time bombs, both for the parties that deal in them and the economic system...derivatives are financial weapons of mass destruction, carrying dangers that, while now latent, are potentially lethal." In systems language, the CDOs cause the simple harmonic motion to expand and contract the money supply fifty times from the beginning money supply level instead of just ten times before CDO manipulation. In other words, whereas previously the Business Cycle was like falling off the Empire State building, CDOs now dropped the economy off Mount Everest. From 2000 to 2007, CDOs exploded in popularity, and turbo-charged money supply expansion and the demand for them caused corresponding housing price inflation. Buffett's "mass destruction" warning proved accurate. The Great Financial Crisis occurred when the money supply and housing prices imploded during the inevitable violent contraction of the Business Cycle.

Jamie Dimon, the CEO of JP Morgan, stated: "The fact is that every five years or so, something bad happens. Nobody ever has a right to not expect the credit cycle to turn."[10] Dimon clearly understood that FRB turns the money supply into a giant slinky that expands and contracts. Even though the money supply is supposed to be the one stable factor in the market, CDO proliferation and the corresponding relaxing of bank reserves expanded the actual size of that slinky, and thus the Business Cycle oscillation that followed was even more extreme. The Great Financial

Crisis of 2007-2008 was the largest boom and bust period in recorded history to that time, and CDOs merely fueled the size of FRB's inherent instability. Moreover, the crisis exposed the fact that the bust would now be felt worldwide due to the Financial Matrix's wholly centralized and interconnected global system. Localized banking issues are a thing of the past. The Financial Matrix has created the biggest and most far-reaching slinky ever. Like a set of dominoes worldwide, one failed bank knocked over another as the money supply began its contraction from five hundred times expansion back toward the original level. Indeed, the crisis began in the U.S. housing market, but it rapidly spread worldwide, first to the United Kingdom, but then almost everywhere, including Iceland, whose banking system collapsed. Of course, the central banks and governments did not let the money supply fall five hundred times but instead interrupted the bust by flowing unimaginable amounts of money into the banking system in order to save those who were "too big to fail." However, it did not and could not solve the root issue—FRB monetary instability. All it did was postpone the reckoning to a future date and guarantee that the magnitude of the bust would be even bigger the next time. The Financial Matrix had used its Fiat Money System to protect the banks while billions of other people paid the price. To repeat a phrase we used earlier, this was a classic case of *privatized gains* and *socialized losses*, meaning that the banks profited on the way up and the people paid when it came crashing down.

### Financial Matrix Record Breaking Profits

This turbo-charged FRB system predictably created profits multiple times higher than before. For instance, according to the US Department of Commerce, in 2008 (during the crisis), the American banking system paid depositors $178.6 billion in total interest while earning a whopping $3.29 trillion on its total loans. At a time when the U.S. government was throwing trillions of dollars at the bankers in order to "save" the banking system, it was making a whopping 1,842 percent return on investment! The FRB could lend money, package it into bonds, and lend it again, to gain returns on investment of over eighteen times. While monopoly profits are always exorbitant, the Financial Matrix is plowing new ground by literally making trillions from billions, leaving every other monopoly in the dust. Even accounting for every bank expense imaginable, an 1,842 percent return is the best proof possible that the system is fraudulent at its core.[11] This book has sought to demonstrate how the Financial Matrix has systematically destroyed the liberty, justice, and dreams of people worldwide, yet is rewarded with the highest profits, the highest executive bonuses, and the highest buildings in every town. These numbers tell the tale.

Nonetheless, without the trillions thrown in by our already hopelessly indebted governments, the 2008 financial crisis, according to the Financial Crisis Inquiry Commission, would have brought down the world's entire financial system:

*For example, as of 2007, the five major investment banks—Bear Stearns, Goldman Sachs, Lehman Brothers, Merrill Lynch, and Morgan Stanley—were operating with extraordinarily thin capital. By one measure, their leverage ratios were as high as 40 to 1, meaning for every $40 in assets, there was only $1 in capital to cover losses. Less than a 3 percent drop in asset values could wipe out a firm. To make matters worse, much of their borrowing was short-term, in the overnight market—meaning the borrowing had to be renewed each and every day...And the leverage was often hidden—in derivatives positions, in off-balance-sheet entities, and through "window dressing" of financial reports available to the investing public.*[12]

The actual leverage ratios during the Great Financial Crisis, even after the banks did everything to protect themselves, were forty times their reserves! This would have bankrupted every single bank in the global FRB cartel. This is why Secretary of the Treasury Hank Paulson at the time told the White House that if Fannie Mae and Freddie Mac (two government sponsored for-profit entities) were not rescued immediately, the troubled housing financial giants would, "I feared, take down the financial system and the global economy with them."[13] The Financial Matrix's socialist money system is not only fraudulent; it's also inefficient and ineffective, but worse, it recklessly risks global financial wellbeing when its carefully orchestrated money manipulations gyrate out of control. However, instead of replacing this catastrophic system with a free market solution, the state props up the very entities that cause the problems in the first place, sending them off unscathed to wreak further havoc in the future.

By looking at the Federal Reserve's growth in total assets, we can see just how badly the monetary system failed during the Great Financial Crisis, and how much the Financial Matrix socialized the losses by passing them on to the people. In an effort to stem the monetary contraction during the bust cycle, and prop up the insolvent banks, the Federal Reserve became not just a "lender of last resort," but also a "buyer of last resort," purchasing inflated (appropriately termed *toxic*) assets from sinking financial institutions in order to provide liquidity (money injections). The assets were valued at only 10 percent of their previous levels, but the Federal Reserve created money to pay the fully inflated prices to not only rescue the bankers but also let them profit. Whereas many private citizens went bankrupt and lost their homes and more during the crisis, most private bankers, when the dust finally settled, wound up profiting. We can see the magnitude of the bailout by noting that for the first fifty-eight years of its existence, the Federal Reserve only had around

# THE RISE OF THE FINANCIAL MATRIX

$100 billion in total assets, but in the next thirty-seven years it surpassed $1 trillion in assets. After the Great Financial Crisis, however, total assets exploded to over $6 trillion as the Federal Reserve bought up toxic assets of every stench to save America's banks. Unsurprisingly, central banks around the world dutifully followed suit. The central banks, in other words, are the Get Out of Jail Free card used by the Financial Matrix and its cronies to help its adherents survive downturns, while those operating outside of their cartel "Do Not Pass Go."

If all this weren't enough, another emergency occurred just over a decade later. Although the full story of what happened to the banking system shortly before the COVID-19 shutdowns may never be known, what we do know is that interest rates in the repo market (where bankers borrow from each other) spiked in mid-September 2019. The rates rose as high as 10 percent intra-day, and even then, financial institutions with excess cash refused to lend to their sister banks. When banks won't lend to banks, rest assured, another FRB contraction cycle has begun because the bankers are the first to feel the pain and know the true value of their inflated assets. As a result, from September up to the COVID-19 shutdowns, the Federal Reserve flowed money into the repo market to ensure the FRB system did not collapse. The global shutdown was incredibly timed to rescue banks on the cusp of another global disintegration. And because banking is now a global system, the failure impacts the whole world, and thus the populist protest that so concerned the Financial Matrix during the financial crisis would have been global in nature, except COVID-19's global shutdown conveniently kept the people locked indoors. Moreover, COVID-19 lockdowns at first ensured people couldn't spend money, which bolstered the banking system's liquidity by greatly increasing savings worldwide. Finally, national governments flowed trillions into the banking system without hardly being questioned because it was all camouflaged as COVID-19 measures.

## FEDERAL RESERVE BALANCE SHEET

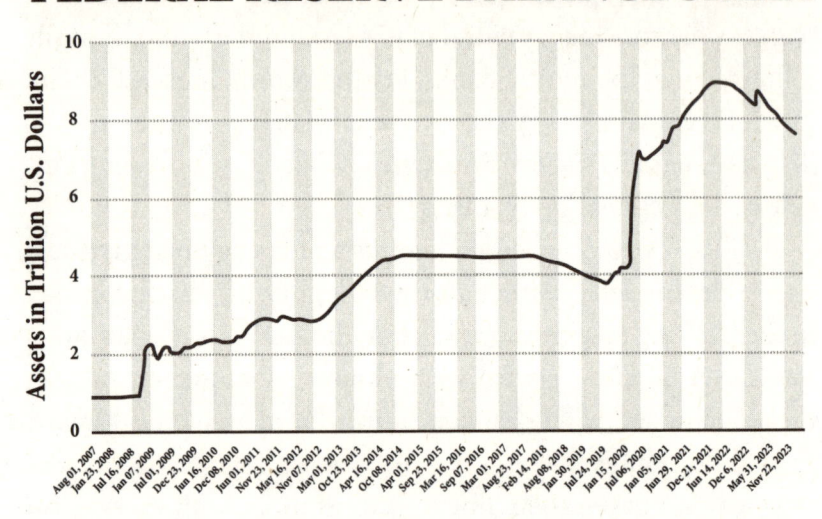

The COVID-19 shutdowns were just about the greatest and timeliest medicine possible for the global banking system. The American government enhanced unemployment benefits (an extra $600 per week) and provided mortgage forbearance plans, each boosting the liquidity of the banking system. According to Mark Zandi of Moody Analytics, without these measures, "an estimated 30 percent of American home loans would have defaulted (about 15 million households)," which would have tanked the highly leveraged FRB system. This would have had a domino effect throughout the world, and not one banking institution would have survived without massive central bank interventions. Not surprisingly, every intervention addressing each new emergency is larger in scale than the one preceding it because the Financial Matrix refuses to let the deflation cycle clear all of the inflation from the exuberant boom cycle. Emergency COVID-19 measures allowed the Financial Matrix to create over $4 trillion in a matter of months. While Elon Musk, the world's wealthiest person, has been an entrepreneur his entire life and today is *only* worth around $250 billion, and the IRS required nearly 75,000 agents to put in countless man hours to collect around $2 trillion, in 2019 the Federal Reserve created over $4 trillion (twice as much money as the IRS raised in a year) in mere nanoseconds.

Nonetheless, no amount of centralized power can escape the laws of economics. Even as the Financial Matrix was publicly promoting how strong the banking system was, it was privately flowing trillions of dollars into it to keep it propped up. For instance, in April of 2020, on CNBC, former Federal Reserve Chair Janet Yellen stated: "We have a strong, well capitalized banking system,"[14] while in reality the banking system was comatose. Veteran Wall Street analyst Pam Martens observed:

> *...the public is increasingly getting curious as to why the New York Fed has had to pump a cumulative $9 trillion in cash to these Wall Street banks, since September 17 of last year* [2019], *if they are so well capitalized. Can big banks actually be well capitalized and have no liquid money to make loans—the key function of a bank? As we have regularly noted, the Fed's trillions of dollars in cash infusions to the banks began months before there was any coronavirus COVID-19 outbreak anywhere in the world.*[15]

The Financial Matrix treats the world economy as its own personal goose that lays golden eggs. The only problem is that the steroids it pumps into the goose are actually killing it. Each time the physical effects start to bring the goose down, they shoot it up with even more steroids. Sooner or later, though, this process ends in destruction. Their goose will be cooked, but the bankers will have their baskets full of golden eggs. This behavior has nothing to do with the free market but instead is a protected socialist practice secured in each nation by following the four step process we will consider next.

*Every lie we tell incurs a debt to the truth.*
*Sooner or later, that debt is paid.*
—*Valery Legasov in the Chernobyl documentary*

# –12–

## Money, Media, Management, and Monopolies
*Don't bite the hand that feeds you.*

Whenever centralized power is achieved, it behaves like a giant star's gravitational field, pulling everything of substance into its orbit. Smaller powers negotiate with the growing absolute power to secure perks and profits for orbiting within its power structure, while those who resist are cast adrift. This hierarchy of subordinate allies, consisting of retainers, bureaucrats, and intellectuals, basks in the absolute power's light, enjoying the benefit of near unlimited power in their field of expertise, as long as they genuflect to the ultimate power. In *The Politics of Obedience*, Étienne de La Boétie describes how it only takes five or six committed retainers to subject an entire country to an absolute dictator's bureaucracy:

*These six manage their chief so successfully that he comes to be held accountable not only for his own misdeeds but even for theirs. The six have six hundred, who profit under them, and with the six hundred they do what they have accomplished with their tyrant. The six hundred maintain under them six thousand, whom they promote in rank, upon whom they confer the government of provinces or the direction of finances...*[1]

The Financial Matrix achieved power by drawing those with ambition and talent—top intellectual, political, and business leaders—into its orbit. What makes the Financial Matrix different from past absolute powers is its global reach. This makes the gravitational pull practically irresistible, even for those who originally opposed it. Alan Greenspan, for instance, as an idealistic young man, was an outspoken opponent of fiat money, stating: "In the absence of the gold standard, there is no way to protect savings from confiscation through inflation. There is no safe store of value. If there were, the government would have to make its holding illegal, as was done in the case of gold."[2] Greenspan later became Chairman of the Federal Reserve—the critic of untethered central power had become its servant. This phenomenon is so common that it has the name "capture," and it is a normal occurrence in the banking world. Like a supernova, the Financial Matrix's gravitational field has captured every nation-state into its orbit and follows a pattern described by the alliteration of Money, Media, Management, and Monopolies. These interconnected areas create a nearly irresistible urge to follow the rules so as to draw closer to their power source. Let's review how the process worked for the Financial Matrix to gain global control over each nation, and since we just completed how it obtained its money monopoly, let's start with the next step: Media.

**Media**

The Financial Matrix uses its money monopoly to purchase the main media sources within each nation. The Media elites who direct public schools, universities, foundations, social media, newspapers, movies, magazines, television, etc. learn quickly that those who play by the rules advance. Most people will not bite the hand that feeds them, even if the hand is doing questionable activities. Through a series of subtle compromises, they will eventually do the Financial Matrix's bidding without the need for coercion. The Financial Matrix owning the media is not even news today, for in 1983 author Ben Bagdikian wrote *The Media Monopoly*, in which he stated, "Fifty corporations dominated almost every mass medium."[3] However, with every rewrite of his book, the number of corporations has dropped from twenty-nine firms in 1987, twenty-three in 1990, fourteen in 1992, to ten in 1997. In fact, according to PBS, by the year 2000, five conglomerates dominated the entire industry. Media critic Mark Crispin Miller noted, "The implications of these mergers for journalism and the arts are enormous. It seems to me that this is, by definition, an undemocratic development. The media system in a democracy should not be inordinately dominated by a few very powerful interests."[4]

Naturally, as the global media centers orbit closer to the Financial Matrix supernova, those who dance to the tune the Financial Matrix is calling will move up the power ladders, and those who don't will not. This self-reinforcing cycle of media figures promoting the approved narrative, agendas, and doctrines becomes so routine that it isn't conspiratorial, but rather cultural. Those who follow the cultural norms advance, and those who don't will eventually leave or be forced out. But actually, there is no need for direct coercion because the carrot works just fine. The Financial Matrix needs the intellectuals to alter the perceptions of the people in order to meekly accept its rule, and the intellectuals need the support of the Financial Matrix to gain personal perks, privileges, and positions, as economist Joseph Salerno described:

*The ruling class, however, confronts one serious and ongoing problem: how to persuade the productive majority, whose tribute or taxes it consumes, that its laws, regulations, and policies are beneficial; that is, that they coincide with "the public interest" or are designed to promote "the common good" or to optimize "social welfare." Given its minority status, failure to solve this problem exposes the political class to serious consequences.*[5]

Media promotes the Financial Matrix, and genuine discussion about free market money and banking is not done, unless in a mocking fashion. Media is less about sharing facts and more about forming the mind. It creates perceptions to, as Plato noted, build "noble lies" that justify the Financial Matrix's economic and political order. The Media is expected to raise issues that divide people because the unwritten rule is that anything polarizing strengthens the Financial Matrix's power. The Financial Matrix also secures economists' support of the economic regime in a number of ways, which journalist Ryan Grim, in a 2009 article titled *Priceless: How the Federal Reserve Bought the Economics Profession*, noted:

*The Federal Reserve, through its extensive network of consultants, visiting scholars, alumni, and staff economists, so thoroughly dominates the field of economics that real criticism of the central bank has become a career liability for members of the profession, an investigation by the Huffington Post has found. This dominance helps explain how, even after the Fed failed to foresee the greatest economic collapse since the Great Depression, the central bank has largely escaped criticism from academic economists…One critical way the Fed exerts control on academic economists is through its relationships with the field's gatekeepers. For instance, at the Journal of Monetary Economics, a must-publish venue for rising economists, more than half of the editorial board members are currently on the Fed payroll—and the rest have been in the past…The Fed also doles out millions of dollars in contracts to economists for consulting assignments, papers, presentations, workshops, and that plum gig known as a visiting scholarship. A Fed spokeswoman says that exact figures for the number of economists contracted with weren't available. But, she says, the Federal Reserve spent $389.2 million in 2008 on "monetary and economic policy," money spent* *on analysis, research, data gathering, and studies on market structure; $433 million is budgeted for 2009.*[6]

The Financial Matrix created the power structure, and the world's top monetary economists gravitated into the Federal Reserve's orbit and obediently blessed it. And because economics is the most important profession needed to legitimize its actions, the Financial Matrix has rolled out the red carpet of profits, power, and perks for its advocates. Author Robert Auerbach, in his book *Deception and Abuse at the Fed*, discovered that in 1992, between the American Economic Association (AEA) and the National Association for Business Economics (NABE), there were approximately 1,000 to 1,500 monetary economists working in America, and over 500 of them were employed by the Federal Reserve. By adding those who previously worked at the Fed, we realize that *nearly every major monetary economist is captured in the Fed's orbit.* Furthermore, many of the editors of prominent academic journals, who review submissions dealing with Fed policy, are also on the Fed payroll. In 2008, the Huffington Post discovered that eighty-four of the top 190 editorial board positions for the top seven journals were connected to the Federal Reserve, which explains why the respectable economists with dreams of tenure write few articles critical of Fed policies and absolutely none that would dare question the Fed's existence.[7]

Of course, this same phenomenon plays out in every field, with the key medical journals now orbiting the pharmaceutical cartel, with the predictable result that these journals will ensure no articles bite the hand of Big Pharma. And let's not forget the federally funded educational system that uses the judicial system, squashing any dissenters, to enforce its uniform worldview in public schools. Similar scenarios occur in every field within the Financial Matrix, where everyone gets along to go along. Ryan Grim, again, described the benefits:

*Being on the Fed payroll isn't just about the money, either. A relationship with the Fed carries prestige; invitations to Fed conferences and offers of visiting scholarships with the bank signal a rising star or an economist who has arrived. Affiliations with the Fed have become the oxygen of academic life for monetary economists. "It's very important, if you are tenure track and don't have tenure, to show that you are valued by the Federal Reserve," says Jane D'Arista, a Fed critic and an economist with the Political Economy Research Institute at the University of Massachusetts, Amherst. And while most academic disciplines and top-tier journals are controlled by some defining paradigm, in an academic field like poetry, that situation can do no harm other than to, perhaps, a forest of trees. Economics, unfortunately, collides with reality—as it did with the Fed's incorrect reading of the housing bubble and failure to regulate financial institutions. Neither was a matter of incompetence, but both resulted from the Fed's unchallenged assumptions about the way the market worked.*[8]

How can a society remain free if those with the knowledge to expose fraud do not have the courage to do so? Unfortunately, when most people are confronted with a choice between principles and pragmatism, the safe bet is a pragmatic sellout. Joseph Salerno, again, explained how the intellectuals are rewarded:

*Here is where the intellectuals come in. It is their task to convince the public to actively submit to State rule because it is beneficial to do so, or at least to passively endure the State's depredations because the alternative is anarchy and chaos. In return for fabricating an ideological cover for its exploitation of the masses of subjects or taxpayers, these "court intellectuals" are rewarded with the power, wealth, and prestige of a junior partnership in the ruling elite. Whereas in pre-industrial times these apologists for State rule were associated with the clergy, in modern times—at least since the Progressive Era in the U.S.—they have been drawn increasingly from the academy. Politicians, bureaucrats, and those whom they subsidize and privilege within the economy thus routinely trumpet lofty ideological motives for their actions in order to conceal from the exploited and plundered citizenry their true motive of economic gain.*[9]

The "court intellectuals" are free to criticize anything except the Financial Matrix. The top leaders in every field who desire to advance must serve the Financial Matrix. Rob Johnson, an economist on the US Senate Committee on Banking, Housing, and Urban Affairs, said consulting gigs should not be looked at "like it's a payoff, like money. I think it's more being one of, part of, a club—being respected, invited to the conferences, having a hearing with the chairman, having all the prestige dimensions, as much as a paycheck."[10] The Fed's hiring of so many economists can be looked at from several vantage points, Johnson said. "You can look at it from a telescope, either direction. One, you can say well they're reaching out, they've got a big budget and what they're doing, I'd say, is canvassing as broad a range of talent," he says. "You might call that the 'healthy hypothesis.'" However, the other hypothesis, Johnson noted, "is that they're essentially using taxpayer money to wrap their arms around everybody that's a critic and therefore muffle or silence the debate. And I would say that probably both dimensions are operative, in reality."[11] The intellectuals love buttered bread, and the Financial Matrix has plenty of butter.

Media *experts* are paid to influence, covertly and overtly. For instance, Walter Lippmann, a two-time Pulitzer Prize-winning journalist, believed the masses were a "great beast" and "bewildered herd" who needed direction.[12] He even coined the term "manufacture of consent" to explain how to manipulate public opinion. The end result, as Media critic Noam Chomsky explained, is intellectuals stampeding the bewildered herd that whimpers: "'We want you to be our leader.' That's because it's a democracy and not a totalitarian state. That's called an election. But once they've lent their weight to one or another member of the specialized class, they're supposed to sink back and become spectators of action, but not participants in a properly functioning democracy."[13] In other words, people are the herd, the intellectuals are the wranglers, and the Financial Matrix owns the ranch. The herd is divided to stampede in all directions, so long as they do not unite to stampede for an escape from the Financial Matrix ranchers.

Napoleon Bonaparte once said, "There are but two powers in the world, the sword and the mind. In the long run, the sword is always beaten by the mind." This directly relates to our earlier discussion about Hobbes' two cardinal virtues of war: force and fraud. Influencing the mind to follow fraudulent practices requires less effort and produces better results than coercing people daily with the force of the sword. People's actions always follow their perceptions. In consequence, when the Financial Matrix changes perceptions, it changes outcomes through metaphysical fraud instead of physical force. This is why many people defend their own enslavement because they believe false perceptions (fraud) of reality and consistently live them out without being conscious of the disconnect. The people are treated like mushrooms—kept in the dark and fed loads of manure. Public relations expert Edward Bernays was proud of this fact:

*The conscious and intelligent manipulation of the organized habits and opinions of the masses is an important element in democratic society. Those who manipulate this unseen mechanism of society constitute an invisible government which is the true ruling power of our country. We are governed, our minds are molded, our tastes formed, our ideas suggested, largely by men we have never heard of. This is a logical result of the way in which our democratic society is organized. Vast numbers of human beings must cooperate in this manner if they are to live together as a smoothly functioning society. Our invisible governors are, in many cases, unaware of the identity of their fellow members in the inner cabinet.*[14]

**Management**

Through its monopoly over Money and now Media, the Financial Matrix has effectively secured control over democratic elections. After all, the two essentials for every democratic political candidate is Money and Media support. If the elected office is considered vital for Financial Matrix rule, the politician must prove willing to orbit around its gravitational field to be considered a viable candidate; otherwise, his chances of election are reduced to zero. All legitimate political candidates of any party running for powerful positions must grovel for the support of the Financial Matrix.

The key for Financial Matrix control is to keep the nation's people evenly divided, and the election process is tailor-made for this process. The right supports conservative values and the Warfare State, while the left supports liberal values and the Welfare State, and these manufactured divisions between people strengthen Financial Matrix control over its Warfare/Welfare State. Interestingly, since 1971 and the final transformation of Financial Power into the full-fledged and global Financial Matrix, the parties have coalesced together as author Noam Chomsky noted: "I mean, what's the elections? You know, two guys, same background, wealth, political influence went to the same elite university, joined the same secret society where you're trained to be a ruler—they both can run because they're financed by the same corporate institutions."[15]

The Management of every nation serves the Financial Matrix, as Antony Sutton, a research fellow at the Hoover Institute, shockingly discovered. Sutton was awarded the highest commendations for his research on Western technology and Soviet economic development, but his continuing research led him to conclude that the West played the key role in building up the Soviet Union's military and technological know-how and had done so from the very beginning. Of course, this made no sense to him at first because the Americans and Soviets were sworn enemies, and it would seemingly be foolish for the Americans to strengthen the military capacity of their enemies. However, if the global banking network controlled both nations and the national conflicts were merely false Hegelian thesis or antithesis constructs, then the true synthesis would conveniently benefit the Financial Matrix. In 1973, Sutton torched his career (but not his character) when he released *National Suicide: Military Aid to the Soviet Union*,[16] a thoroughly researched work that showed the Cold War was not fought to restrain communism but instead to generate multibillion-dollar armaments contracts. Sutton clearly demonstrated that the global financial system centered in the United States had loaned billions of dollars to the Soviet Union to arm both sides directly and indirectly in the Korean and Vietnam wars. In a 1972 testimony before Subcommittee VII of the Platform Committee of the Republican Party, Sutton summarized his discoveries:

*In a few words: there is no such thing as Soviet technology. Almost all—perhaps 90–95 percent—came directly or indirectly from the United States and its allies. In effect the United States and the NATO countries have built the Soviet Union. Its industrial and its military capabilities. This massive construction job has taken 50 years. Since the Revolution in 1917. It has been carried out through trade and the sale of plants, equipment, and technical assistance.*[17]

# MONEY, MEDIA, MANAGEMENT, AND MONOPOLIES

This was way too much truth to be shared during the Cold War, so in reward for his candor, he was dismissed from his prestigious position at the Hoover Institute and had any further research defunded. Today, Sutton's conclusions are slightly less astonishing because, after the collapse of the Soviet Union, the lies of its economic system were exposed. The Soviets could not even feed themselves, and after the nuclear disaster at Chernobyl, even their supposedly vaunted technical know-how was revealed as farcical. Thus, the only way for the Cold War to be believed, and then promoted and escalated, was for the Financial Matrix to lend the Soviets money to buy Western technology so they could appear to be a viable and even scary opponent. Sutton wrestled to understand why America would allow its military-industrial complex to fund and build the military system used against its own soldiers. The paradox was resolved when he realized he had it backward. *The financial system didn't serve the American state, but rather, the American state served the financial system.* Sutton, in short, discovered what I have been communicating throughout this book—namely, that the true rulers of the modern world are not national powers, but the international Financial Matrix to which they report. The American and Soviet states borrowed from the Financial Matrix to purchase weapons from the same military-industrial complex, in a futile effort to defend themselves against a false enemy while obeying the true enemy. The result of the Cold War was bankruptcy for the Soviet Union, deep debt-dependence for America, and absolute power for the Financial Matrix.

**Monopoly**

Finally, once the Financial Matrix controls the Money, Media, and Management of each nation-state, it uses the state to build, expand, and regulate its worldwide Monopolies. The Financial Matrix directs its subservient ruling elites in each nation to gain profits by building national monopolies and international cartels. Debora Mackenzie, in a *New Scientist* article intriguingly titled *Revealed: The Capitalist Network that Runs the World*, shared how, in a study of over forty-three thousand transnational corporations (TNCs), a relatively small number of companies, mainly banks, had a "disproportionate power over the global economy." The study was conducted by three systems theorists at the Swiss Federal Institute of Technology in Zurich and claims to be the first to go beyond ideology to specifically verify a network of power. Through a combination of mathematics, modeling, and mountains of corporate data, the network of ownership and control was mapped out. One of the researchers, James Glattfelder, stated, "Reality is so complex, we must move away from dogma, whether it's conspiracy theories or free market. Our analysis is reality-based."[18] This empirical research totally verifies that absolute power is the gravitational field that draws all other powers to it. The Financial Matrix has drawn practically every other corporate power, like planets orbiting the sun, into its gravitational field. Mackenzie reported:

*From Orbis 2007, a database listing 37 million companies and investors worldwide, they pulled out all 43,060 TNCs and the shared ownerships linking them. Then they constructed a model of which companies controlled others through shareholding networks, coupled with each company's operating revenues, to map the structure of economic power. The investigation exposed a core of 1318 companies with interlocking ownerships. Each of the 1318 had ties to two or more other companies, and on average they were connected to twenty. What's more, although they represented 20 percent of global operating revenues, the 1318 appeared to collectively own through their shares the majority of the world's large blue-chip and manufacturing firms—the "real" economy—representing a further 60 percent of global revenues. When the team further un-*

*tangled the web of ownership, it found much of it tracked back to a "super-entity" of 147 even more tightly knit companies—all of their ownership was held by other members of the super-entity—that controlled 40 percent of the total wealth in the network.*[19]

"In effect, less than 1 percent of the companies were able to control 40 percent of the entire network," says Glattfelder, and in reality, if the true interconnectedness of seemingly independent financial entities were known, we would discover even higher levels of corporate centralization.[20] Now the complete picture is coming into view. The Financial Matrix started with its absolute power over Money to control the worldwide Media system, which led to control over elections to select the Management of nations, culminating in its international corporate Monopoly. The pursuit of monopoly is a wildly profitable business strategy. As author Federic C. Howe admitted, "These are the rules of big business. They have superseded the teachings of our parents and are reducible to a simple maxim: Get a monopoly; let society work for you; and remember that the best of all business is politics, for a legislative grant, franchise, subsidy, or tax exemption is worth more than a Kimberly or Comstock [gold mines] lode, since it does not require any labor, either mental or physical, for its exploitation."[21]

The Financial Matrix understands that true competition is disorderly and unpredictable, as economist Joseph Schumpeter concluded when he wrote that the "gale of creative destruction" was the "process of industrial mutation that continuously revolutionizes the economic structure from within, incessantly destroying the old one, incessantly creating a new one."[22] Similar to how the Wright brothers beat out a much better funded and staffed military/university group in becoming the first to achieve powered flight, bureaucracies struggle to compete against nimbler competitors, constantly threatening to creatively destroy the old methods and replace them with better ones. This is what happens in a free market. "Little guys" with a better idea are free to rise up and topple "bigger guys" who have grown stodgy and fat from profits. Despite the politicians who like to throw around the word progress and claim credit for any advancements, it's the rough-and-tumble jungle of free competition that actually drives society forward. The Financial Matrix cartels could not let such amazing forces run loose under their carefully constructed house of cards. Thus they declared economic war, knowing that they couldn't compete with creative upstarts popping up everywhere, so they instead got creative in deploying tools of mass suppression to stop them, including regulations, licenses, fees, approvals, inspections, and taxes. Through the crushing weight of government regulations and barriers to entry, smaller startup firms collapse under the added weight, while the larger established firms are dutifully protected from pesky competition. In short, monopolies increase government regulations, not, as alleged, to protect the people from monopolies but rather to protect the monopolies from competition. Historian Gabriel Kolko stated the case almost exactly:

> *Ironically, contrary to the consensus of historians, it was not the existence of monopoly that caused the federal government to intervene in the economy, but the lack of it...Despite the large number of mergers, and the growth in the absolute size of many corporations, the dominant tendency in the American economy at the beginning of* [the twentieth] *century was toward growing competition. Competition was unacceptable . . . it was not the existence of monopoly that caused the federal government to intervene in the economy, but the lack of it.*[23]

To summarize, the Financial Matrix proceeded from Money to Media to Management, finally using its Management of national power to build a network of Monopolies and cartels. This has turned the law from an instrument of justice into one of injustice, as Frédéric Bastiat warned: "The law perverted! The law—and, in its wake, all the collective forces of the nation—the law, I say, not only diverted from its proper direction, but made to pursue one entirely contrary! The law becomes the tool of every kind of avarice, instead of being its check! The law is guilty of that very iniquity which it was its mission to punish!"[24] Economist Mark Perry of the American Enterprise Institute produced what some have called the "chart of the century" because it reveals just how costly it is to live in the Financial Matrix economy with its monopolies and cartels.

## PRICE CHANGES (JANUARY 1998 TO DECEMBER 2019)
### SELECTED US CONSUMER GOODS & SERVICES, WAGES

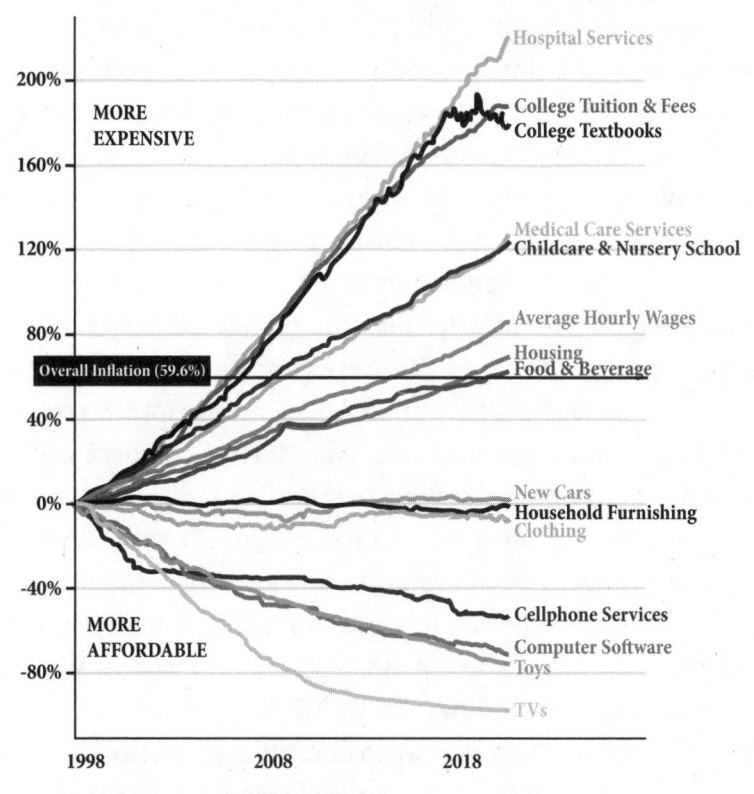

**Source: Bureau of Labor Statistics**

On one hand, the government-protected cartels provide the so-called non-tradables, things not subject to market competition (hospital stays, medical care, and college tuition), which have increased prices two to three times (or more) faster than the rate of inflation. On the other hand, the prices of goods subject to competition (toys, televisions, and mobile phones, for instance) have decreased over the past two decades. This clearly shows that free markets and actual competition benefit consumers. In other words, the "more affordable" lines represent free market pricing, while the "more expensive" lines represent government-supported cartel pricing.

The Financial Matrix apparently has more difficulty maintaining high prices internationally due to competition amongst nations, but where the government can intervene (in medical care and university education), the price increases are sky-high. Without an international state to enforce its monopolistic policies, the Financial Matrix resorts to a more ancient and clumsy method of threats and intimidation to plunder the people, backed, if necessary, by military force. Major General Smedley Darlington Butler, one of the most decorated Marines in American history (the only person awarded a Marine Corps Brevet Medal and a Medal of Honor for two separate military actions), was one of the first to express concerns over the military's mafia-like tactics overseas. Butler was an American patriot who served throughout Central America and, at age forty-eight, became one of the Marines' youngest major generals. In a 1933 speech, however, he objected to the misuse of the military: "I wouldn't go to war again as I have done to protect some lousy investment of the bankers. There are only two things we should fight for. One is the defense of our homes, and the other is the Bill of Rights. War for any other reason is simply a racket."[25]

After World War I, Butler began questioning U.S. involvement in foreign conflicts because he realized war was less about protecting people and more about protecting profits. Disgusted by the senseless endangerment of military personnel to defend monopoly or cartel profits, he became an unrelenting voice against the business of war, stating:

> *I spent most of my time being a high class muscleman for Big Business, for Wall Street, and for the Bankers. In short, I was a racketeer, a gangster...I helped make Mexico, and especially Tampico safe for American oil interests in 1914. I helped make Haiti and Cuba a decent place for the National City Bank boys to collect revenues in. I helped in the raping of half a dozen Central American republics for the benefit of Wall Street. I helped purify Nicaragua for the International Banking House of Brown Brothers in 1902-1912. I brought light to the Dominican Republic for the American sugar interests in 1916. I helped make Honduras right for the American fruit companies in 1903. In China in 1927, I helped see to it that Standard Oil went on its way unmolested.* **Looking back on it, I might have given Al Capone a few hints. The best he could do was to operate his racket in three districts. I operated on three continents [emphasis added].**[26]

If anything, the problem is even worse today than in Major General Butler's time. For instance, according to CNN, America today has military personnel in 150 countries, certainly at least suggesting the military focus is more offensive than defensive.[27] This is the result of the Financial Matrix capturing the management of the nation-states and using the military as its private police force (in this case, paid for by American taxpayers) to protect its international Monopolies and cartels. Fortunately, there is a workable plan to restore free market principles to money and banking, which would provide liberty and justice for all. This is the subject of the next chapter.

*Sound money and free banking are not impossible; they are merely illegal.*
—*Hans F. Sennholz*

# –13–

## Free Banking and the Bitcoin Standard
*Better late than never.*

For most of this book, we have talked about one monetary fraud after another, culminating in the birth of the Financial Matrix. The good news is that we now get to talk about solutions. Just as the problem was the centralization of power directed by FRB fraud, the answer must involve the decentralization of power directed by the free market. Ultimately, the Financial Matrix cannot survive. Like a supernova, absolute power draws everything into the center until it gains too much mass, detonates, and flies apart. Power is addictive, but it never satisfies. As power over others increases, the desire to increase it even more becomes consuming. The human heart is a contradictory mixture of good and bad elements, which is why good leaders reject absolute power and bad leaders covet it. The truth is that absolute power should not be entrusted to anyone because it corrupts the very humanity of its holder. This is why the Financial Matrix is systemically evil, for it corrupts those at its helm and in its orbit. It's also why "throwing the bums out" will not accomplish anything, as long as the underlying system that endlessly recruits and entices new "bums" remains. Aleksandr Solzhenitsyn explained, "If only there were evil people somewhere insidiously committing evil deeds, and it were necessary only to separate them from the rest of us and destroy them. But the line dividing good and evil cuts through the heart of every human being."[1] In other words, if the Financial Matrix system rewards the evil within human hearts, we should not be surprised that there is a steady stream of people willing to partner with it. As a result, the key to ending the Financial Matrix is to focus on changing the *systems* so that those systems don't take advantage of the corruptible nature within us. In a good political system, power checks power, and likewise, in a good economic system, the market checks power. Sadly, as we have seen, the Financial Matrix has reversed this and uses power to check the markets instead.

The ever-expanding Financial Matrix is the natural result of centralized power growing unchecked within our political and economic systems, centralizing subsidiary powers to orbit around and serve it. Since absolute power is a parasite that seeks to reap where it has not sown, when it controls governments, the laws of those states are inverted from protecting liberty and justice for all to trampling liberty and plundering all. Economist Frédéric Bastiat said, "Man can live and satisfy his wants only by ceaseless labor; by the ceaseless application of his faculties to natural resources. This process is the origin of property. But it is also true that a man may live and satisfy his wants by seizing and consuming the products of the labor of others. This process is the origin of plunder. Now since man is naturally inclined to avoid pain—and since labor is pain in itself—it follows that men will resort to plunder whenever plunder is easier than work."[2] Although Bastiat wrote *The Law* back in 1848, few have since described any better how tyranny and oppression grow systemically when absolute power controls the state's political and economic systems. Today the Financial Matrix is international and controls nearly every state, and its absolute power is growing through systemic tyranny and oppression over the world's political and economic systems. Since the Financial Matrix is a triumph of systematic centralized control, its unwinding must come through systematic decentralized replacement.

## Free Market Money: Gold Versus Bitcoin

The first step toward dismantling the Financial Matrix is to return to free market money, ending the legal tender laws that force people to use its monopoly money. Free market money must begin with whatever is the most marketable commodity and whatever the free market chooses (whether precious metal money, Bitcoin, or some other alternative). The key is that money must be freely chosen by the people in the market. Unlike fiat money, gold has endured as a store of value since ancient times, and the gold used back then can still be exchanged today. On the contrary, no fiat money system has endured beyond the state that birthed it, and all fiat money has returned to its true marketable value, which is zero. Indeed, of the hundreds of mandated monies, none have survived. Whereas free market money has legitimate market demand to back up its value, government money has only government force behind it. Therefore, just as the path to absolute power began with fraudulent FRB mandated money, so the path to freedom must begin with honest free market money. This is essentially a heart transplant accompanied by a complete blood transfusion, removing the core of the problem and replacing it with an organ of freedom and justice that will transform the beast from the inside. At the present time, the two main contenders for the future of free market money appear to be gold and Bitcoin.

## What is Bitcoin?

Bitcoin is a decentralized, distributed, digital virtual currency created in 2009 as a direct result of the housing market crash and is considered by many to be analogous to digital gold. It was created by the pseudonymous Satoshi Nakamoto and follows the protocols outlined in the white paper issued during its release. The real identity of the person (or persons) who created the technology is still a mystery to this day.

According to Austrian economist Saifedean Ammous, Bitcoin is a potential free market money that is "an invention leveraging the technological possibilities of the digital age to solve a problem that has persisted for all of humanity's existence: how to move economic value across time and space."[3] Bitcoin offers the promise of international money transfers around the globe at a much lower cost than traditional money transfer mechanisms. Moreover, it is operated by a decentralized, distributed authority mechanism, unlike the Financial Matrix's centrally issued currencies. Very importantly, the total number of bitcoins is limited by its program to 21 million. As Chris Brady wrote in *The Bitcoin Bride*, "This immutable finiteness makes bitcoin the absolute scarcest thing in human existence outside of our own time."[4]

Throughout this book we've talked about the need for stable money. The world has never seen a "money" this stable. And, since bitcoins are digital, there are no physical coins; only balances and transactions are transparently displayed on a public ledger. Furthermore, since bitcoins are decentralized and are not issued or backed by any government or bank, no entity can control their creation, transfer, or value. Instead, bitcoins have a market price because, like all goods and services, the market values them. In fact, the value of Bitcoin is growing as people realize the level of fraud the Financial Matrix has committed against them by noticing the ever-shrinking purchasing power of their national currencies. As governments overborrow and overspend, they inflate their currencies and thereby devalue them, invisibly stealing from their citizens. Bitcoin is a financial safe haven that more and more people are utilizing to protect the fruits of their labor. Essentially, Bitcoin is a grassroots movement aimed at the creation of free market money, entirely separate from the Financial Matrix.

The idea of free market money is not new, nor is the desire for stable or digital money. However, what makes Bitcoin so revolutionary is its elegant solutions to time-honored problems, all accomplished in one invention. One of the biggest obstacles to creating something like Bitcoin was the problem often referred to as the Byzantine Generals Problem (BGP), which software entrepreneur Marc Andreessen described:

> *Bitcoin is the first practical solution to a longstanding problem in computer science called the Byzantine Generals Problem (BGP). To quote from the original paper defining the BGP: "[Imagine] a group of generals of the Byzantine army camped with their troops around an enemy city. Communicating only by messenger, the generals must agree upon a common battle plan. However, one or more of them may be traitors who will try to confuse the others. The problem is to find an algorithm to ensure that the loyal generals will reach agreement.*[5]

The BGP, in other words, asks how to identify trustworthy actions from fraudulent ones, and thereby establishes a basis for trust in a decentralized network of unrelated parties like the Internet. Satoshi Nakamoto's technological solution created, for the first time in world history, the ability to transfer value between distant peoples without relying on a trusted centralized intermediary, and as a result, neither banks nor governments are needed to successfully complete transactions. Indeed, the ramifications of Bitcoin's core technologies are so profound that it has rightfully been suggested that Satoshi Nakamoto is a worthy recipient of both the Nobel Prize for economics and the Turing Award for advances in computer science.

### Essential Characteristics of Money

The technological innovations created in Bitcoin have the essential characteristics of money, money that is scarce (only twenty-one million bitcoins will ever be created), durable (being digital, they don't degrade), portable (the digital signature allows bitcoins to travel with you anywhere and to be transmitted electronically), divisible (into individual units one hundred millionths of a full bitcoin, called Satoshis), verifiable (through the public blockchain), easy to store (paper or electronic), fungible (each bitcoin is equal in value and fully interchangeable), difficult to counterfeit (cryptographically impossible), and achieving widespread acceptance within the marketplace, with many top technologists and programmers working overtime to improve it. The following chart from MAXIMALIST indicates how Bitcoin stacks up against other potential moneys.

| TRAITS OF MONEY | GOLD | FIAT | BITCOIN | "CRYPTO" |
|---|---|---|---|---|
| Fungible (Interchangeable) | High | High | High | High |
| Non-Consumable | High | High | High | High |
| Portability | Moderate | High | High | High |
| Durable | High | Moderate | High | Moderate |
| Highly Divisible | Moderate | Moderate | High | High |
| Secure (Cannot be Counterfeited) | Moderate | Moderate | High | Moderate |
| Easily Transactable | Low | High | High | Moderate |
| Scarce (Predictable Supply) | Moderate | Low | High | Moderate |
| Sovereign (Government Issued) | Low | High | Low | Low |
| Decentralized | Low | Low | High | Low |
| Smart (Programmable) | Low | Low | High | Low |

Source: Best Bitcoin Buyers Maximalist

Money, according to economist William Stanley Jevons, becomes money by progressing through four particular stages:

**1. Collectible:** First, people collect the item because it has a peculiar and special value to them—that is, they may like the way the shells, beads, or precious metals look and feel, choosing to save the items of interest.

**2. Store of value:** Soon enough, people demand that the peculiar item be recognized as an acceptable means of keeping and storing value. The more people recognize the perceived value of the former collectible, the more purchasing power increases as more people begin collecting it as a store of value, until a plateau of stored value is reached.

**3. Medium of exchange:** Now, the new money is fully recognized as a store of value, and its purchasing power has stabilized, thus making it a suitable medium of exchange. Interestingly, the famous story of the man who, in the early years of Bitcoin, traded ten thousand bitcoins (worth hundreds of millions in bitcoins today) for two pizzas indicates that the four-step money progression was not clearly understood, pushing the new collectible into a medium of exchange before its monetary value had plateaued and significantly overpaying for those pizzas!

**4. Unit of account:** The last stage of money progression is when money becomes widely used as the medium of exchange and all other goods and services are priced in terms of that new money. Bitcoins, for instance, are not at this stage yet because items purchased with bitcoins are just the dollar (or national currency) price charged by the merchant and then converted into Bitcoin terms at the current market exchange rate. Indeed, bitcoins will not become the unit of account until merchants accept them for payment without regard to bitcoins' exchange rate against other currencies.[6]

Bitcoin is currently a legitimate store of value, and the world is witnessing the birth of a potentially new free market money. Naturally, it will take time to progress from a store of value to a true medium of exchange, and the path is unpredictable; however, the speed at which the dollar and other fiat currencies are inflating could cause Bitcoin to progress faster than most people think. Of course, Bitcoin may never progress beyond a store of value similar to gold. After all, just as banks can create symbols on top of gold's value, they could also do similarly with Bitcoin's value, but there is one enormous monetary advantage with Bitcoin compared to gold: digital Bitcoin is a much easier transfer of value than physical gold.

The progression from a store of value to a medium of exchange took gold many centuries, and since a new money is not a common occurrence, no one can accurately predict how all of this will play out or if Bitcoin becoming a medium of exchange is even necessary. After all, Bitcoin will never be as fast as centralized digital money transfers, and I doubt if people will wait even a couple of minutes to transfer Bitcoin money to buy a coffee or shirt. At the individual level, transaction speed is very important. There are solutions for this already in place, such as the lightning network. But the big point is that bankers can wait a minute or two to settle accounts with every competing bank, and that's really the level at which Bitcoin can transform the financial system from the inside out. Transferring Bitcoin is way easier for banks than transferring physical gold from one location to another. It's difficult to forecast the future, but what we know for sure is that Bitcoin has progressed from a techno-cyberpunk collectible to an established store of value worldwide, and its value has increased significantly as the market becomes more comfortable with the technology.

Because Bitcoin is limited to a grand total of twenty-one million bitcoins, all displayed on the blockchain's public ledger, unlike the Federal Reserve fiat money system, its total supply will never increase, and anyone attempting to fraudulently duplicate bitcoins would be rejected by the blockchain network. Bitcoin has solved a key aspect that led the banks to start committing fraud, namely, the metaphysical-symbols-to-physical-reality fraud. Because gold is difficult to transfer around the globe, bankers created symbols and exchanged them while gold remained in their vaults. This opened the door to creating more metaphysical symbols than the physical gold it supposedly represented. Bitcoin, however, is both the symbol and the value in one, and thus, even though fraudsters can create fake symbols, they cannot create fake bitcoins. And since, unlike gold, Bitcoin can be reliably transferred from bank-to-bank at any distance at an extremely low cost, the fraudulent creation of symbols not backed by legitimate bitcoin reserves will be quickly uncovered.

As a result, banks on a Bitcoin Standard could each create symbols representing Bitcoin to serve their customers' money transaction needs and, more importantly, settle accounts daily with their banking counterparties by closing any balance of money differences between banks in Bitcoin. Those who created more symbols than Bitcoin would still have to transfer Bitcoin to settle the interbank differences, where they would be found out and, if persisting, would not only be bankrupted but also face government enforcement of commercial codes against fraud. And because settlements occur every twenty-four hours and the blockchain ledger is public, fraudulent banks would be exposed quickly. In short, banking would behave like every other free market business, which must settle its accounts promptly or go out of business. Notice the turnabout with such a system: fraudulent activities would not only be punished by the market, but also no longer *protected* by government and instead *prosecuted* by them. Simply stated, the Bitcoin Standard would end the Financial Matrix by restoring stable money and Free Banking. The same market forces that disciplined central bankers in Hume's "international price-specie flow mechanism" to not inflate beyond other central banks would now apply in what we could coin as the "inter-banking price-bitcoin flow mechanism," wherein market forces themselves are sufficient to ensure each bank does not inflate the money supply. Free Banking under a Bitcoin Standard, in other words, effectively ends FRB, the banker's original sin, and would eradicate it from the money and banking world. Rarely in the history of insidious frauds has a solution so neatly and readily been at hand.

**Free Banking is Free Market Banking under a Free Money Standard**

For this discussion, I am going to use Bitcoin as the free market money because of its settlement advantages; however, if another money is used by the free market, the specific techniques may change, but the underlying principles will not. Free Banking under the Bitcoin Standard indirectly causes banks to respond to David Hume's price-specie flow mechanism market forces, but without the need for central authorities to direct the banks' behavior. It would create the most open, decentralized, and competitive money and banking system ever. By mandating all banks globally settle accounts with each other every twenty-four hours using Bitcoin, the FRB fraud would no longer be viable. Due to Bitcoin connecting the symbol and reality (the metaphysical and physical aspects) of money programmatically, competitive banks could no longer inflate money symbols beyond the Bitcoin value held without overnight exposure. This is due to the fact that every day, Bitcoin can and must be moved to settle accounts with competing banks worldwide. The FRB fraud, trading money symbols while leaving gold safely in the vaults, would not fly under such a Bitcoin Standard. Free market money and banking would end government mandated money, fractional reserve banking fraud, central bank socialism, and the Financial Matrix tyranny—every single intervention that created the global monetary crisis we suffer under today. Alas, the free market is the principle, and Bitcoin Standard is the path to end the Financial Matrix and finally restore liberty, justice, and prosperity for all.

## Central Banks Versus Free Banking

Under a Free Banking Bitcoin Standard there would be no need for central banks (no cartel) because each bank would be in competition with other banks, and such a system would also be non-inflationary (no FRB) due to its nightly account settlements. This provides a truly stable money supply with no more Business Cycles. Recall that central banks were created to benefit the state-bank partnership. Through that mechanism state rulers gained access to more loans in an effort to increase their power, and the banks gained a 'lender of last resort' to protect against the downside risk of FRB. Neither of these is justified or needed in a Free Banking Bitcoin Standard model. Governments would be forced into budget discipline, like all other entities, and nightly bank settlements would ensure the FRB system is a thing of the past. Governments, in other words, could no longer recklessly borrow their way out of every financial constraint as they do today. Economist Vera Smith, a student of Nobel Prize-winning Austrian economist Friedrich von Hayek, described Free Banking as:

*A régime where note-issuing banks are allowed to set up in the same way as any other type of business enterprise, so long as they comply with the general company law. The requirement for their establishment is not special conditional authorization from a Government authority but the ability to raise sufficient capital and public confidence to gain acceptance for their notes and ensure the profitability of the undertaking. Under such a system, all banks would not only be allowed the same rights, but would also be subjected to the same responsibilities as other business enterprises. If they failed to meet their obligations, they would be declared bankrupt and put into liquidation, and their assets used to meet the claims of their creditors, in which case the shareholders would lose the whole or part of their capital, and the penalty for failure would be paid, at least for the most part, by those responsible for the policy of the bank...No bank would have the right to call on the Government or on any other institution for special help in time of need. No bank would be able to give its notes forced currency by declaring them to be legal tender for all payments....* [7]

Free banking is not a new idea, and before the era of central banks, there was much less FRB inflation because each bank feared having insufficient reserves to cover customer withdrawals. However, the central bank construct allowed banks to work as a cartel to inflate the money supply for profit because they knew there was a 'lender of last resort' waiting to bail them out. Free banking advocate Kevin Dowd noted:

*Free banking is—or at least ought to be—one of the key economic issues of our time. There is mounting evidence that the monetary instability created by the Federal Reserve—persistent and often erratic inflation, the unpredictable shifts of Federal Reserve monetary policy, and the gyrating interest rates that accompany both inflation and the monetary policy that creates it—have inflicted colossal damage on the US economy and on the fabric of American society more generally.*[8]

**Free Banking with 100 Percent Reserves**

The Bitcoin Standard Free Banking model follows Ludwig von Mises' proposal in *Human Action*: "What is needed to prevent any further credit expansion is to place the banking business under the general rules of commercial and civil laws, compelling every individual and firm to fulfill all obligations in full compliance with the terms of the contract."[9] Whereas Mises emphasized the importance of bank competition under general commercial law, he later, like Murray Rothbard, went one step further, suggesting that fractional reserve, since it is fraud against the consumer, should also be protected under the commercial code, explaining:

# FREE BANKING AND THE BITCOIN STANDARD

"The answer to fraud, then, is not administrative regulation, but prohibition of tort and fraud under general law."[10] Thus, these two great economic minds arrived at free market banking with 100 percent mandated reserves, operating under general commercial law, all of which is achieved by a Bitcoin Standard as described. Mises explained the benefits of Free Banking over the current travesty:

> Free banking is the only method available for the prevention of the dangers inherent in credit expansion. It would, it is true, not hinder a slow credit expansion, kept within very narrow limits, on the part of cautious banks which provide the public with all information required about their financial status. But under free banking, it would have been impossible for credit expansion with all its inevitable consequences to have developed into a regular—one is tempted to say normal—feature of the economic system. Only free banking would have rendered the market economy secure against crises and depressions.[11]

Banks would not only keep 100 percent money reserves on hand as mandated by law but would also do so of their own accord to ensure they remained solvent. Successful long-term bankers would be those who established trust by consistently doing the right thing, which would readily be noticed and rewarded by the free market. On the other hand, the free market is so quick and efficient that it would be able to punish fraudulent banks long before the government would even be aware that FRB fraud was committed. The misbehaving institutions would quickly be excommunicated by fellow bankers and abandoned by customers in an environment that allowed all actions to have their consequences. Without the protection racket run by today's mafioso central banks, misbehaving banks would become extinct under such swift forces of free market justice.

FRB, for all practical purposes, would be eliminated under Free Banking competition, even without the 100 percent reserve requirement. But like legal suspenders to go along with a free competition belt, even if some wily banker were to discover a novel method of using fractional reserve banking, it's doubtful many would risk prison sentences to do so. In 1994, after he had retired, former Federal Reserve Chair Paul Volcker, perhaps the most fiscally conservative person ever to hold the position, admitted:

*It is a sobering fact that the prominence of central banks in this century has coincided with a general tendency towards more inflation, not less. If the overriding objective is price stability, we did better with the nineteenth-century gold standard and passive central banks, with currency boards, or even with "free banking." The truly unique power of a central bank, after all, is the power to create money, and ultimately the power to create is the power to destroy.*[12]

With free market banking and the end of central banks, importantly, banks would then have to convince customers (with competitive interest rates) to forgo access to their money in order to loan it to others. The money supply would not expand because the depositor and borrower would not have access to the same money at the same time. No more having multiple claim checks for one jacket. Additionally, Free Banking would be much more efficient, performed at a fraction of the cost, and at reasonable (instead of exorbitant) profits because the banks would no longer be able to create more symbols than the Bitcoin held in reserve.

Depositor money would always be secure (without the need for a central bank lender of last resort), the money supply would be stable (and selected by the free market), and inflation would be a thing of the past (banks no longer expanding the money supply). As such, the Free Banking structure would allow banks to pursue whatever business ventures they deemed profitable so long as they had 100% reserves to protect customer deposits.

Moreover, anyone would be able to enter the field of banking instead of groveling for a charter before the Financial Matrix gatekeepers. To succeed, they would be required to earn customer deposits by building trust. The interest rates on loans and securities would be determined by the supply and demand for money on the free market, which would then determine the market price (the interest rate) of money. There would be no more pronouncements of what the interest rate was being "set at" from central planners in their ivory tower.

Free Banking would allow independent banks to open and close branches wherever they believed they could or couldn't compete effectively. Finally, there would be no need for FDIC insurance or any other excessive regulations since FRB is illegal, and the competition among banks would ensure that building trust would be the only way banks could stay in business. To compete, banks would have to impress upon customers that their deposits were secure and impress upon competitive banking institutions that their banknotes were as good as gold (or Bitcoin, in our proposal).

Free Banking is merely the consistent application of free market principles to money and banking. Period. It would allow free people to enjoy the blessing of the free market's ability to produce spiritual, political, and economic liberty. It would represent the total deregulation of the banking industry and lead to the following benefits:

1. A stable free market money.
2. The end of fractional reserve banking.
3. Competition and innovation in the banking profession.

4. No more central banks and their creation of fiat money out of thin air.
5. Governments would have to budget because they could not borrow unlimited amounts of fiat money.
6. No more inflation or deflation of the money supply.
7. No more boom or bust business cycles.
8. Banks would pay customers interest for saving money.
9. Prosperity would increase for all producers.
10. Financial manipulators could no longer unjustly profit from people's production.
11. Rebirth of liberty.
12. Reduced international meddling due to limited state funds.

Free Banking advocate Larry Sechrest concluded:

*As long as money remains a tool of the state, that tool will continue to serve the state as a wellspring of income redistribution, social engineering, and military adventurism. A laissez-faire [Free Market] approach to money and banking is more than merely conducive to efficiency and stability. It is likely to prove to be the necessary precondition for prosperity, justice, and peace.*[13]

Of course, free market money and banking are only possible economically when we also ensure the state is limited politically. Otherwise, the absolute state would quickly intervene in money and banking and begin fraudulent processes all over again. Therefore, a limited state is an essential aspect of a sustainable free market money and banking system. In fact, one major purpose of the political system would be to protect the free market economic system. Not surprisingly, the most effective way to limit power in a state is by limiting access to its funding. This is why the FRB system is so insidious, because with practically unlimited fraudulent money, Financial Power can and will gradually buy and corrupt the state, bending it to its will and wielding it for protection. However, without FRB fraud, the government cannot borrow money at will, and thus is only as energetic as its ability to tax, since it takes money to run the government.

This book has focused on systemic money fraud and how it produced absolute economic and political power for the Financial Matrix. In a future book, the objective will be to address how to ensure the political system has checks and balances to protect against the corrupting influence of money and power. I have sought to expose the force and fraud practiced in our economic and political spheres to, first, inform people of what is truly going on in our society and, second, summon those good men and women out there who won't just complain or bury their heads in the sand but instead help restore economic freedom. For starters, every individual can choose to right their own financial ship, extract themselves from the debt deception so prevalent in our FRB system, and effectively defund the Financial Matrix one person at a time.

# STUDY QUESTIONS

**Preface:**
1. What is the Financial Matrix, and what are its similarities and differences from *The Matrix* movie?
2. What are the two cardinal virtues of war, and how does the Financial Matrix use them to oppress the world?

**Introduction:**
1. "Orrin, you promised me," was my wake-up call to learn the truth about money and success. What was your wake-up call that started you on the learning journey?
2. How is success like walking through a minefield?
3. What are the Golden Rule and Power Rule economic philosophies?

**Chapter 1:**
1. How is going into debt like the Boiling Frog Syndrome?
2. Why is counterfeiting money illegal for everyone but banks?
3. What is the Cantillon Effect?
4. How does inflation benefit the few at the expense of the many?
5. Name the three big groups that borrow money from the Financial Matrix, all of which must be paid for by the people.

# STUDY QUESTIONS

**Chapter 2:**
1. Is there a moral element to economics? Why or why not?
2. What was Bertrand de Jouevenal's key economic insight?
3. What is the Free Market Mechanism, and how does it model the dynamic nature of the free market?
4. What does Say's Law communicate about the balanced economy, and why did Keynes seek to refute it?
5. How does the economy self-regulate and balance itself without the need for centralized control, and why is it not possible for any centralized group to achieve similar results?

**Chapter 3:**
1. What is the definition of free market money, and what has historically been the preferred money source?
2. How was free market money measured?
3. What was the first monetary fraud that expanded the money supply?
4. How does the expansion of the money supply affect the prices of products and services?
5. Is money a commodity or merely a symbol or sign? Explain why this matters.

**Chapter 4:**
1. What is the difference between legitimate and illegitimate banks?
2. What is usury?
3. Why is the confusion of terms (usury, FRB, and capitalism) so beneficial to fraudulent bankers?
4. Who said compound interest is the "eighth wonder of the world," and why?
5. Why was the transition from monarchies to democracies so profitable for the bankers?

**Chapter 5:**
1. What is fractional reserve banking, and is it fraudulent?
2. How is FRB like the medieval-age alchemists?
3. With 10 percent FRB reserves, how much can the money supply be expanded?
4. What is the root cause of the FRB money supply's inherent instability that causes the expansion and contraction cycles?
5. Why would the banks still use FRB as the money supply when it has proven to be wholly unstable and incapable of providing the one thing the money supply must provide, namely, a stable measure of value?

**Chapter 6:**
1. In what ways is the borrower a slave to the lender?
2. Why is Machiavelli considered the patron saint of the Financial Matrix?
3. How did early bankers corrupt government and church officials?
4. How did bankers use the state to protect their business interests?
5. How were bankers involved in the Reformation?

**Chapter 7:**
1. What is the simplest way to end the FRB money supply instability?
2. Why is the FRB money supply an oscillating wave?
3. How does the FRB system reinforcing loop flipping from expansion to contraction account for the "cluster of errors" entrepreneurs experience during Business Cycles?
4. How does the FRB flipping from expansion to contraction account for consumer goods slowing down but capital goods effectively collapsing?

# STUDY QUESTIONS

5. How is the oscillating wave of the FRB money supply related to the oscillating wave of the Business Cycle?

**Chapter 8:**
1. How are the terms "moral hazard," "shift the burden," and "lender of last resort" related to central banks?
2. How do central banks increase the money supply many times higher than the amount of gold, even though they are allegedly on the gold standard?
3. Are central banks part of the free market or a socialist intervention?
4. How did the Second National Bank seek to corrupt the United States government?
5. Explain how free market money died when Abraham Lincoln created State Power "Greenbacks," and what did Financial Power do in response?

**Chapter 9:**
1. Define the three types of money: 1) Free Market, 2) Financial Power, and 3) State Power.
2. How did the private Financial Power money use the gold standard to hammer public State Power money?
3. Why is Financial Power money the most destructive type of money?
4. How did Ben Franklin propose to implement State Power money in colonial Pennsylvania?
5. Explain why America, which won its independence using State Power money, shortly afterward returned to Financial Power debt-money.

**Chapter 10:**
1. Why was Napoleon such a threat to Financial Power bankers?

2. Why did President Lincoln call the Greenbacks "the greatest blessing the American people have ever had"?
3. What did Financial Power gain at the end of World War I?
4. How did the German government restore full employment while the rest of the world continued to suffer mass unemployment during the Great Depression?
5. Why did Financial Power insist upon 'unconditional surrender' to its State Power opponents during World War II?

**Chapter 11:**
1. How did Bretton Woods increase the money supply from one hundred times the gold supply base to one thousand times?
2. How did Financial Power drive President Nixon to go off the gold standard completely in 1971 to create a new global fiat money regime?
3. How did Collateralized Debt Obligations increase the money supply five times more?
4. How have modern central banks become 'buyers of last resort' to protect the Financial Matrix?
5. Even though productivity has continued to rise since 1971, why have people's wages flatlined after accounting for inflation?

**Chapter 12:**
1. What role does mainstream Media play in ensuring Financial Power's rule?
2. How does Financial Power maintain influence over the economics profession?
3. What are the two things necessary for a modern politician to be democratically elected, and who controls these two necessities?

# STUDY QUESTIONS

4. Why would Financial Power fund both sides of the Cold War?
5. Why do centralized money and a centralized state naturally lead to centralized monopolies?

**Chapter 13:**
1. What is the first step in restoring freedom to return to free market money, whether that is gold, silver, or Bitcoin?
2. Why is Bitcoin a possible improvement upon the "classical" gold standard?
3. How could Free Banking, like the "price-specie flow" mechanism between nations under the classical gold standard, settle the balance of payments among competing banks using the 'price-bitcoin flow' mechanism to end FRB?
4. Why are central banks not needed under a Free Banking system with an overnight balance of trade settlements between competing banks?
5. Why haven't the people insisted upon a return to Free Banking and free market money since it would end the Financial Matrix by terminating the FRB symbol fraud, central banks socialist interventions, and the Business Cycle?

# ACKNOWLEDGMENTS

While writing demands many hours alone to study, think, and construct the various lines of thought into a rough draft, the final product can only be achieved by a team effort. Fortunately, I am surrounded by a world-class team, one that is just as committed to setting the world free from the Financial Matrix as I am.

This team begins at home, where I have been blessed beyond measure with my amazing wife, Laurie Woodward. Not only is she lovely, loving, and loyal, but her willingness to go the extra mile in practically every area allowed me the time necessary to tackle a project of this magnitude. She never complained about the extra workload; she never criticized her husband's reclusive behavior; and she never wavered in her support. Moreover, Laurie, along with our adult children, Jordan, Christina and her husband Alex, Lance and his fiancé Marissa, and Jeremiah, should be given an award for subjecting themselves to my Financial Matrix ramblings during our weekly family call. If it were not for my family's continued belief, encouragement, and support, this book would never have seen the light of day.

The second part of this team is my lifetime friendship and business partnership with Chris Brady. I could not fathom writing this book without his input. Not only did he read every word of the manuscript, but he took "providing feedback" to a whole new level. Sure, he suggested edits to nearly every paragraph to ensure I said clearly what I intended to say, but he also challenged any unsupported assumptions, which drove me to better source my conclusions with the historical evidence. This resulted in the

## ACKNOWLEDGMENTS

dots being connected more clearly in a step-by-step fashion to help the readers draw their own conclusions from the data and facts presented. Brady even proposed sentence rewrites when his friend's writing became overly verbose. Alas, for the CEO of a multi-million dollar company to dedicate hours per day for several months to improve this book without complaint, fanfare, or any agenda besides seeing the book communicate its message, clearly makes me forever in my friend's debt.

I would also like to thank the Life community for sharing their stories of how the Financial Matrix has impacted them. It is because of your inspiration that this book was written. A special shout-out goes to Pastor Scott VanderPloeg, whose biblical insights on money and work helped clarify my thinking on the Financial Matrix, while his constant encouragement helped me push to the finish line. My brother John Woodward also stepped up by reading an early draft of the book and encouraging me to press on to completion. Next, I would like to thank the corporate staff at Life. COO Rob Hallstrand and his team, including Steve Kendall and Jordan Woodward, are a joy to work with and turned this book around in record time.

Finally, none of this would have been possible without the love and mercy of my Lord and Savior, Jesus Christ. To Him be all the glory and honor!

# END NOTES

**Preface**
1. Lana Wachowski and Lilly Wachowski, directors, *The Matrix*, Burbank, CA: Warner Bros., 1999
2. Lana Wachowski and Lilly Wachowski, directors, *The Matrix*, Burbank, CA: Warner Bros., 1999.
3. John Perkin, *Confessions of an Economic Hit Man*, 3rd ed. (Plume, 2005).
4. Open Culture, "'The only thing necessary for the triumph of evil is for good men to do nothing,' a Quote Falsely Attributed to Edmund Burke." Open Culture, March 13, 2016, www.openculture.com/2016/03/edmund-burkeon-in-action.html.
5. Buckminster Fuller, *A Fuller View* (Studio City, CA: Michael Wiese Productions, 2012).

**Chapter 1**
1. IMF Blog. "Global Debt Reaches a Record $226 Trillion," December 15, 2021, https://www.imf.org/en/Blogs/Articles/2021/12/15/blog-global-debt-reaches-a-record-226-trillion.
2. Ezra Pound, "Seven Quotes from Ezra Pound." Exploring Your Mind, March 30, 2020, www.exploringyourmind.com/seven-quotes-from-ezra-pound/.
3. Jonathan Newman, "Four Charts That Show Cantillon Effects," *Mises Institute*, February 1, 2024, https://mises.org/mises-wire/four-charts-show-cantillon-effects.

# END NOTES

4. Abraham Lincoln, 1861 Annual Message to Congress.
5. Ernest Hemingway, *The Sun Also Rises* (Scribner, 2006).
6. Jack Caporal, "Total Household Debt by Type," The Motley Fool, February 22, 2024, https://www.fool.com/the-ascent/research/average-household-debt/.
7. Torsten Sløk, "Monthly Payments for New Mortgages," Apollo Academy, June 21, 2023, https://www.apollo-academy.com/monthly-payments-for-new-mortgages/.
8. Matt Schulz, "2024 Credit Card Debt Statistics," LendingTree, March 13, 2024, https://www.lendingtree.com/credit-cards/credit-card-debt-statistics/.
9. Claire Tsosie, "How Credit Card Issuers Calculate Minimum Payments," NerdWallet, May 31, 2023, https://www.nerdwallet.com/article/credit-cards/credit-card-issuer-minimum-payment.
10. William J. Bennett, "Opinion | Our Greedy Colleges," *The New York Times*, February 18, 1987, sec. Opinion, https://www.nytimes.com/1987/02/18/opinion/our-greedy-colleges.html.
11. Drozdowski, Mark J. 2023. "What Caused the $1.8 Trillion Student Debt Crisis? | BestColleges." www.bestcolleges.com. August 14, 2023.https://www.bestcolleges.com/news/analysis/what-caused-the-student-debt-crisis/
12. FRED, "Motor Vehicle Loans Owned and Securitized," Federal Reserve Bank of St. Louis, March 7, 2024, https://fred.stlouisfed.org/series/MVLOAS.
13. Jasmin Suknanan, "54% of People Believe a Partner With Debt Is a Reason to Consider Divorce—Here Are Other Ways Debt May Affect Your Marriage," *CNBC*, 2023. https://www.cnbc.com/select/national-debt-relief-survey-debt-reason-for-divorce/.
14. Ashley Kirzinger, Liz Hamel, Cailey Muñana, Audrey Kearney, and Mollyann Brodie Published. "KFF Health

Tracking Poll—Late April 2020: Economic and Mental Health Impacts of Coronavirus - 9447," KFF, April 24, 2020, https://www.kff.org/report-section/kff-health-tracking-poll-late-april-2020-economic-and-mental-health-impacts-of-coronavirus/#:~:text=About%20two%2Dthirds%20of%20those.

## Chapter 2
1. Augustine, *The City of God* (Peabody, MA: Hendrickson Publishers, 2009).
2. Mises, Ludwig von, *Omnipotent Government* (New Haven, CT: Yale University Press, 1944).
3. Albert Jay Nock, *Our Enemy the State* (North Stratford, NH: Ayer Publishing Co., 1972).
4. Franz Oppenheimer, *The State* (New York: B. W. Huebsch Publishing, 1992).
5. Albert Jay Nock, *Our Enemy the State* (North Stratford, NH: Ayer Publishing Co., 1972).
6. Bertrand de Jouvenel, *The Ethics of Redistribution* (New York: Cambridge University Press, 1951).
7. Richard Ebeling, "The Free Market and the Interventionist State," Imprimis, August 1, 1997. https://imprimis.hillsdale.edu/the-free-market-and-the-interventionist-state/.
8. Jean-Baptise Say, *A Treatise on Political Economy* (1803).
9. Ludwig von Mises, "The Freeman" October 30th 1950 https://mises.org/mises-daily/lord-keynes-and-says-law

## Chapter 3
1. Murray Rothbard, "Money: Its Importance, Origins, and Operations," Mises.org, 1983, https://mises.org/mises-daily/money-its-importance-origins-and-operations.

# END NOTES

2. John Flynn, *Men of Wealth* (Kessinger Publishing, 2010).
3. Richard Ehrenberg, *Capital and Finance and the Age of the Renaissance* (New York: A.M. Kelly, 1963).
4. Milton Friedman, *The Counter-Revolution and Monetary Theory* (London: Institute of Economic Affairs, 1970).
5. David Hawke, *The Culture of Usury in Renaissance England* (Springer, 2010).

## Chapter 4

1. Aristotle, *The Politics Part 1* (London: Penguin, 1981).
2. Chad Brand, "Usury in the Gospels," Tifwe.org, June 28, 2023. https://tifwe.org/usury-in-the-gospels/.
3. Goodreads.com, "A Quote by Albert Einstein." Goodreads.com, n.d., www.goodreads.com/quotes/76863-compound-interest-is-the-eighth-wonder-of-the-world-he.
4. Tami Luhby, "Interest Payments on the Nation's Debt Are Soaring. It's Only Going to Get Worse. CNN Politics," *CNN*. November 16, 2023. https://www.cnn.com/2023/11/16/politics/interest-payments-federal-government-debt/index.html

## Chapter 5

1. F.A. Hayek, *The Fatal Conceit: The Errors of Socialism* (University of Chicago Press, 2011).
2. David Hawke, *The Culture of Usury in Renaissance England* (Springer, 2010).
3. Murray Rothbard, *The Case for 100 Percent Gold* (Ludwig von Mises Institute, 1962).
4. Jack Weatherford, *History of Money* (New York: Three Rivers Press, 1997).

5. Minnesota State Law Library, "Credit River Case," Minnesota State Law Library, 1969, www.mn.gov/law-library/legal-topics/credit-river-case.jsp.
6. Murray Rothbard, *The Mystery of Banking* (Ludwig von Mises Institute, 2008).

**Chapter 6**
1. David Hawke, *The Culture of Usury in Renaissance England* (Springer, 2010).
2. Bradley Birzer, "Machiavelli: The Prince of Darkness?" The Imaginative Conservative, May 2, 2021, https://theimaginativeconservative.org/2021/05/machiavelli-prince-darkness-russell-kirk-bradley-birzer-timeless.html.
3. Niccolò Machiavelli, *The Prince* (New York: New American Library, 1952).
4. Christopher Hibbert, *The Rise and Fall of the House of Medici*, (London: Penguin, 2001).
5. Greg Steinmetz, *The Richest Man Who Ever Lived* (New York; Toronto: Simon and Schuster, 2016).
6. Vespasiano da Bisticci, William George, and Emily Waters, *The Vespasiano Memoirs: Lives of Illustrious Men of the XVth Century* (University of Toronto Press, 1971).
7. Tim Parks, *Medici Money: Banking, Metaphysics, and Art in Fifteenth Century Florence* (W. W. Norton & Company, 2006).
8. Tim Parks, *Medici Money: Banking, Metaphysics, and Art in Fifteenth Century Florence* (W. W. Norton & Company, 2006).
9. Tim Parks, *Medici Money: Banking, Metaphysics, and Art in Fifteenth Century Florence* (W. W. Norton & Company, 2006).

# END NOTES

10. Tim Parks, *Medici Money: Banking, Metaphysics, and Art in Fifteenth Century Florence* (W. W. Norton & Company, 2006).
11. Richard Ehrenberg, *Capital and Finance and the Age of the Renaissance* (New York: A. M. Kelley, 1963).
12. Greg Steinmetz, *The Richest Man Who Ever Lived* (New York; Toronto: Simon and Schuster, 2016).
13. Greg Steinmetz, *The Richest Man Who Ever Lived* (New York; Toronto: Simon and Schuster, 2016).

## Chapter 7

1. David Fischer and James McPherson, Foreward to *Rainbow's: The Crash of 1929*, by Maury Klein, (Oxford Press, 2003).
2. Peter Senge, *The Fifth Discipline: The Art & Practice of The Learning Organization.*
3. Koshy Mathai, "Monetary Policy: Stabilizing Prices and Output," IMF Article, https://www.imf.org/en/Publications/fandd/issues/Series/Back-to-Basics/Monetary-Policy#:~:text=In%20a%20recession%2C%20for%20example,country%27s%20exports%20may%20also%20fall.
4. Murray Rothbard, *America's Great Depression* (Quoting Frank Graham), (Ludwig von Mises Institute, 1972).
5. R.G. Hawtrey, *Currency and Credit* (Hardpress Publishing, 2012).
6. Hugh Rockoff, *Coping With Financial Crises* (Springer, 2017).
7. Hugh Rockoff, *Coping With Financial Crises* (Springer, 2017).
8. Murray Rothbard, *America's Great Depression* (Quoting Frank Graham), (Ludwig von Mises Institute, 1972).

9. National Bureau of Economic Research, "US Business Cycle Expansions and Contractions," National Bureau of Economic Research, July 19, 2021. https://www.nber.org/research/data/us-business-cycle-expansions-and-contractions
10. Hans Sennholz, "The Great Depression," Mises Institute, December 21, 2020. https://mises.org/mises-daily/great-depression.

## Chapter 8

1. Murray Rothbard, *Mystery of Banking* (AL: Ludwig Von Mises Institute, 2008).
2. Murray Rothbard, *History of Money and Banking* (AL: Ludwig Von Mises Institute, 2005).
3. Alice Beagley, "Why Was the Bank of England Founded?" Bank of England Museum, 2021, https://www.bankofengland.co.uk/museum/online-collections/blog/why-was-the-bank-of-england-founded.
4. Karl Marx and Frederick Engels, *Communist Manifesto* (Penguin Classics).
5. Ron Paul, "Central Banking Is Socialism: Ron Paul," *Orange County Register*, March 9, 2020, https://www.ocregister.com/2020/03/09/central-banking-is-socialism-ron-paul/.
6. F. A. Hayek, *The Fatal Conceit* (University of Chicago Press, 2011).
7. Murray Rothbard, *History of Money and Banking* (AL: Ludwig Von Mises Institute, 2005).
8. Franklin Roosevelt, Letter to Col. Edward Mandell House, 21 November 1933, as quoted in *F.D.R.: His Personal Letters, 1928-1945*, by Franklin Roosevelt, edited by Elliott Roosevelt, (New York: Duell, Sloan and Pearce, 1950), 373.

# END NOTES

9. Arthur M. Schlesinger, *The Age of Jackson* (New York: Little, Brown Publishing, 1945).
10. Arthur M. Schlesinger, *The Age of Jackson* (New York: Little, Brown Publishing, 1945).
11. Andrew Jackson, "Bank Veto Message (1832)," https://constitutioncenter.org/the-constitution/historic-document-library/detail/andrew-jackson-bank-veto-message-1832.
12. Nicholas Biddle, *Nicholas Biddle Papers*. Library of Congress. https://lccn.loc.gov/mm78012690.
13. Bray Hammond, "Jackson's Fight with the 'Money Power,'" *American Heritage*, June 1956, www.americanheritage.com/jacksons-fight-money-power.
14. Bray Hammond, "Jackson's Fight with the 'Money Power,'" *American Heritage*, June 1956, www.americanheritage.com/jacksons-fight-money-power.
15. The Lerhman Institute "History - Essays", https://lehrmaninstitute.org/history/Andrew-Jackson-1837.html
16. H. W. Brands, , *Andrew Jackson: His Life and Times* (New York: Anchor Books, 2005).
17. Arthur M. Schlesinger, *The Age of Jackson* (New York: Little, Brown Publishing, 1945).
18. Arthur M. Schlesinger, *The Age of Jackson* (New York: Little, Brown Publishing, 1945).
19. Arthur M. Schlesinger, *The Age of Jackson* (New York: Little, Brown Publishing, 1945).
20. Gary North, "Defenders of Crony Capitalism: Why Historians Ridicule Andrew Jackson," August 13, 2016, www.garynorth.com/HistoriansJackson.pdf.
21. Andrew Wolstenholme, "Never Waste A Good Crisis (Wolstenholme Report)," 2009.
22. Federal Reserve History. "National Banking Acts of 1863 and 1864," July 31, 2022, https://www.federalreservehis-

tory.org/essays/national-banking-acts#:~:text=In%20 1863%2C%20the%20United%20States,blown%20 military%20and%20industrial%20endeavor.
23. Doris Goodwin Kearns, *Team of Rivals* (Simon and Schuster, 2006).
24. Ron Paul, "The Origins of the Fed," Mises Institute, 2011, https://mises.org/mises-daily/origins-fed.
25. David Hume, *On the Balance of Trade* (1752).
26. Richard Cooper, *The Gold Standard: Historical Facts and Future Prospects* (The Johns Hopkins University Press, 1982), https://www.brookings.edu/wp-content/uploads/1982/01/1982a_bpea_cooper_dornbusch_hall.pdf.

## Chapter 9

1. Ryan McMaken, "How the Classical Gold Standard Fueled the Rise of the State," Mises Institute, 2021, https://mises.org/mises-wire/how-classical-gold-standard-fueled-rise-state.
2. Marc Flandreau, *Glitter of Gold* (Oxford University Press, 2004).
3. Ryan McMaken, "How the Classical Gold Standard Fueled the Rise of the State," Mises Institute, 2021, https://mises.org/mises-wire/how-classical-gold-standard-fueled-rise-state.
4. F.A. Hayek, *Denationalisation of Money* (Institute of Economic Affairs, 1976).
5. Thomas Edison, Commenting on Henry Ford's currency plan in "Ford Sees Wealth in Muscle Shoals," *New York Times*, 6 December 1921, 6
6. A.K. Chesterton, *Candour Magazine*.
7. Farley Grubb, "Benjamin Franklin and the Birth of a Paper Money Economy" (The Library Company of

Philadelphia, 2006), https://www.philadelphiafed.org/-/media/frbp/assets/institutional/education/publications/benjamin-franklin-and-paper-money-economy.pdf

8. Sara Whitford, "The Currency Act (1764) – the Ugly, Old Cousin of the Federal Reserve Act," Adam Fletcher Adventure Series by Sara Whitford, (October 18, 2022). https://www.adamfletcherseries.com/the-currency-act-of-1764/#:~:text=It%20is%20called%20Colonial%20Scrip,interest%20to%20pay%20no%20one.%E2%80%9D

9. Sara Whitford, "The Currency Act (1764) – the Ugly, Old Cousin of the Federal Reserve Act," Adam Fletcher Adventure Series by Sara Whitford, (October 18, 2022). https://www.adamfletcherseries.com/the-currency-act-of-1764/#:~:text=It%20is%20called%20Colonial%20

10. CURIOSity Collections, "Continental Currency," American Currency—CURIOSity Digital Collections. https://curiosity.lib.harvard.edu/american-currency/feature/continental-currency

11. Joshua Rapp Learn, "How Benjamin Franklin Fought Money Counterfeiters," (Science News. July 18, 2023), https://www.sciencenews.org/article/benjamin-franklin-money-counterfeiter.

12. Kenneth Scott, *Counterfeiting In Colonial America* (University of Pennsylvania Press, 2009), 258.

13. Thomas J. Dilorenzo, *Hamilton's Curse: How Jefferson's Arch Enemy Betrayed the American Revolution--and What It Means for Americans Today* (Crown's Publishing Group, 2009).

14. Thomas J. Dilorenzo, *Hamilton's Curse: How Jefferson's Arch Enemy Betrayed the American Revolution--and What It Means for Americans Today* (Crown's Publishing Group, 2009).

## Chapter 10

1. James Narron and David Skeie, "Crisis Chronicles: The Collapse of the French Assignat and Its Link to Virtual Currencies Today," Liberty Street Economics, July 11, 2014, https://libertystreeteconomics.newyorkfed.org/2014/07/crisis-chronicles-the-collapse-of-the-french-assignat-and-its-link-to-virtual-currencies-today/.
2. Alice Girard, "The French Revolution, the Assignats, and the Counterfeiters," Numiscorner.com (blog). September 19, 2019, https://www.numiscorner.com/blogs/news/the-french-revolution-the-assignats-and-the-counterfeiters.
3. Banqeu De France, "The History of the Banque de France," (n.d.), https://www.banque-france.fr/en/banque-de-france/institution-rooted-history/founding-history-banque-de-france#:~:text=The%20Banque%20de%20France%20is%20founded%20on%2018%20January%201800,the%20discounting%20of%20commercial%20bills.
4. libertytree.ca., "Napoleon Bonaparte Quote," LibertyQuotes. (n.d.), http://libertytree.ca/quotes/Napoleon.Bonaparte.Quote.0D4B.
5. Henry Dundas in the Introduction, *The Coalitions against Napolean*, by William Nester. (Everand, 2023), https://www.everand.com/book/642162287/The-Coalitions-Against-Napoleon-How-British-Money-Manufacturing-and-Military-Power-Forged-the-Alliances-that-Achieved-Victory.
6. William Nester, *The Coalitions Against Napoleon* (Pen and Sword, 2023).
7. Neil Gale, "President Abraham Lincoln Institutes a Centralized Banking System to Fund the Union in the Civil War, With Notes by Lincoln on Banking in His Own Words." December 30, 2018, https://drloihjournal.blogspot.com/2018/12/

# END NOTES

   abraham-lincoln-institutes-centralized-banking-system-to-fund-union-in-civil-war.html.
8. libertytree.ca., "Quotation by Abraham Lincoln," LibertyQuotes, http://libertytree.ca/quotes/Abraham.Lincoln.Quote.9495.
9. quotefancy.com, "Abraham Lincoln Quote: 'I Have Two Great Enemies, the Southern Army in Front of Me and the Bankers in the Rear. Of the Two, the One at My Rear I...'", https://quotefancy.com/quote/760176/Abraham-Lincoln-I-have-two-great-enemies-the-Southern-Army-in-front-of-me-and-the-bankers.
10. Richard Cooper, "The Gold Standard: Historical Facts and Future Prospects," *Brookings Papers on Economic Activity*, https://www.brookings.edu/wp-content/uploads/1982/01/1982a_bpea_cooper_dornbusch_hall.pdf.
11. Bradford Tax Institute, "History of Federal Income Tax Rates: 1913-2024." https://bradfordtaxinstitute.com/Free_Resources/Federal-Income-Tax-Rates.aspx#:~:text=In%20order%20to%20finance%20U.S.,War%20is%20expensive.
12. Franklin D. Roosevelt Presidential Library and Museum, "Great Depression Facts - FDR Presidential Library & Museum," https://www.fdrlibrary.org/great-depression-facts#:~:text=throughout%20the%201920s.-,At%20the%20height%20of%20the%20Depression%20in%201933%2C%2024.9%25%20of,42.5%25%20between%201929%20and%201933.
13. Henry Hazlitt, *Economics in One Lesson* (New York: Harper & Bros, 1946).
14. Pilkingtonphil, "Hjalmar Schacht, Mefo Bills and the Restoration of the German Economy 1933-1939," Fixing the Economist, December 11, 2013, https://

fixingtheeconomists.wordpress.com/2013/12/11/hjalmar-schacht-mefo-bills-and-the-restoration-of-the-german-economy-1933-1939/

15. Paul M. Sparrow, "The Casablanca Conference – Unconditional Surrender," Forward With Roosevelt, (FRD National Archives, January 10, 2017), https://fdr.blogs.archives.gov/2017/01/10/the-casablanca-conference-unconditional-surrender/

**Chapter 11**

1. Federal Reserve History, *Creation of the Bretton Woods System*, https://www.federalreservehistory.org/essays/bretton-woods-created#:~:text=July%201944,became%20the%20World%20Bank%20Group.
2. Murray Rothbard, *The Mystery of Banking*.
3. Carrol Quigley, *Tragedy and Hope Quotes*.
4. Barry Eichengreen, *Exorbitant Privilege: The Rise and Fall of the Dollar and the Future of the International Monetary System*.
5. Peter Senge, *The Fifth Discipline: The Art & Practice of The Learning Organization*.
6. Mises, Ludwig von. *The Causes of the Economic Crisis*. Auburn, AL: Ludwig von Mises Institute, 2006.
7. Powell, Jerome. 60 Minutes. CBS News [video], May 17, 2020. www.cbsnews.com/news/full-transcript-fed-chair-jerome-powell-60-minutes-interview-economic-recovery-from-coronavirus-pandemic.
8. Michael T. Snyder, *Guess How Many Nations In The World Do Not Have A Central Bank?* https://www.investing.com/analysis/guess-how-many-nations-in-the-world-do-not-have-a-central-bank-254385.
9. Bethany McLean and Joe Nocera, *All the Devils Are Here* (2010).

# END NOTES

10. Jamie Dimon, https://quotefancy.com/quote/1164421/Jamie-Dimon-No-one-has-the-right-to-not-assume-that-the-business-cycle-will-turn-Every\
11. The source was Federal Reserve Economic Data, but has been removed since I first captured the data. https://fred.stlouisfed.org/.
12. George M. Noceti, "What Really Caused the Financial Crisis? 11 Conclusions Every Investor Should Read," 2013.
13. Paulson, Henry M. Jr. *On the Brink* (Business Plus, 2010).
14. Yellen, Janet. CNBC [video], April 6, 2020. www.cnbc.com/video/2020/04/06/watch-cnbcs-full-interview-with-former-fed-chair-janet-yellen.html.
15. Pam Martens and Russ Martens. "The Fed Does Not Ride to the Rescue of Wall Street Yesterday: What's Up?" Wall Street on Parade, September 9, 2020. www.wallstreetonparade.com/2020/09/the-fed-does-not-ride-to-the-rescue-of-wall-street-yesterday-whats-up/.

## Chapter 12

1. Étienne de La Boétie, *The Politics of Obedience: The Discourse of Voluntary Servitude* (Auburn, AL: Ludwig von Mises Institute, 2015).
2. Ayn Rand et al. *Capitalism: The Unknown Ideal.* Chapter 6 *Gold & Economic Freedom;* Alan Greenspan. (New York: New American Library, 1966).
3. Ben Bagdikian, *The New Media Monopoly* (Boston: Beacon Press, 1983).
4. Norman Solomon, *Cover of Media Mergers*, Quote by Mark Crispin Miller, www.niemanreports.org/articles/coverage-of-media-mergers/.

5. Rothbard, Murray. *The History of Money and Banking: Colonial Era—WWll*; Introduction by Joseph Salerno. Auburn, AL: Ludwig von Mises Institute, 2002.
6. Grim, Ryan. "Priceless: How the Federal Reserve Bought the Economics Profession." HuffPost, May 13, 2013. www.huffpost.com/entry/priceless-how-the-federal_n_278805.
7. Auerbach, Robert D. *Deception and Abuse at the Fed*. Austin: University of Texas Press, 2008.
8. Grim, Ryan. "Priceless: How the Federal Reserve Bought the Economics Profession." HuffPost, May 13, 2013. www.huffpost.com/entry/priceless-how-the-federal_n_278805.
9. Rothbard, Murray. *The History of Money and Banking: Colonial Era—WWll*; Introduction by Joseph Salerno. Auburn, AL: Ludwig von Mises Institute, 2002.
10. Grim, Ryan. "Priceless: How the Federal Reserve Bought the Economics Profession." HuffPost, May 13, 2013. www.huffpost.com/entry/priceless-how-the-federal_n_278805.
11. Grim, Ryan. "Priceless: How the Federal Reserve Bought the Economics Profession." HuffPost, May 13, 2013. www.huffpost.com/entry/priceless-how-the-federal_n_278805.
12. Walter Lippman, *Opinion* (San Diego: Harcourt, 1922).
13. Noam Chomsky, *Media Control* (New York: Seven Stories Press, 1991).
14. Edward Bernays, *Propaganda* (Brooklyn, New York: Ig Publishing, 1928).
15. Noam Chomsky, "On the State of the Nation, Iraq and the Election." *Democracy Now*, October 21, 2004, www.chomsky.info/20041021/.

## END NOTES

16. Antony C. Sutton, *National Suicide: Military Aid to the Soviet Union* (New Rochelle, NY: Arlington House, 1973).
17. Antony C. Sutton,, "Testimony of the Sutton Before Subcommittee VII of the Platform Committee of the Republican Party," 1972.
18. Debora Mackenzie, and Andy Coghlan. "Revealed—The Capitalist Network that Runs the World," *New Scientist*, October 19, 2011. www.newscientist.com/article/mg21228354-500-revealed-the-capitalist-network-that-runs-the-world/.
19. Debora Mackenzie, and Andy Coghlan. "Revealed—The Capitalist Network that Runs the World," *New Scientist*, October 19, 2011. www.newscientist.com/article/mg21228354-500-revealed-the-capitalist-network-that-runs-the-world/.
20. Debora Mackenzie, and Andy Coghlan. "Revealed—The Capitalist Network that Runs the World," *New Scientist*, October 19, 2011. www.newscientist.com/article/mg21228354-500-revealed-the-capitalist-network-that-runs-the-world/.
21. Frédéric C. Howe, *The Confessions of a Monopolist* (Chicago: Public Publishing Co., 1906).
22. Joseph A. Schumpeter, *Capitalism, Socialism and Democracy* (New York: Harper Perennial, 1950).
23. Gabriel Kolko, *The Triumph of Conservatism* (New York: Simon and Schuster, 2008).
24. Frédéric Bastiat, *The Law* (Auburn, AL: Ludwig von Mises Institute, 2007).
25. Butler, Smedley D. *War Is a Racket*. Los Angeles, CA: Feral House, 1935.
26. Butler, Smedley D. *War Is a Racket*. Los Angeles, CA: Feral House, 1935.
27. CNN [article], April 4, 2012. www.cnn.com/interactive/2012/04/us/table.military.troops/.

## Chapter 13

1. Aleksandr Solzhenitsyn, *The Gulag Archipelago* (New York: Harper and Row, 1973).
2. Frédéric Bastiat, *The Law* (Auburn, AL: Ludwig von Mises Institute, 2007).
3. Saifedean Ammous, *The Bitcoin Standard* (2018).
4. Chris Brady, *The Bitcoin Bride* (2021).
5. Marc Andreessen, "Why Bitcoin Matters," *New York Times*, January 21, 2014. dealbook.nytimes.com/2014/01/21/why-bitcoin-matters/.
6. William Stanley Jevons, *The Theory of Political Economy* (New York: MacMillan and Co., 1871.)
7. Vera C. Smith, *The Rationale of Central Banking and the Free Banking Alternative* (Indianapolis, IN: Liberty Fund, 1990).
8. Larry Sechrest, *Free Banking: Theory, History and a Laissez-Faire Model* (Auburn, AL: Ludwig von Mises Institute, 2008).
9. Ludwig von Mises, *Human Action* (Auburn, AL: Ludwig von Mises Institute, 1999).
10. Murray Rothbard "Review of Austrian Economics" 1988 https://mises.org/mises-daily/myth-free-banking-scotland
11. Ludwig von Mises, *Human Action* (Auburn, AL: Ludwig von Mises Institute, 1999).
12. Central Banking, "Lifetime Achievement Award Paul Volcker," January 18, 2014. www.centralbanking.com/central-banking-journal/feature/2321715/lifetime-achievement-award-paul-volcker.
13. Larry Sechrest, *Free Banking: Theory, History and a Laissez-Faire Model* (Auburn, AL: Ludwig von Mises Institute, 2008).